CRITICAL CHOICES

A JOURNEY WITH THE FILIPINO PEOPLE

Dorothy Friesen

WILLIAM B. EERDMANS PUBLISHING COMPANY
GRAND RAPIDS, MICHIGAN

The author and publisher gratefully acknowledge permission to reprint
the following, originally published elsewhere:

a portion of Chapter 9 from "Low Intensity Conflict in the Philippines," first published in the February 1, 1988, issue of *Christianity and Crisis*

a portion of Chapter 13, first published as "Vigilantes Resurgent";
adapted by permission of *The Progressive*, 409 E. Main St., Madison, WI 53703. Copyright © 1987 by The Progressive, Inc.

a portion of Chapter 14 from "Leandro Alejandro: Victim of Growing Militarism in the Philippines," first published in *The Christian
Century*

The proceeds of all royalties on the sale of this book will go to Synapses,
Inc., 1821 W. Cullerton, Chicago, IL 60608.

Library of Congress Cataloging-in-Publication Data

Friesen, Dorothy.
    Critical Choices.

    1. Philippines—History—1946–1986. 2. Philippines—History—
1986–   . I. Title.
DS686.5.F75   1988   959.9'04 88-21401

ISBN 0-8028-0371-7

Contents

Acknowledgments

Though there is only one author's name on this book, it could never have been completed without the generous help of many friends and colleagues, both in the United States and in the Philippines. Special thanks are due to Carol Heise, Len Abesamis, and to my husband, Gene Stoltzfus, for their encouragement and help throughout this project. Carol painstakingly read and commented on every draft of every chapter. In addition to making useful suggestions on the manuscript, Gene shouldered many of my household tasks.

I am grateful to the volunteer staff of Synapses—Kryss Chupp, Reynaldo Lopez, Gene Stoltzfus, and Eileen Fay—for their helpful comments and for their cheerfully doing double duty at the office for a much longer time than originally planned. Thanks to Joan Gerig and Orlando Redekopp, who gave both material and moral support, and to Perry and Elizabeth Yoder, who opened their house to me and patiently taught me how to use their word processor.

I also want to acknowledge the help of Dale Suderman, Miriam Weinstein, Cheryl Payer, Myrna Arceo, Arche Ligo, Al Manrique, Vir Montecastro, Myrla Baldonado, Ben Montecastro, Ian Lind, John Howard Yoder, Carol Rose, and Leo Constantino, who offered ideas and information or commented on certain chapters of the manuscript. For security reasons some of the Philippine friends and colleagues who were most helpful must go unnamed; they know who they are.

To Katherine Epp Friesen and Elmer Stoltzfus
who embody the politics of empathy
in their daily lives

1

First Impressions

The 747 jumbo jet flights to the Philippines from Tokyo, Hong Kong, and Honolulu all seem to land and disgorge their passengers simultaneously at the Manila International Airport. The result is a daily mob scene worthy of a movie set. Hundreds of people race around the airport, children in tow, waving down porters and competing frantically for the few luggage carts. The pack then gathers in the luggage area, waiting to pounce on the gigantic cardboard boxes and suitcases as they snake along on the sporadically functioning conveyor belt.

My husband, Gene, and I ventured into this chaos in August 1977, five years after Philippine president Ferdinand Marcos had declared martial law. We came with one-way tickets and a list of possible contacts to introduce us to life in the Philippines. We joined the crowd at the conveyor belt and, after an interminable wait, retrieved our suitcases, almost miniature size in comparison to the mammoth boxes labeled "Balikbayan." *Balikbayan* is the term for Filipinos returning to their country after a long time abroad. In 1977, most came only for a visit, bringing "stateside" gifts for all the relatives and members of the extended family.

Because we had heard horror stories about Metro Manila's congested traffic, we resolved to start calling people as soon as we left the bedlam of the airport. We wanted to set up appointments in an organized manner. Patience and flexibility are important virtues to cultivate anywhere; they are crucial for survival in the Philippines.

By our second day in Manila, we had worked our way to the front of the telephone queue at the Christian Guesthouse, only to encounter busy signals, dead connections, and raspy recordings telling us the number we dialed was not yet in service. The telephone service became worse in the early 1980s as the economic crisis deepened and more trained Filipino operators and technicians left for the Middle East to find better-paying jobs.

When we finally managed to reach people on our list, it became clear that a lively network existed within church, human rights, and community organizing circles in Manila. The third person we called already knew our name and our story.

We had arrived in Manila unannounced and unheralded. Around the same time, two famous American visitors with round-trip tickets arrived and were warmly welcomed by Ferdinand and Imelda Marcos. One was evangelist Billy Graham; the other was United Farm Worker (UFW) founder Cesar Chavez.

Chavez was scheduled to meet farm workers, business representatives, and church people. The Filipino-Americans in the UFW in California are almost all from the Ilocos region of the Philippines, the home province of Ferdinand Marcos. Fierce regional loyalty meant political loyalty to the dictator and so Cesar Chavez, the champion of the oppressed in the United States, was a guest of the Marcos dictatorship in the Philippines.

The Wednesday Forum, a group of progressive church and human rights people, planned to host Chavez for a discussion and invited us to attend the meeting. On Tuesday night before his scheduled appearance, the leaders of the Forum visited our Guesthouse. "We have canceled Chavez's appearance tomorrow because everywhere he goes, he is accompanied by military people who record all the proceedings. Some members of our Forum are former political detainees, others are being watched right now by government intelligence. We won't be able to have an open discussion with him," they told us. "Actually," they added, "we can't even contact him at all. So maybe the government already canceled his appearance."

"We can't find another speaker on such short notice," continued the Wednesday Forum coordinators. "Can you fill in?" My husband, Gene, with wisdom gained in ten years of work in Asia, declined. Lacking his experience and wisdom, I welcomed the opportunity to help out our new-found friends. It takes a certain degree of naive *chutzpah* to talk before church leaders, former senators, and political detainees after being in the country one week. I did not even have the good sense to be nervous as we walked to the church to join the Forum the next day.

Cosmopolitan Church, a leading Protestant congregation in the city, anchors a busy corner on Taft Avenue. Colorful jeepneys (army jeep engines with elongated bodies, which serve as public passenger vehicles) stream past the church belching black diesel smoke. Passengers dart in and out of traffic to jump on the jeepneys. The first impression on the streets is one of sheer beauty. Faces reflect a combination of Malay, Chinese, and European features. Hair is black and straight, often flowing or cut in the latest styles. Slender frames, graceful movements, and smiles add to the general charm of the people.

Vendors have set up their wares—newspapers, cigarettes, roasted peanuts, sunglasses—along the sidewalk facing the church. The noon crowds overflow into the streets. The sights, sounds, and smells combine into a vibrant festival of life and at every opportunity I stopped like an enraptured child to imbibe the street scene more fully.

Rev. Cirilo Rigos, the pastor of Ellinwood Church, another prestigious Protestant congregation in the neighborhood, was our host. By the time we climbed the stairs together to the foyer leading to the meeting room, the ladies were already serving lunch buffet-style on long shaky tables. Ceiling fans languidly stirred above us, circulating the warm air. I tried to wipe the sweat beads from my face with the back of my hand and push my glasses back up my nose before accepting the plastic plate offered to me. I discovered that my hand was black with soot from the jeepney smoke. My glasses were fogged up from my perspiration.

In the midst of this discomfort, I smiled weakly at the women behind the table and wondered to myself whether men ever serve the food at these gatherings. I was to learn from Filipina feminists that before the Spanish incursion into the country in 1521, women in this Pacific archipelago carried an active responsibility for spiritual, economic, and political life. The economic customs contributed to the autonomous stature of women within society. Precolonial Philippines was also marked by a relative sexual egalitarianism. Spanish law, however, stressed male superiority and emphasized that women belonged at home. The Roman Catholic Church taught passivity and piety as the proper traits for women. Furthermore, the American colonial experience reinforced economic control by men. Much of the pre-Hispanic culture is deeply overlaid by colonial culture. Thus, even at gatherings of people committed to justice women still quietly serve in the background.

Over fifty people were already seated at the long tables inside the room. "This is a semipublic, private gathering," explained Rigos, as he introduced us to each person in our path as we angled our way toward some empty chairs. The faces became a blur as indistinguishable as the mumbled names.

With unscreened windows wide open, the street noises competed with the steady whir of the ceiling fans and the muted conversations at every table. I realize only in retrospect how difficult it is to find a quiet meeting room in Manila or anywhere in the Philippines except for the remote barrios. Somehow the Filipinos I met had an ability to screen out distractions like honking horns, vehicles with defective or nonexistent mufflers, screeching brakes, blaring music, noisy fans, loud air conditioners, other peoples' conversations, squealing pigs, and crowing roosters. It took me several years to develop that knack.

The chairperson of the Wednesday Forum adjusted the makeshift podium and then explained to the gathering why Cesar Chavez could not be present. The room buzzed with discussion. "But we are fortunate to have found a substitute at such short notice—a Mennonite from the United States who has just visited Indonesia." More buzz. Mennonites at that point were not one of the 350 registered mission agencies in the Philippines. No one knew of the Mennonites. They thought he said Mormon.

I made a brief opening statement, as I had been instructed, about my work as a community organizer in the United States and my observations of Indonesia. The questions poured out— "What is the goal of community organizing in the United States? What tangible evidence do you see that your new president, Jimmy Carter, cares about human rights? Who really makes decisions about foreign policy in your government? Will the U.S. government apply an Indonesian solution to the Philippines?" (In 1965 a military coup toppled nationalist Indonesian president Sukarno and millions were charged with communism and killed or imprisoned.) "Why does your government support dictators? Did Watergate make a difference in the way government is conducted?"

It dawned on me very quickly that this audience was knowledgeable in world affairs, well acquainted with the American political scene, and steeped in the experience of struggle in their own country. Though I have boycotted grapes and lettuce faithfully and urged others to do the same, I was clearly no substitute for Cesar Chavez in this room.

As I cast about for a graceful exit, an older gentleman, with smiling face and hand half raised, caught my attention. He had slipped in late, missed the food and most of my comments. He began with a quiet question from his seat, about democracy, but he soon rose to his feet and delivered an impassioned speech on the need for liberation from dictatorship. A burst of applause and a standing ovation followed. "We have just heard the Thomas Jefferson of the Philippines," whispered my husband as I sank behind the podium to let this man take over.

The orator was Jovita Salonga, a former Philippine senator in the pre–martial law days, author of a prominent text on international law, and legal counsel for Senator Benigno Aquino when he was arrested by Marcos in 1972. In 1971 Salonga himself was a victim of a bombing at the Plaza Miranda during a political rally. He was blinded in one eye and still carries shrapnel within his body. In the 1980s, Salonga was placed under arrest, too—charged, ironically, with conspiracy to bomb President Marcos. "Jovy," as he is known by his friends, was released after three months to the custody of his wife. They went into exile in the United States. "From martial law to marital law" he often joked.

Salonga returned to the Philippines in 1985 and became a leading member of the Conveners Group—opposition politicians who put together a unified platform and pledged to support a common candidate to challenge Marcos in the February 1986 presidential elections. That candidate was Mrs. Aquino, widow of the late Senator Benigno Aquino.

When Mrs. Aquino took office, Salonga headed the newly-formed Commission on Good Government, charged with recovering the hidden wealth of Marcos and his business cronies. Salonga's diligent investigative work, even during the

Marcos years, laid the groundwork for solid negotiations with foreign governments and banks, especially in Switzerland where much of the Marcos wealth is hidden.

In 1987 he resigned from the commission to run for the Senate; for the third time in his political career he won the largest number of votes of any candidate (in the Philippines the entire country votes for each senator). Salonga was elected president of the Senate by his peers when Congress opened in July 1987. Like Defense Minister Gen. Fidel Ramos, Salonga is Protestant and a member of the Cosmopolitan Church. Unlike Ramos, Salonga is an active church member and a participant in World Council of Churches commissions.

In 1977, when we were first introduced, Salonga insisted that he be addressed as "Senator," since he had not yet completed the term of office to which the people had elected him. When President Marcos declared martial law in September 1972, he dissolved the Congress. Years later when I met Jovy in exile in the United States, I was impressed with his implacable confidence that one day he would be back in political favor in the Philippines. His burning intensity at the Cosmopolitan Church gave a glimpse into the motivation that kept him and many others hoping and working during the dark days of the Marcos dictatorship.

Filipinos are famous for their graciousness and hospitality. The Wednesday Forum participants were no exception. At the end of the meeting, almost every person thanked me or invited me to visit their house or office. My favorite comment came from a young man who smiled, shook my hand, and said with great sincerity, "You are very open for a Mormon." The scene in the church was fascinating for me, having come directly from Indonesia, a neighboring Southeast Asian country. Indonesia lives up to all the fantasies about an exotic Asian country. In the villages, people dress in distinctively Malay style. English is not used. The entire island of Java reeks of the unforgettable aroma of clove cigarettes. In contrast, the Wednesday Forum participants dress in western clothes; they speak English; they are acquainted with the latest styles, news, and entertainment of the United States. They are representative of middle-class educated urban Filipinos, with the exception of their strong nationalist stance.

Even a cursory reading of Philippine history makes it painfully clear why nationalist Filipinos concerned about justice and prosperity in their country find it necessary to be knowledgeable about American politics. Laws passed by the U.S. Congress, commissions sent by the Department of State, and appointments by the president from the turn of the century until the present profoundly affect the Philippines. Its economy has been systematically tied into the American economy.

For example, in 1903, William Howard Taft, president of the Philippine Commission and later president of the United States, proclaimed "Philippines for the Filipinos," a popular policy echoed in later years by nationalist Filipinos. However, a deeper reading of Taft's rationale leaves a somewhat different impression of his real intent. "The carrying out of the principle, 'Philippines for the Filipinos' in first promoting the welfare, material, spiritual and intellectual of the people of these islands is the one course which can create any market here among the people for American goods and American supplies that will make the relation of the United States to the Philippines a profitable one for our merchants and manufacturers."[1]

His commission recommended the urgent enactment of land and franchise laws that would facilitate the entry of major exporters and give them maximum opportunities for profitable investments. This included the textile industry and major investors like the railroad, public utility, mining, sugar, and construction companies. In 1899 the Philippines purchased only 9 percent of its total imports from the United States; by 1933 that figure had risen to 64 percent.

In 1945, after the Pacific War, while preparations were being made for Philippine independence, Congress passed the Bell Trade Act, which provided for continued free trade between the two countries. That meant unlimited entry of American goods into the Philippines, but Philippine sugar, cordage, tobacco, and coconut oil exported to the United States were subjected to quotas. Senator Millard Tydings, who sponsored the bill in the Senate, admitted that "most of the people who favor the bill are opposed to independence. . . . Their whole philosophy is to keep the Philippines economically even though we lose them politically."[2]

1. Renato Constantino, *The Philippines: A Past Revisited* (Manila: Tala Publishing Services, 1975), p. 292.

2. Renato and Letizia Constantino, *The Philippines: The Continuing Past* (Manila: Foundation for Nationalist Studies, 1978), p. 201.

Senator Tydings's and William Howard Taft's goals have been accomplished. The penetration of multinational corporations into the everyday life and the psyche of the Philippines is phenomenal. Many popular items are referred to by their brand names. Children whose chins barely reach the countertop of the local sari-sari store (a neighborhood all-purpose shop, often just shelves and a counter) ordering soft drinks say, "Give me a coke, the orange one." Razors are referred to as gillettes; toothpaste is called colgate; refrigerators are called frigidaires. Children seeing our cameras yell, "Kodak me. Kodak me."

Even the staunchest nationalist cannot escape the clutches of foreign goods. During our first month in the country, we visited the Task Force Detainees, an organization founded in 1974 by the Association of the Major Religious Superiors to document human rights abuses and act as an advocate for victims of this abuse. We sat down to chat and within minutes, as Filipino hospitality customs dictate, the coffee jar, cups, and saltine crackers appeared. Someone took a picture of the gathering around the table and we used it to accompany an article for American church papers. Within weeks I received questioning letters from friends in the United States. "Why are you sitting behind a big jar of Nescafé? In a Third World country, of all places! You know there's been a boycott for years!" It's hard to explain to someone eight thousand miles away, but the most committed and politically sophisticated groups in 1977 had not transferred their nationalist commitments to their personal consumption habits. During the 1980s, consumer groups were formed that connected personal consumption with nationalist economics, but their influence was not widespread.

Ten years later I witnessed an advanced stage of foreign corporate penetration—a Coca-Cola singing contest in Zamboanga City. Schools and colleges from all around the city competed to see who could perform the latest Coca-Cola jingle the most creatively. Fifteen groups sang and danced with a multitude of ingenious props to an approving throng of ten thousand young people and their parents. One entry, the choir of Ateneo de Zamboanga, the prestigious Jesuit-run college, translated the jingle into Chubacano, the native dialect, and released white doves during their performance.

Just the night before I had interviewed the Ateneo choir

director and other teachers who had participated quite courageously on behalf of Cory Aquino during the presidential campaign. These obviously bright people had no second thoughts about their participation in this Coca-Cola extravaganza, which featured a Filipina teenage singing idol and speeches by Coca-Cola executives extolling their contribution to the Philippines, with the Marines in full combat uniform acting as security guards. The Ateneo director's only concern was with winning the contest, which offered a five thousand peso prize. I asked one Marine sergeant why his men had to carry M-16s to do the job that school security guards should be doing. "Oh, ma'am, the children are so excited to see the star of the Coca-Cola ad. They won't stay behind the ropes if it's just security guards."

"It's a blessing and a curse" says Charito Planas, a nationalist politician, describing the American-Philippine relationships. "We all learned 'A is for apple' in first grade, but we have no homegrown apples in the Philippines. You know we have the most wonderful fruit here—mangoes, nangka, pineapples, rambutan, durian. Hundreds of kinds of fruit, but we spend a dollar for an imported apple at Christmas, because the American textbooks set the standard for what is desirable."

Charito ran for the Batasang Pambansa (the Marcos parliament) in 1978 on the opposition ticket with Benigno Aquino, who campaigned from his cell. Her life threatened by Marcos, she sought asylum—where else but the United States. She returned to the Philippines when Marcos was forced out of the country in 1986.

Not only do many Filipinos visit or emigrate to the United States; the reverse process is also true. There are thousands of long-term foreign residents in the Philippines—with the church, the media, international development agencies, in business, in universities and colleges. A religious directory lists more than 350 separately organized Christian churches or associations. Many of these have foreign links, either in the form of financial aid or personnel or with parallel structures to an American or European counterpart. Protestant churches have registered 1,380 expatriate missionaries working in the Philippines, while the Catholic church lists 1,800 foreign priests. Hundreds of religious teachers and evangelists simply apply for tourist visas and thus slip in without registering.

However, famous evangelists like Billy Graham do not just

slip in. Preparations for the Billy Graham Crusade, which included careful training of counselors and Bible study leaders and the assembling of a five thousand–voice choir, were in process for over a year before he arrived. A school of evangelism to be held concurrently with the crusade was planned for the plush International Convention Center, part of a complex that includes theaters, a cultural center, and a hotel—one of Imelda Marcos's projects.

As the plans unfolded, some Filipino Christian leaders raised questions about the appropriateness of such efforts. In a letter to Billy Graham before he arrived in November 1977, the church leaders wrote,

> You are coming here as an evangelist with the sole purpose of spreading the word of God. And if God's word is to touch the lives of our people, should not God's messenger seek the people's welcome by trying to understand the fears which haunt them, the pains which try them, the hopes that sustain them? But in your case, you will be billeted in one of the best hotels and your reception will be as grand as the reception given to monarchs and kings. In short you will be isolated from the very people you seek to lead to the saving knowledge of our Lord.

Rev. Rigos showed us the letter and explained why many Protestant leaders signed it, though the more usual Filipino style is to promote smooth interpersonal relations and avoid confrontation. The final paragraph of the letter summarized the church's dilemma.

> In a country beset with economic and social problems, there is increasing attraction to communist alternatives because of the concern for the welfare of the poorest people. The church is under particular pressure to live out the love of God in concrete ways among the people. This crusade will be seen as a symbol of the church's collusion with continued American influence and affluence in the Philippines. Like you, we believe in the cause of evangelism. But your style is something we cannot afford.

In November 1977, Mr. and Mrs. Marcos met Billy Graham at the airport; the picture of that welcome, complete with leis, was duly recorded in the national media. Rev. Graham's statement that "no one in the Philippines is in prison for their faith" received front page coverage in the *Bulletin Today*, a leading

Philippine daily during the Marcos's time. The Task Force Detainees of the Philippines estimated that two thousand prisoners of conscience were being held throughout the country at the time of Graham's statement.

The Philippine Protestant sensitivity to inappropriate links with the United States is related to the history of the religious justification of the United States' conquest of the Philippines at the turn of the century. Amid a national controversy about America's attempt to take over the Philippines, President William McKinley told a visiting delegation of Methodist church leaders in 1899,

> I am not ashamed to tell you gentlemen that I went down on my knees and prayed almighty God for light and guidance more than one night. And one night late, it came to me this way . . . 1. That we could not give them back to Spain—that would be cowardly and dishonorable. 2. That we could not turn them over to France and Germany—our commercial rivals in the Orient—that would be bad business and discreditable. 3. That we could not leave them to themselves—they were unfit for self-government—and they would soon have anarchy and misrule over there worse than Spain's was. 4. There was nothing left for us to do but to take them and to educate the Filipinos and up-lift and civilize and Christianize them and by God's grace do the very best we could by them, as our fellow-men for whom Christ also died. And then I went to bed and went to sleep and slept soundly.[3]

While some of the Wednesday Forum members battled to keep the church from living in the shadow of the American eagle and from legitimizing Marcos's dictatorship, a few members had already shifted their allegiance to the underground revolutionary movement. "You cannot hope to understand what is happening in this country without acquainting yourself with the goals and practice of the underground. They provide the direction and the energy for change. They are trying to construct an economy and a culture which is truly Filipino," said one church figure as he invited Gene and me to go "to the countryside" to meet members of the underground.

Despite the attractiveness of the invitation, we declined.

3. Daniel B. Schirmer and Stephen Rosskamm Shalom, *The Philippines Reader* (Boston: South End Press, 1987), p. 23.

We turned away from the possibility of revolutionary adventures and spent the next two years observing the effects of American economics and politics on the lives of ordinary Filipinos, on rural and urban communities, and on national political life. We knew that we must first understand the situation Filipinos face before we could really comprehend why some people, at risk to their lives, choose to join or support an underground movement for change.

Over the next ten years, deepening friendships with Filipinos became the cornerstone of our conviction that the beleaguered poor of the country were yearning for peace and were desperate to find a way to survive economically.

2

Life in Agdao Barrio

FORMATION OF A POINT OF VIEW

The quest to understand another country, its people, culture, and economic and political life is never done in a vacuum. The experiences and assumptions we bring helps to determine what we are open to see and what we absorb. As church workers, Gene and I came with questions like: Where is the Spirit of God at work in this country? Where are the significant signs of hope?

For foreigners, a particular boon of living in another society, like that of the Philippines, is the added social mobility—both upward and downward. We were accepted among people in the upper strata—an experience we never encountered in Canada or the United States. But this experience was not unique to us. In September 1987, Philippine columnist Hilarion M. Henares, Jr., commented angrily in the national daily newspaper, the *Philippine Inquirer*,

> Americans play gods because we let them. . . . Low-level American officials are granted access to our high-level officials. They mingle officially and socially with our senators, congressmen, Cabinet secretaries, with the President herself. . . . And no Filipino—writer or student or professor—can get the information that an ordinary American student making his thesis, can get.

Henares is right. We knew that middle-class Filipinos would probably not receive that same welcome in upper-class America or in government circles in Washington. For my part, when I returned from the Philippines, I did not wander around the Cabrini Green Public Housing Project in Chicago without a specific invitation from a resident. In the Philippines, however, we visited the urban slums without the same apprehension that affected some Filipino acquaintances who were more attuned to the nuanced signals of class differences within their own society. We felt a general warmth in rural barrios and urban slums and a willingness on the part of residents to talk with us. In our attempt to accommodate to the cultural differences, our accommodation between class parameters was also stretched. We realized that our sojourn in the Philippines was a particular gift of grace in this regard and we needed to treasure and use this gift wisely.

Theoretically, an external situation exists that everyone can view, but there is usually a cacophony of contradictory voices to interpret the situation. For example, a coconut corporation executive told us that farmers are poor because they are lazy. A labor union representative told us that the management was skimming company profits into private pockets while claiming the company could not afford to raise wages. A sugar *hacendero* (plantation owner) told us that landowners should make decisions because they know how to handle authority and administration. A squatter community leader told us he held the World Bank responsible for his dire poverty. The list of voices is endless. To whom do we listen?

Who do we think is making an important contribution to history? The president or prime minister, a general, the street sweepers, bar girls? Soon after we arrived, a Filipino friend gave us a book by nationalist historian Renato Constantino and wrote in the flyleaf, "So you may be able to see our future through our past—properly." Constantino discusses the proper subjects of history:

> The individuals who made history colorful could not have made history without the people. While it is true that the inarticulate as individuals cannot have deeds recorded in history, their collective effort can and should be chronicled and given its deserved importance. But since the articulate having assumed the responsibility and privilege of writing history, have done so from their point of view, the resulting accounts present an incomplete and distorted picture which unduly projects individual *men* [sic] while disregarding the dynamic role of the masses.[1]

1. Renato Constantino, *The Philippines: A Past Revisited* (Manila: Tala Publishing Services, 1975), p. 5.

The question of whom to listen to brings us to the core of our values. Whether consciously or unconsciously chosen, whom we listen to reflects on our understanding of the overarching question of who we think God is. Deciding how to assess the various voices in the society became a key component of our attempt to understand the Philippines.

I knew from biblical material that God uses the weak, the inarticulate, and the socially unacceptable to get things done. During our first year in the Philippines I reread some of those accounts—like the story in the Book of Joshua about the fall of Jericho. One of the main characters in the story was Rahab.

Rahab, a prostitute, was living in Jericho at the time that Israel was finally ready to cross over the Jordan River to the promised land of Canaan. Before the Israelite soldiers marched on Jericho, their military leader, Joshua, sent two spies to explore the land. The spies went to Jericho and stayed at Rahab's house. The passage does not explain why they stayed with a prostitute, but there were probably several considerations. Since they were unwelcome strangers in town, one of the safest places for them would undoubtedly be a prostitute's house. Customers do not usually have to identify themselves clearly and the anonymity would serve their purpose well. Someone like Rahab, who herself was not part of respectable society, would not have to determine whether her customers were worthy of her services.

The people in Jericho had already heard stories about the God of Israel. Rahab, who had no personal investment in defending the gods of Jericho, was psychologically freer to consider other points of view. So, when her own townspeople came to her house to ask whether she had seen the two spies, she protected the men by saying that they had already left. She risked her own life to protect theirs, telling them, "I know that God has given you this land" (Josh. 2:8). When her prediction came true and the walls of Jericho fell and Israel took over the city, only Rahab and her family were saved. Her ability to see the future more clearly was not unconnected to her being at the periphery of her society.

The story does not end simply with the safety of Rahab and her family, however. Rahab's name surfaces in the New Testament list of Jesus' ancestors, a predominantly male genealogy recorded in the Gospel of Matthew. Her actions are mentioned in the Book of Hebrews in a list of the people of faith like Abraham, Moses, David, and Jacob. The commentary that follows her name says, "It was faith that kept the prostitute Rahab from being killed with those who disobeyed God, for she gave the Israelite spies a friendly welcome." So Rahab, the foreign prostitute, becomes part of the liberation history of the Israelites and part of church history.

Rahab was just a footnote to the principal event of the New Testament—Jesus. But the main point of Jesus' story was not so different. With Jesus came the ultimate weakness and incoherence—a revolutionary who could not keep his supporters together even for a little skirmish, a dissident who staged a makeshift parade for children in the capital city, a prisoner who had no articulate defense and who did not organize a groundswell of public support to agitate for a retrial after he was sentenced to death. And yet, Jesus' story had and continues to have a tremendous impact across the world, twenty centuries later.

The theme haunts me—the unrespectable, the unimportant, and the inarticulate seem to be a key part of real history making.

God purposely chose what the world considers nonsense in order to shame the wise and God chose what the world considers weak in order to shame the powerful. God chose what the world looks down on and despises and thinks is nothing in order to destroy what the world thinks is important. (1 Cor 1:27-28)

My experiences in community organizing in the United States reinforced this line of thinking. I learned at the expense of an often bruised ego that the disenfranchised can carry a wisdom tested in bitter circumstances that is unavailable to a mainstream person. The result of being on the bottom can be a clearer view of the whole scene and a stronger ability to empathize with the situation of other human beings.[2]

Added to the notion about God's bias toward the weak and despised, Gene and I also carried the influence of American democratic customs, which pointed to the will of the majority as a key factor in deciding a country's direction. Thus in our

2. Gloria Steinem makes a compelling case for adopting the ethics of empathy as a guideline for American public life in an article entitled "If Moral Decay Is the Question, Is a Feminist Ethic the Answer?" *Ms.* September 1987.

inquiry into life in the Philippines, we decided to listen to everyone, but we agreed that our plumb line for testing events and ideas would be what actually served the interest of the majority in the country—the poor and the marginalized. We knew we would need direct experience in order to use that plumb line with integrity and skill.

After a period of travel and exploration of the Philippine islands, we settled in Davao, the third largest city in the Philippines in population and the largest in the world in land mass. Stories of a vibrant church office involved in work with farmers, fisherfolk, tribal Filipinos, and urban poor attracted us to this southern Mindanao city.

Unfortunately, we came to Davao without the benefit of proper introductions from the social action offices in Manila. Almost all social action programs in the 1970s were sponsored by the Catholic church. We knew that the cathedral is always located on the town square opposite the city hall with its obligatory statue of the national hero, Jose Rizal. Armed with that knowledge, we proceeded to San Pedro Cathedral in Davao. However, we soon found out that Davao had gained prominence in social action work in spite of the presiding archbishop, Antonio Mabutas, who did not approve of the direction this church apostolate was taking. The feeble social action center at the cathedral was about to close its doors permanently when we arrived.

We did find one enthusiastic worker left at the center—Enrique Vasquez. Because he did not know us and we had no letter of introduction, Enrique began awkwardly, shuffling his feet and hunting for the appropriate questions to ask us. We sat in the shadow of the gigantic cathedral and tried to get to the topics that mattered to all of us. I could tell from looking in Enrique's eyes that he was trying to decide if he should trust these "gringos" who had just wandered into his life. The church bells tolled and Enrique's eyes lit up, "It's lunch time. I know a nice restaurant where it will be easier to talk."

Enrique led us to a premier Chinese restaurant, ordered an exquisite meal, and explained that the real church social action was not at the local cathedral, but at a Mindanao-wide organization called Mindanao-Sulu Pastoral Conference, with offices not far from San Pedro. At the end of the meal, Enrique pushed back his chair and said, "Now, if you come to work with us, no more meals like this. You will have to eat simply."

At some undetermined point in our conversation Enrique had decided to trust us and soon he began to introduce us to others in the network for peace and justice. One such person was a charming, intense woman named Leonora. "Her whole family is committed," said Enrique, "even the dog." Leonora agreed and described some of her encounters with the military in the course of her work with tribal Filipinos in the provinces bordering Davao City. Another person in the network was Virgilio Montecastro, a poultry farmer–electronics expert–photographer, who had a rare bone disease that doctors had predicted would fell him by age seven. He was still determinedly hobbling about his business at age forty-five when we met him.

We decided to stay in Davao, to eat simply as Enrique predicted, and to learn to view the Philippine scene from the perspective of an urban poor barrio. "Urban poor" is a term used in the Philippines to denote people who live in impoverished communities, often along the shoreline in the cities. We moved into a quiet section of a community known as Agdao, which sprawled across the waterfront and stretched to the local market and into a commercial section toward the city center. The shanties closest to the waterfront were built on posts above the water with no sanitation provisions except the murky brown liquid underneath the houses. Some of the residents of Agdao were squatters—over the years, they had moved onto the land surreptitiously and constructed their houses. Some of them built up the shoreline by manually hauling rocks and gravel to the water's edge.

Further from the shore more substantial houses were interspersed with makeshift huts. It was never quite clear to us who owned what. We paid rent in a six-month lump sum to a young Filipino couple who moved out of the house and stayed with relatives. They told us they were using our rent money to start a piggery. We never found out if they also owned the land on which the house was constructed. We didn't ask any questions; we were thankful to settle down finally in a hospitable barrio after months of travel within the Philippines.

Agdao was a mosaic of vibrant life. The residents were to experience turmoil and violence later with the appearance of armed vigilantes, but in 1978 when we moved in, the neighborhood was relatively peaceful. The sights and sounds common to barrio life surrounded us. Before dawn while we were still lying on our *benig* (woven mats traditionally placed on the floor and used as "mattresses"), we could hear the flipflop of the vendors' thongs as they hurried past our house to get their wares to market. Next came the roar of the jeepney engine right outside our window as the vehicle strained to navigate the narrow corner along a road that was originally intended as a footpath.

By six in the morning, children in the neighboring houses began scrubbing the floors with the *bunot*, a halved coconut husk. The swish of the fibres of the husk against the floors acted as a gentle alarm clock. We seemed to be the last in the neighborhood to wake up. By the time we emerged from our house, mothers and children were already lined up to wash at a community pump. Directly behind our house, the Philippine national anthem blared out daily over the loudspeaker at Holy Cross of Agdao School. Our neighbor's roosters then crowed, announcing the rising sun only a few hours after the fact.

Throughout the day, pigs tied to an adjacent tree squealed while children played with their homemade toys nearby. Morning and evening we could hear the local *tuba* man whistling as he climbed the coconut trees to collect the juice to make the cheap alcoholic beverage. On a bench a few feet from our front door, the youths amused themselves by strumming their guitars and occasionally breaking into a song. Good sounds. The sounds of life.

During our travels, we had stayed in *conventos* (parish houses) or *pensions* (hostels) or with friends and had thus avoided the direct experience of the chores and routines of mundane life in the Philippines. Life in Agdao changed that.

Keeping a healthy house in the tropics was a constant battle against nature. Leave a pile of papers in a drawer for a few days and some mouse will shred them to provide a nest for her babies. Out comes the mousetrap—but the mice in this land are of a superior intelligence and know how to grab the bait without tripping the trap. We could just imagine them in some hideout holding seminars on successful bait grabbing! If we turned on the light at night, we could watch the cockroaches frolicking on the bathroom walls. One night of neglecting to spray all the possible openings seemed to multiply the creatures tenfold. I developed an instinctive fear of turning on the light at night and surprising some temperamental cockroach from his perch on the toilet paper.

And the ants! Black ants formed convoys across the walls and ceilings the minute one crumb was left anywhere. Other smaller varieties clustered around the sugar jar hoping that by the process of osmosis a granule would ooze out of the glass. We rushed through dinner so we could quickly wash the dishes before the troops mobilized in overwhelming numbers. The worst scourge were red ants gathering around the cooking oil, crumbs, or even the smell of garlic. In a split second as we wiped them off the table, they clambered onto our hands and bit us in revenge for disturbing their meal. Painful red swellings on hands and feet reminded us to treat this enemy with extreme caution.

The experience was something like having a perpetual picnic on an anthill. Nothing was safe. The parental warnings not to eat in the living room and bedroom made sense in this context. One crumb not cleaned up would be detected by our ants and for the rest of the night they would swarm around, hoping for another windfall. The psychological effect of this battle was the constant feeling of ants crawling over, tickling, and biting one when in fact there were none at all.

When we looked for a place to live, I had told my Filipino companions I wanted a simple house where we could experience the everyday life of ordinary Filipinos. I didn't anticipate the painful daily confrontation I had with my own lifestyle, since I had never considered myself affluent or an active participant in the American consumer society. It wasn't always the glaring differences but rather the little assumptions that often struck me most deeply.

We spent a great deal of time on household activities like cooking, cleaning, washing clothes, and visiting the market daily since there was no refrigerator to store excess supplies. Food spoils quickly in the tropics. "Why are you doing this work yourselves?" visitors would ask. "Everyone in the Philippines has a helper." *Helper* is a nice word for servant. But not everyone in the Philippines has a helper. For example, helpers don't have helpers. None of our neighbors had helpers, either.

A community well directly in front of our house provided the brackish water we used for flushing the toilet, washing clothes, or taking a bath. We collected the rainwater that ran off our tin roof into a large tank with a spout leading into the house. We used this water for drinking, cooking, and washing dishes. If there was no rain, we would have to buy our water.

A water truck delivered water once every few days to our community where one enterprising neighbor stored it in a large tank and then sold it to the rest of us when we needed it.

We always boiled our water, even when we bought spring water, because we didn't know what kind of bugs were in our neighbor's storage tank. None of the other neighbors did. "Are you used to the germs here? Is that why you don't boil your drinking water?" I asked one day as we gathered around the well to draw our water. "No, we don't want to use our fuel for that" was the reply.

Gracious entertaining was precarious if we hadn't checked our water supply. Just one overnight guest could disturb the equilibrium of the water-hauling routine. Though the well was close to our house, it required some effort to dip the pail deep into the well, haul it up, fill our bucket, carry it through the house, and pour the water into our large plastic barrel in the bathroom—a process that had to be repeated at least ten times until the barrel was filled. A visitor, used to easy access to an unlimited water supply, could easily deplete our barrel with just one long carefree bath. Thus, we strongly advocated the dip and pour method of bathing to conserve water and we supplied a small dipper beside the barrel to encourage conservation.

Electricity was an on-again, off-again proposition, so keeping plenty of candles on hand was a must. Electricity is often not available in the rural barrios, but we were living in Davao City, third largest population center in the Philippines. Using an electric typewriter was a dubious undertaking, for without warning a "brownout" could occur. Our electric fan suffered an early demise, done in by the numerous cuts in current as it valiantly tried to keep air moving during the hot afternoons. I described to my neighbor how the screens on our windows seemed to cut out any possibility of a breeze in the afternoon and asked her what she would do. "I don't have that problem," she said. When I looked a little closer, I realized that most houses in the neighborhood did not have screens.

Most of our neighbors cooked "dirty kitchen" style, which refers to cooking over an open wood or charcoal fire, usually at the back of the house. We bought a small tank of fuelane gas to use for cooking, which was attached to a two-burner open flame hotplate. There was no way to gauge when the fuel was used up, so I was caught on several occasions with no gas in the midst of preparing a meal for guests. I then had to unhook the tank, drag it a quarter mile out to the road, hail a tricycle (a motorcycle with a side car used for public transport) and ride down to the fuelane supply shop to trade in my tank for a new one. I could haul it all the way home and discover that the pin on the opening was malfunctioning and the gas wasn't being released. Then I would repeat the trip all over again. One day I complained to my neighbor about the hassle and asked her what she would advise. She just looked at me and finally said, "I don't know." Later, when she got to know me better, she told me that most people gather firewood where they can find it, because they cannot afford gas.

A key institution in our little community was the *sari-sari* store—a local all-purpose shop with shelves and a counter for customers to lean on while ordering their supplies. It was a good place to catch up on neighborhood rumors and reports. People loved to exchange *tsismis*, as they call their light-hearted gossip. With the exception of *tuba*, the native coconut-based alcoholic beverage made in the barrio, almost everything else in the store was foreign. My favorite shop was Lita's Sari-Sari Store, which we had to pass every day on our way out of the barrio. Lita was a toothpick-thin thirty-year-old woman with several children hanging on to her skirts as she served her customers. She always had a cheerful smile for anyone passing by.

Lita's store, one of the few in the community with a refrigerator, sold ice in narrow plastic bags. She seemed to have an uncanny knowledge about when we would be receiving guests. She always made sure her nephews filled the five-inch-long plastic bags with water in ample time to freeze before I would show up at the store and ask for cokes and ice. Lita knew that the warm coke customarily served to guests in the rural areas was anathema in the house of the "cana" (Americana).

I knew I could depend on Lita or any of the other shopkeepers to shepherd guests to our place. The houses in the neighborhood had grown up in an unruly fashion and the path between them on the way to the outside road was circuitous. Tricycle drivers would drive from the Agdao market, veer off the main road, and stop at the front gate of the Holy Cross school where the road ended, and then vaguely point in the general direction of our house. Inevitably, Lita's family would take charge of hospitality and guide the bewildered visitors to our door. One of the reasons for what seemed like a constant stream of visitors was that Davao was a transfer point between other towns and cities, but public transportation did not run all night. In the tropics the sun goes down by six in the afternoon, so the wisest thing to do is to find a place to stay overnight and begin the journey the next day.

At first our immediate neighbors were suspicious about all the visitors. What aroused suspicions in this family-oriented society more than anything else, however, was the fact that we did not have children. What kind of happily married couple does not have children? The women were very curious. I began with long explanations about life in America being different— sometimes choices have to be made between work and family because support systems for childcare are inadequate. All I got was more suspicious looks and advice on fertility. The stock answer I finally developed was "God has not blessed us yet."

Suspicion lifted when my parents came for a visit. This friendly white-haired couple visiting the sari-sari store, walking around the neighborhood, hauling water at the well, and potting plants in front of the house provided a context for me in the neighbors' minds. I may not have children, but at least I had parents. People in the Philippines have had four hundred years of experience of nuns and priests, eighty years of long-term Protestant missionaries, two decades of experience with Peace Corps volunteers, and more recent experience with Mormon missionaries and short visits by progressive foreigners on study tours. We did not quite fit any of the categories, but our neighbors in Agdao tried desperately to find a suitable slot for us.

Friends made an effort to share their perception of life with my parents during their visit. One evening, for example, Father Ben, a priest who worked in the squatter community of Piapi, tried to explain the problems of martial law and the Marcoses to my father, a fundamentalist Christian. I left them to their discussion around the table while I began heating the water for dishwashing. Father Ben had just finished his explanation when I rejoined them. After some silence my father said, "But we are instructed to pray for our government." "Oh, we do," said Ben in all sincerity. "We pray they will get their just deserts."

During the time we lived in Agdao, an added feature of Marcos's New Society (martial law) was introduced to supplement the paramilitary defense forces. The Ministry of Local Government and Community Development initiated the concept of a civilian defense force at the smallest unit of local government—the *barangay*. Provincial officials and mayors were called to Manila for a month-long training. Then seminars were held at the barangay level throughout the country. Physical exercise, repetition of New Society slogans, and silent meditation on the meaning of the New Society were all part of the week-long regimen. Members of a local Barangay Brigade described their graduation ceremony to us. "We were escorted at night, blindfolded, to the cathedral. Our blindfolds were taken off and lights were turned up on a picture of Ferdinand and Imelda Marcos and the Philippine flag. We were led up to the front of the church where we think we signed a pledge of allegiance to the New Society. It was in English, so we don't really know what we signed."

While some clergy worried that a cult of the Marcoses was being built, others laughed it off. Father Ben noted that where there was a strong Basic Christian Community, the Barangay Brigade did not affect the people. In Agdao, the youth formed a volunteer nightly guard in response to the seminar they had attended. A month later, the guard was disbanded. "We get very tired staying up all night. It's hard to go to work the next morning," explained one youth.

One important business enterprise in Agdao, as elsewhere around the country, was comic book rental. Comic books are probably the most popular reading material in the Philippines. The majority were written in Tagalog or Pilipino, the national language, and then translated into other languages of the Philippines. Cebuano was the most common language spoken in Agdao, for many people came from Cebu or surrounding Visayan islands. For fifteen centavos (about two American cents in early 1979) comic book aficionados could indulge their habit. Friends in the know told us that comic writers and publishers were strongly urged by the Marcos government censors to include a few favorable comments about the New Society in the story line.

Another feature in Agdao, common to most communities around the Philippines, was the presence of a small bread called *pandesal*. Little corner bakeries keep the pandesal hot for their customers. Children, helpers, or heads of households can be seen in the early morning line-up at the bake shop. Our neighbor, a pandesal vendor, came by at 5 A.M. with a giant version of this bun, which she left at our doorstep on her way to sell the remainder at the market. The size of her pandesal was unusual. Most pandesal were shrinking annually, reflecting the state of the economy, according to local punsters.

Many Agdao residents were vendors at the local markets. Others worked at the port or in the plywood factories. Several of our neighbors were jeepney drivers. The jeepneys in our neighborhood tended to be of the smaller size with virtually no decoration, whose routes were restricted to Davao City proper.

The section of Agdao we lived in was poor but certainly not the most depressed or desperate area in the city. In keeping with our neighbors' habits, we made a concerted effort to use everything and recycle as much as possible. Nevertheless, since the city did not provide sewage and garbage collection, we dug a little hole behind our house in which we threw whatever could not be recycled. Not every neighbor did that, but there did not seem to be a problem with garbage piling up.

People used extra newsprint as toilet paper. The vendors wrapped their goods in old newspaper. Backyard industries utilizing recycled materials abounded in the neighborhood. Old tires were cut into flowerpots. Little bottles were designed into mini kerosene lamps. One old man collected bottles to sell to a bottling plant. Another family kept a pig that fed on vegetable peelings and other discarded food.

I became even more sensitive about our wasteful habits after one particularly jarring event. Immediately after burning our garbage beside our house one day, I went inside, began to cry, and wrote in my journal:

> In a weekly ritual I separate the jars and tins, set aside the old envelopes to write on (we read somewhere that is what Gandhi did), give the stamps to a friend and fold up any plastic or paper bags. Then I walk with my cardboard box half full of waste to our garbage hole and light a match. Instantly a ring of children forms around the garbage hole, "Sayang! Sayang!" (What a pity, what a shame!) they murmur as they gaze longingly into the hole. Anxiously I peer into the flames. What have I thrown away that was so pre-

cious? All I can see are some leaflets with writing on both sides so I can't use them as scrap paper. One child kneels down and gingerly sticks her hand into the flame to retrieve the Kodak film cardboard container.

"Huwag!" (Don't!) I yell, "You'll burn yourself." The children look at me silently, reproachfully. I am burning valuable items, something their parents can use or they could play with and I have the nerve to yell at them. We stand together, they watching the flame as though it were a funeral pyre and I watching them to make sure they don't try to retrieve anything else. It seems to take forever.

Am I really throwing away so much? Angry that these children have come to expose my wastefulness and the wastefulness of the society from which I come, angry at the inequity which makes them careful and me wasteful, I want the moment to end, but the fire continues. A little boy goes past with a tin can nailed to a stick, probably recovered from my garbage pile. He proudly pushes it along the ground as though it were the latest model toy car. I want the children to go home, but how can I dismiss people at a wake, mourning my death producing habits of consumption?

It became patently clear to me that some of our neighbors lived on the edge of economic survival. Added to this hardship was the imminent danger of the demolition of their homes. During October and November of 1978, the government stepped up demolitions of "squatter" houses, including some in Agdao. Many of the people accused of being squatters were in reality tenants who for over ten years had been paying rent. Their landlords began refusing rent payments in order to accuse the tenants of squatting, so they could force them to leave and then develop the area into a modern shopping center.

Our neighbor, Alfredo, a gentle, soft-spoken man, was watching a demolition scene one day in November in another section of Agdao. People who refused to move from their houses were chased by police authorities. When one of the property owners began flourishing a gun and shooting into the air, Alfredo took down his name. By law, civilians are not supposed to be handling firearms. The owner then turned on Alfredo and he was hauled away to the police station for two hours of questioning and roughing up.

During the questioning Alfredo repeated that he was innocent; he had just taken pity on those whose houses were being destroyed. Before he was released, Alfredo was forced to sign a paper attesting to the fact that his human rights were not violated. This event took place only a few weeks before the official celebration of International Human Rights Day on December 10, in a year when President Carter's undersecretary for human rights, Pat Derian, was scheduled to pay a visit to the Philippines.

This was not Alfredo's first run-in with the authorities. Only months before, he had been given a conditional release after spending two years in prison. "They say I violated Republic Act 1700, the Anti-Subversion law. That means," Alfredo said, "that I have the wrong version of what is happening in our society. My sub-version is to create community where people care for each other and there is no oppression. The version of the ruling class is to exploit people for their personal gain. I know I should try to stay out of trouble since I just got out of jail, but how can I pretend to be deaf, blind, and speechless? "

As I listened to Alfredo's story, I remembered Rahab's subversion of her own city, Jericho. From her position at the periphery of her society, she was able to sense which way history was moving and she decided to take a chance with the two strangers against the Jericho establishment. She saved her life and that of her family. Deciding whose version of events to trust can be a life-and-death matter.

During the demolitions, I discovered that many families in Agdao and other urban poor communities were actually recent immigrants from the rural areas. Some, like Lita's family, had come to Davao from neighboring provinces when they were evicted from their land. Their version of life was bulldozed crops on the farm and bulldozed houses in the city. I realized I could not understand their present situation without looking at where they had come from. My friendship with Lita and Alfredo and others in Agdao pushed me into looking more closely at who controls the land and who controls commerce.

Our minuscule taste of life in an urban poor barrio was not an end in itself; the economic desperation of neighbors became a prod for us to grapple with the reasons why the people of Agdao and communities like it across the Philippines are forced to live the way they do.

3

Land

LIFEBLOOD OF THE FILIPINO PEOPLE

*Snat, one of the first men in the world, lived in a boat
with his companions. When the land was created and
Snat died, his companions got off the boat and buried
Snat. After a long while, rice began to grow from his
stomach. Reeds grew from his hair, corn grew from his
molar teeth, thick bamboo from his thighs and thin
bamboo from his legs. From Snat's head, grew coconut
trees. So, you see all plants come from Snat.*

—T'Boli tribal elder, Lake Sebu, South Cotabato

*Land reform programs by the government are launched
only when there is an insurgency. Insurgency is the
solution, not the problem.*

—Abe Padilla, Philippine anthropologist

*Fearful forces still haunt
Our hopes, half won and half aborted
Listen, there will be no peace
Till we reclaim our land.*

—KMP—Mindanao

Land forms the basis for livelihood for a large percentage of
Filipinos. The Philippine Constitutional Convention of 1981
found that 10 percent of the population owns 90 percent of
the land and 90 percent of the population is left with 10 percent of the land. For many of the tribal Filipinos across the
archipelago, land is not only a means of livelihood but also a

spiritual resource and a means of maintaining connectedness with their ancestors.

For example, in northern Luzon the Bontoc have struggled against a World Bank–funded dam that threatened to destroy their rice terraces and the land where the bones of their ancestors were buried. In the south, the T'Boli, a Filipino tribal group in Mindanao, faced the same prospect of destruction and countered with their own explanation of the meaning of land and development.

The homeland of the T'Boli is among three interconnected lakes—Lake Sebu, Lake Selotan, and Lake Lahit, seven hundred meters above sea level in the province of South Cotabato, a few hours' drive from the Dole plantations. Though most T'Boli do not hold legal title to this land, they have occupied it since long before the Philippine government, which now issues titles, ever existed. The T'Bolis trace their roots in the area back to creation, and their legend about Snat, one of the first men in the world, underlines the intimate relationship between the T'Boli and their ancestors—and the lakes and the land. The security of this relationship has helped to nurture T'Boli creativity, which is expressed in their music, dances, and crafts. The beauty of the people is in tune with the beauty of the land.

But this scenic paradise has not been undisturbed. Poor settlers from other islands, looking for land and a better life in Mindanao, have taken over fertile land around the lakes. One method of acquiring the land is to allow the T'Bolis to run up debts in the stores and offices and then require the land as payment. The T'Boli are forced to cultivate the steep hillsides, adding to the erosion already started by the indiscriminate logging practices of companies who have timber concessions in the mountains surrounding the lakes. Lowlanders from the neighboring town of Surallah have fenced off Lake Sebu for their duckeries and fishpens. Thus the lake, which the T'Boli believe was given into their care by God, is no longer accessible to them.

In 1977 some T'Boli spotted National Power Corporation trucks and surveyors around the lakes. They were told that the riceland between the lakes would be flooded to form a reservoir for a hydroelectric dam fifty-six meters high. Though the plans were already in printed form, this was the first news the T'Boli received about the project. The project planners claimed that the development of Lake Sebu would not entail significant dislocation of population in the project area.

T'Boli leaders discussed the consequences of the project and decided it was not beneficial at this time for their people. They sent a petition to President Marcos and to the Asia Development Bank, which was funding the project. "If this land is flooded and our food supply destroyed, it will certainly kill us and our children, for where shall we go, since our brothers from the lowlands have already taken the choice lands that God had first given us?"

Only then did the national planners pay some attention to the fact that the land around the lakes was inhabited. A series of meetings took place between government officials and the T'Boli, during which the officials explained the benefits of the dam. "With electricity you can fry tilapia fish on an electric stove instead of an open fire. You can wash your clothes in an electric washing machine instead of in the river." The T'Bolis replied, "Where will we hang the lightbulbs? In the trees? We will have no houses if we are driven from the land." The average per capita income of the T'Boli is thirty dollars a year.

The government officials continued, "Electricity means progress and development. It will bring tourists, hotels, and cinemas." But the T'Bolis disagreed: "We have no need for tourists and hotels. We need roads—roads to get our products to market, so we can make a living for our families. We need hospitals for our sick." Twenty-five percent of T'Boli children do not survive beyond five years of age. Over 50 percent of them suffer from malnutrition.

"We would rather kill ourselves and our children than to witness the terrible destruction this dam would bring," said the T'Boli, brandishing their *bolos* during the meeting with government planners. Bolos are long curved knives that are the all-purpose tool for tribal Filipinos as well as lowland Filipino farmers.

Though funding for the dam is international, the T'Boli were most immediately pitted against other Filipinos who have wholeheartedly accepted the capital-intensive, technical model of development. So the T'Boli are viewed as an obstacle to progress. However, their misgivings about the dam are substantiated by the results of hydroelectric and irrigation projects elsewhere in the country.

For example, the people displaced by the Pantabangan dam project in northern Luzon are living in poverty on barren hillsides, despite many assurances from the government.

During public discussions, the government technocrats defended their projects, saying, "It's unfortunate, but the few must be sacrificed for the benefit of the majority." These Manila-based technocrats who plan the infrastructure and development projects are, in effect, sacrificing the majority, the ordinary Filipino, for the benefit of the few foreign-controlled corporations and industries.

The T'Boli, through their petition, pointed to a different process of development. "We do think that real development has to be realized with the free participation of the common people, no matter how poor they are. Do we not have rights? Are we not Filipino citizens, capable of planning for our own future?"

Over fifty ethno-linguistic groups like the T'Boli were the least influenced by Christianity and Spanish culture and thus have sustained the closest links with their pre-Hispanic cultural heritage. These groups number about six million people, the majority of whom are still intimately tied to the land. In fact, more than 60 percent of all Filipinos are still rural based.

According to the 1985 study by the Philippine National Census and Statistics Office, of the 21.6 million Filipinos in the labor force, 10 million are employed in agriculture. Of these, 5 million are landless workers, 2 million are tenants, 1.5 million own the lands they are tilling, while another 1.5 million farm public lands without the benefit of a title.

A government study conducted by the National Economic and Development Authority also found that the average six-month family income of the bottom 30 percent of farm families was 5,151 pesos (20 pesos = 1 dollar). The expenditure for the same period was 5,931 pesos. So, every six months, these families are 780 pesos deeper in debt as they try to meet their basic needs.

The inequity in land ownership and the resulting poverty of rural Filipinos forms the basis for agrarian unrest and discontent. The majority of the armed insurgents in the Philippines come from the rural peasant population. The founder of the Communist Party of the Philippines, Jose Maria Sison, who was released from prison when Mrs. Aquino came to power in 1986, said at that time that if the government instituted a solid land reform program, there would be no reason for the insurgents to continue fighting.

What is the genesis of this uneven control and use of land? What are the possibilities for a shift in ownership and use?

The Spanish explorer Ferdinand Magellan arrived in 1521 at Mactan, an island that was part of the Pacific archipelago south of China later to be named the "Philippines" after Spanish King Philip II. The actual colonization of the islands began over forty years later in 1565 with a Spanish expedition headed by Miguel Lopez de Legazpi. The Spaniards found and subdued generally small communities, known as *barangays*, headed by village chiefs called *datus*, who acted as administrative leaders. These communities were at various stages of transition when the Spanish arrived.

Below the datus and their families in status were the nobles or *maharlika*. Filipino historian Renato Constantino uses the term *freemen* to describe the layer of society below the chiefs. Freemen assisted the administrative leader in tasks that often involved the welfare of the community. Below the freemen was the *dependent population*, a term that connotes a gentler version of debt peonage—laborers bound in servitude because of a debt. The early Spaniards misleadingly called these people slaves, but the relationship was much more like a family with an authoritarian father. The debt was not simply economic, but psychological as well. It formed the basis of what has come to be known as *utang na loob*, a debt of gratitude that still binds some tenants to their landlords.[1]

The Spanish built upon these emerging feudal structures and incorporated them into their colonial apparatus. They established *encomiendas*, geographically based administrative units whose purpose was to extract tribute from the natives. By 1572, when he died, Legazpi had assigned 143 encomiendas to his men. Each *encomendero*, in whose care a native settlement was entrusted, was to maintain peace and order, support the missionary work, and help in the defense of the colony. To finance these obligations, tribute was collected from the natives within the territory, usually by the native chiefs who then would forward it to the encomendero.[2]

Spanish colonial rule helped to deepen and solidify the emerging class divisions. For example, the *bandala* was the

1. Renato Constantino, *The Philippines: A Past Revisited* (Manila: Tala Publishing Services, 1975), pp. 24-43. Also helpful for data during the Spanish rule is John Leddy Phelan, *The Hispanization of the Philippines: Spanish Aims and Filipino Responses, 1565–1700* (Madison: University of Wisconsin Press, 1959).

2. Constantino, *The Philippines: A Past Revisited*, pp. 40-41.

assignment of an annual quota to each province for the compulsory sale of products to the government. Even if there was a bad harvest, people were forced to sell their quota to the government. This meant that each household had to purchase rice in order to give it to the government on credit. The excessive assessments forced many natives to become indebted to the village chiefs from whom they borrowed. This more indirect rule by the Spanish in the Philippines was in contrast to their colonial style in Mexico. The class structure in native Filipino society thus remained more cohesive than in Mexico with the result that the village chief's economic and social position became even more entrenched.[3]

The native chieftains not only acted as intermediaries between the material demands of the Spanish regime and the productive capacities of the people, but they also became the local political administrators. Thus in the Spanish colonial exploitation process, the Filipino chieftains played a high-profile role. They continued that role during the American colonial period and during the Japanese occupation in the 1940s. After the country's flag independence in 1946, the Filipino elite acted not simply as intermediaries but also as representatives or junior partners of the international businesses that moved into the country to exploit natural resources and cheap labor.

For the first two hundred years of Spanish rule, the Philippine colony remained largely a missionary and military way station for Spain. Manila was essentially a trans-shipment port for the trade between Mexico and China. Philippine products were not in great demand in China or Mexico, so Philippine Spaniards did not find it profitable to develop local products for export. The friars, members of various Roman Catholic orders, most notably the Augustinian and Dominican, acquired land through royal bequest, purchase, and outright land-grabbing early in the colonizing process. By 1800 rural society was characterized by a three-tiered hierarchy consisting of Spanish priest, the families of the village chiefs, and the masses.

Various landlaws provided for an easy way of registering land and obtaining title, as well as giving legal sanction to land-grabbing. Landholders were given one year within which

3. This is John Leddy Phelan's argument in *The Hispanization of the Philippines*, based on comparative studies of the effects of Spanish colonialism in Mexico.

to register and secure a legal title. After the deadline, untitled lands were deemed forfeit. Naturally, only those who knew about the decrees could take advantage of the law and register their land. The traditional village chiefs were quick to take advantage of the opportunities opened to them by the concept of private property that the Spanish introduced. *In the late 1800s, at least four hundred thousand persons lost their lands because they failed to acquire title to them.*[4]

Vast tracts of land were amassed not only through land-grabbing, expedited by the landlaws, but also through royal grants. Two large haciendas (estates or plantations) were established by royal grant in Luzon. The most famous one, Hacienda Luisita, is still owned by Cory Cojuangco Aquino's family. The Cojuangcos, like many of the leading economic and political families in the Philippines, are Chinese mestizos—products of intermarriage between Filipino natives and Chinese people and between the Spanish and Chinese. The Chinese from the mainland moved to the Philippines during the first two hundred years of Spanish rule when trade between China and Mexico flourished. The Chinese mestizos began by acquiring many of the smaller parcels of land and by the twentieth century had replaced the Spaniards as owners of the large haciendas.

Though the establishment of the haciendas and their style of management were rooted in the original religious estates controlled by the friars, some customs were modified to accomodate the new capitalist developments. For example, a fundamental transformation of Philippine economic life took place during the period from 1820 to 1870, with the development of an export crop economy featuring tobacco from the north, sugar from western Visayas, and abaca from the Bicol region.

The successful economic position of the Chinese mestizos provided them with the social status to take the leadership of the emerging Filipino society. From their ranks came many *illustrados*—wealthy, educated liberals who played an important role in the movement for reform and revolution. These children of the wealthy Chinese-Spanish had a liberal education in Spain, a country whose intellectual life was in-

---

4. Donald E. Douglas, "Historical Survey of Land Tenure Situation in the Philippines," Solidarity Publication, Manila, the Philippines (July 1970).

fluenced by the French revolution. The illustrados were deeply aware of the Spanish exploitation and, unlike other classes in society, had the means at their disposal to challenge the colonizers.

These shifts and changes within the economic and political life of the Spanish colony affected only those Filipinos living in the coastal cities and towns. Others simply moved further into the interior and higher into the mountains, away from the control of the church, which was the principal means of colonial control in the latter period of Spanish colonial rule.

The tribal Filipinos in the interior, like the T'Boli, continue to hold their land in a somewhat communal fashion, practicing swidden agriculture. Farmers slash and burn the underbrush, plant crops, and then move as a community to another plot within a large, but somewhat bounded area. Within a generation, sometimes within a matter of years, the farmers return to the first area they planted, which is again overgrown, and they begin the process once more. This gives the delicate ecology of the rain forest and the thin layer of topsoil a chance to replenish itself between plantings. The groups practicing this lifestyle assume that those who till the soil reap the fruits of their labor. The western concept of private property is somewhat alien to them.

For example, in the 1970s when Herminio Disini, a Marcos crony, was given forest rights in Abra to supply his Cellophil Corporation with logs, the native people of the province, the Tingguian, objected. The story is told that Disini's spokesman showed the Tingguian leaders his title to the land. They looked at it for awhile and replied, "Fine, the piece of paper is yours to use; the forest is ours to use."

When the American colonizers took over the country at the turn of this century, they built on the existing political and economic structures left by the Spanish. In order to encourage export crop production, agricultural land was underassessed and undertaxed and agricultural products were exempted from tax assessment. These exemptions again strengthened the Filipino landed elite. Their enhanced prosperity gave them a definite stake in the American colonial set-up and thus they became the most stable allies of American colonialism. Many were recruited into the colonial bureaucracy and into political office. Filipino historian Renato Constantino explains the economic result for the Philippines of this American strategy:

The demand for export crops was a powerful stimulus for more purchases by landowners. Hacenderos enlarged their holdings and intensified exploitation to take fuller advantage of the demand for their products under free trade conditions. Thus the hacienda system that had been born as a result of capitalist linkage during the Spanish occupation was strengthened under the American rule. The tenancy problem worsened during the same period.[5]

In the first decades of American rule, the economy of the Philippines was rapidly integrated into the American economy. In 1899 the Philippines purchased only 9 percent of its total imports from the United States. By 1933 the proportion had risen to 64 percent. In 1899, 18 percent of Philippine exports went to the United States. By 1933, exports to the United States had risen to 83 percent, the majority of which were agricultural products.

The knitting together of the two economies was interrupted by the Japanese takeover of the Philippines during the Second World War. American carpet bombing of areas of the country left the Philippines and its economy in ruins by the end of the war. Political economist Cheryl Payer views the interruption as an opportunity for the Philippines to have rebuilt its economy along diversified industrial lines.

The Japanese occupation had severed the umbilical cord of free trade which had tied the Philippines to the United States since 1909 and had tailored the output and the consumption of the Philippine economy to American markets and American supplies. The effect of thirty years as an American colony had been the creation of the classical colonial relationship with the Philippines supplying raw materials, mostly agricultural—sugar, coconut products, hemp, cordage—and importing industrial products from the mother country.[6]

This opportunity to build a diversified economy that would not have to rely on agricultural exports did not materialize. The Filipino elite continued to dominate the political decision-making process in the newly independent republic. Philippine president Manuel Roxas, convinced that the Philippines could

5. Constantino, *The Philippines: A Past Revisited*, p. 300.
6. Cheryl Payer, *The Debt Trap: The International Monetary Fund and the Third World* (New York: Monthly Review, 1974), p. 50.

not survive, much less rehabilitate its economy, without American aid and investment, journeyed to Washington in 1946 to make his appeal. He told Americans,

> Although the color of our skin is brown, the temper of our mind and heart is almost identical with yours. . . . You have in us a protagonist of your political and economic system—a broadcasting station for Americanism.[7]

The American Congress and administration exacted a high price for the aid that Roxas requested. A provision was tacked onto the Philippine Rehabilitation Act prohibiting war damage compensation pending the Philippine Congress's acceptance of the Bell Trade Act. This act reimposed free trade, granted U.S. citizens the same rights as Filipinos in the exploitation of natural resources in the country, and pegged Philippine currency to the American dollar, which effectively took fiscal control out of the hands of the Philippine government.

The relationships between the main players—the American government, American business, the Filipino elite leadership, and the Filipino people—were essentially the same after independence as they had been during the colonial period. The Filipino elite cooperated with the foreign power—Spanish, American, or Japanese—in exchange for some political or economic benefit to themselves. The victims of these relationships were the majority of the people in the Philippines—those whom Renato Constantino called the "dependent population" at the time of the Spanish incursion.

Though the elite made their peace with the Americans, the Filipino masses, most notably the peasants of Central Luzon, followed their own course of action. The land tenure system was probably the most compelling reason for the unrest. Though there were sporadic and halfhearted attempts by the American regime to help the landless, the tenancy rate in the central plains increased sharply in the twentieth century—from 38 percent in 1903 to 67 percent of all Pampango farms in 1939.[8]

7. Renato and Letizia Constantino, *The Philippines: The Continuing Past* (Manila: Foundation for Nationalist Studies, 1978), p. 201.

8. Eduardo Lachica, *Huk: Philippine Agrarian Society in Revolt* (Manila: Solideridad Publishing House, 1971), p. 41. The peasant resistance before and after the Second World War centered in Pampanga, Central Luzon.

A communist-led militant peasants group popularly known as "Huks," who before the war had confronted oppressive land-lords in Central Luzon, formed guerrilla resistance units against the Japanese during the occupation from 1941 to 1945. After the Japanese had been driven out and Gen. Douglas MacArthur returned to the Philippines, there was an attempt to disarm the Huk squadrons and imprison some of their leaders. However, the *Hukbo ng Bayan Laban sa Hapon* (Army of Resistance against Japan) became the *Hukbong Magpapalaya ng Bayan* (People's Liberation Army), still "Huk" in popular parlance.

The Huks opposed the agreements made with the American government by President Roxas and the Philippine Congress through parliamentary means. When that proved unsuccessful—the Democratic Alliance with whom the Huks aligned were outmaneuvered and their duly elected representatives were unseated—the Huks shifted to more exclusively armed struggle. In early 1950, the Huks were at the height of their strength and posed a real threat to the arrangements made by the Philippine and American governments and business.

Luis Taruc, son of Pampangan peasants and a Socialist leader in the coalition of groups that formed the Huk resistance, explained the basic reason for their struggle:

> For centuries "land for the landless" has been the peasants' cry and the peasants' hunger for land has been our nation's most pressing problem. This has led to the common saying among our people that social justice can be achieved only by one of two ways; either a land reform or a revolution. Our history of the past four centuries is one of successive uprisings and their basic cause has always been the peasants' hunger for land.[9]

American advisors in the Philippines in the late 1940s preferred land reform to revolution, after watching China become communist in 1949 and seeing the French colonial power threatened in Vietnam. Their hope was that some internal land reform could head off a revolution that might threaten American investments, trade, or use of military installations.

9. Lachica, *Huk*, p. 41, citing Philippine Senator Manuel Manahan's report by the Committee on National Defense and Security to the Sixth Congress of the Philippines, May 1967.

The U.S. Mutual Security Administration's land tenure specialist, Robert S. Hardie, studied the problem in order to make recommendations for the Philippines. The Hardie Report recommended no less than the abolition of the institution of tenancy. The Philippine elite, many of whom were in the Philippine Congress, were concerned with the preservation of their own property interests. They bitterly opposed the Hardie recommendations. The speaker of the Philippine House of Representatives denounced Hardie as a communist.

As a result of the counterinsurgency program designed by CIA operative Edward Lansdale and implemented by Philippine secretary of national defense and later president, Ramon Magsaysay, the Huk threat receded. The United States was then willing to accommodate its Philippine allies by discarding the Hardie Report. Hardie was recalled from Manila in August 1953.[10]

What contributed to the defeat of the Huk insurgency, in addition to a revitalized military, was the appearance of reform and the illusion of social change. Magsaysay was able to capture the Huk's image of land for the landless through his Economic Development Corps (EDCOR). EDCOR was ostensibly designed to resettle Huk surrenderees in public lands, providing them with some initial assistance.

This program was heralded with much fanfare, but only 1,000 families were resettled and only 246 of them were ex-Huks. Many of the others were retired military personnel. Philippine historian Renato Constantino says,

> As a program to help the landless, EDCOR's impact was negligible, but as propoganda it was a big success. Magsaysay's well publicized visits (he personally accompanied the first settlers to Mindanao), the posters, pamphlets and films depicted EDCOR farms as the promised land—all these offered hope to poor tenants everywhere and to Huk supporters in particular.[11]

In tandem with the cosmetic land reform program, Magsaysay instituted rural community development plans. The Americans saw this program as a more effective and immediate way

10. Stephen R. Shalom, "Counter-Insurgency in the Philippines," in Daniel B. Schirmer and Stephen Rosskamm Shalom, eds., *The Philippines Reader* (Boston: South End Press, 1987), pp. 111-23.

11. Constantino, *The Philippines: A Past Revisited,* p. 241.

of attaining their objectives. The CIA recruited Gabriel Kaplan, a New York lawyer and businessman, to help CIA operative Edward Lansdale elect Ramon Magsaysay president of the Philippines. Kaplan steered some of "his boys," as he called them, into community development. One of those "boys" was Jaime Ferrer, who began organizing community centers in 1953. Ferrer had earlier headed the National Movement for Free Elections (NAMFREL) created by the CIA to help elect Magsaysay.

In his memoirs concerning the 1950 period, CIA official Joseph Burkholder Smith describes the financial backing for one CIA community development scheme, the Presidential Assistant for Community Development (PACD). The U.S. aid mission approved $4.2 million for this community development, which the CIA directed.

> An ingenious scheme was worked out whereby the United States foreign aid agency supplied the bulk of the funds for the project while CIA paid the key officials and provided special funds for certain selective activities designed to build up future political leaders upon whom we could count.[12]

EDCOR, the land reform program with plenty of publicity and very little substance, together with community development funds from the U.S. government, effectively undercut the Huk insurgency. Philippine anthropologist Abe Padilla aptly describes one side of the 1950s land reform efforts: "Land reform programs are launched by the government only when there is an insurgency." In the 1950s the more insidious side of this program was the conscious use of a reform package to reach into the internal affairs of a supposedly sovereign nation and manipulate its local political process.

Thirty-four years after completing his work in local community development for the CIA, Jaime Ferrer was appointed minister of local government in the Aquino administration, a key position from which he worked to create vigilante groups across the country to fight communism. The result has been terrifying human rights abuses, including beheadings of civilians by these local vigilantes. Filipino nationalist groups are more aware of CIA manipulations in the 1980s, having had

---

12. Joseph Burkholder Smith, *Portrait of a Cold Warrior* (New York: G. P. Putnam's Sons, 1976), pp. 252-53.

the benefit of the 1950 machinations publicized through the CIA officers' memoirs.

The land issue in the Philippines is never very far from the political process, whether it be democracy or dictatorship. It was the promise of land reform if he had a free hand to implement it that gave Mr. Marcos his primary excuse for the imposition of martial law. Marcos proclaimed martial law on September 21, 1972, promising that land reform would be the cornerstone of the New Society (Bagong Lipunan). His agrarian program applied only to rice and corn lands, seven hectares or larger, and required farmers to pay over a twenty-five-year amortization period. Many large landowners switched from rice and corn to other crops to avoid losing their land through the land reform act. Later in the decade, Marcos required corporations to grow rice and corn in order to help meet the need for these crops. Seven hundred twenty-two large, mostly foreign firms held 216 hectares each in corporate farms (1 ha. = 2.2 acres).

Under the Marcos land reform program, almost 90 percent of its beneficiaries—small farmers—defaulted on their payments because of the high amortization rate. The program resulted in the transfer of 1,500 hectares of rice and corn lands to some sixteen hundred tenants. As a result of the corporate farming program, however, 47,801 hectares were transferred to seventy corporate farms. Tenants in these lands were displaced to accommodate the incursion of the corporate farms, both foreign and domestic.[13] When it soon became clear that the New Society land reform program was without substance, the peasants formed the backbone of the early opposition to the Marcos regime.

Militant peasant organizations, local and regional and even national at some points, have existed for centuries with varying success. At various times in Philippine history when the peasants have aligned with the illustrados, the educated liberal upper and middle class, they have been abandoned when the elite decided they could benefit from cooperating with a foreign power.

Thus the founding of a National Peasants Union, the Kilusang Magbubukid ng Pilipinas (KMP), on July 27, 1985,

13. Ernst Feder, Perverse Development (Manila: Foundation for Nationalist Studies, 1983), pp. 119-24.

marked a quantum leap in organizational reach and political intensity in the peasant movement. The KMP has a membership of 750,000 peasants organized in twelve regional and thirty-nine provincial chapters. There are seventy-three provinces and ten million agricultural workers in the Philippines.

Through a combination of militant action and concrete alternative programs, the KMP, a legally registered organization, has been able to reduce land rent by almost 50 percent in most of its organized areas. Interest payments to usurers have been reduced 30-50 percent, according to KMP estimates. The KMP has held week-long marches to Manila in order to present their demands and to negotiate with government ministries of agriculture and agrarian reform. Peasants walk for days from north and south to join together in the capital city.

In October 1985, thousands of farmers massed in the city, camping on the steps of some of the stately government buildings near Luneta Park. I was in Manila at the time with a Mennonite Central Committee study tour. We went to speak with the farmers one evening. The only light was provided by torches perched on long poles spread throughout the crowd. Faces of men, women, and young people near the torches could be seen in outline and flickering form. The entire expanse of the majestic steps leading to the main entrances of the stone building was filled with huddled bodies. A crackling loudspeaker based on the flatbed of a truck was used to announce the arrival of the various provincial chapters from around the country.

"Are these the insurgents?" asked one Mennonite pastor rather nervously. "No, this is an unarmed national citizen organization of peasants, but I will bet anything that you will read about them as subversives in the newspapers within the next few days."

Fortunately for the pastor, Mennonites don't engage in betting. The next day, as the farmers marched down Taft Avenue, they were shot at by unidentified men from a rapid transit platform. A police van moved directly into the marchers, separating the leadership at the front of the march from the bulk of the farmers. Farmers threw stones at the police to keep them at bay, while some of their rank tried to pull their wounded to safety. The headlines in the paper and the television news reported the incident as proof of communist subversion in the country.

Joel Rodriguez, executive director of the Forum for Rural Concerns and deputy secretary general of the KMP, points to a different perspective on the reasons for the farmers' militancy:

> It was mainly through their [the farmers'] silent labor that the Philippines ranked fourteenth among the world's largest food producers in 1985. Their combined production tonnage was more than enough to feed our present population for one whole year. . . . However statistics show that the average urban income is 60% higher than the average rural income. Eighty-five per cent of rural households live below the poverty level. . . . Much of the problem is traced back to landlessness or lack of sufficient land. In Mindanao, 80% of the tillers are non-owners. In the Visayas, seven out of 10 farmers do not own land. In Central Luzon—the show window of all past regimes' land reform programs—five out of 10 rice farmers still do not own the land.[14]

When Cory Aquino became president on February 25, 1986, the farmers' union was hopeful that their lot in society would improve. Jaime Tadeo, the president of the KMP, said,

> When Cory Aquino came to power, we were strongly convinced that she will implement genuine land reform. . . . I remember when we were preparing the KMP's program for genuine land reform, we invited Mr. Angel Baking, a former peasant leader and guerrilla (Huk period), as a guest speaker to comment on our program and on President Aquino. . . . Mr. Baking posed a question to us: "Do you think Cory Aquino can afford to be a traitor to her own class?" As you know her family owns one of the biggest sugar estates in the country, the Hacienda Luisita. . . . The question then was hard to answer because we perceived Cory as a genuine and honest leader who really cares for the common people.[15]

Based on the assumption of Cory's care for the common people, the KMP initiated dialogue with her Ministry of Agrar-

14. Joel Rodriguez, lecture delivered at De La Salle University, February 18, 1987.
15. Interview with Jaime Tadeo by *SIMBAYAN (Church for the People) Newsmagazine*, published by the Ecumenical Center for Development, first quarter, 1987.

ian Reform. Thousands of peasants came to the ministry offices in January to press for a firm land reform program.

On January 22, 1987, the farmers marched to Malacanang Palace to try to meet with Mrs. Aquino, after they felt that their attempts to negotiate with the Minister of Agrarian Reform, Heherson Alvarez, were unsatisfactory. They were met at Mendiola Bridge, which leads to the palace, by the police and military, who opened fire on the crowd. Twenty-two farmers and supporters were killed and at least sixty were wounded. Televison clips on the evening news showed police in their vehicles pursuing the fleeing farmers and shooting. Foreign journalists and visiting international church people provided eyewitness accounts of the police aggression. The nation was shocked at the open brutality against unarmed civilians.

A booklet published by the National Council of Churches in the Philippines explains the impasse leading up to the Mendiola massacre:

> Relations between the government and the KMP soured most visibly in the period of January 15-21, 1987. . . . In the cross purposes of intent and timing, negotiations went badly. . . . Where the KMP was earnest and impatient, the MAR [Ministry of Agrarian Reform] was busy and a trifle wary. The KMP was used to organizing its grievances into pressure politics. Many of its members had already taken over abandoned lands—with the benefit of only their sense of right and wrong. Bureaucracies bored them. They understood only concrete action. The MAR on the other hand . . . did not lift a decisive hand without consulting, coordinating or cooperating with some government agency, bureau, department or ministry.[16]

President Aquino ordered an investigation into the killings, but the KMP became even further disillusioned when the investigating committee found Jaime Tadeo guilty of provocation. Officers testified that they could not identify their men in the photos foreign journalists had taken of police aiming pistols at the crowd.

Tadeo, expressing the desperation of the farmers, said, "While officials talk, we go hungry. While they make us wait for due process, we die every day." However, as a direct result

---

16. Jo-Ann Maglipon, ed., *The Mendiola Tragedy* (Manila: National Council of Churches–Philippines, 1987), p. xxvii.

of the January 22 killings, Malacanang Palace opened its doors to a dialogue with the KMP on their Minimum Program for Land Reform.

The Aquino government's Agrarian Reform Ministry had begun in 1986 by simply accelerating the Marcos land reform program. The KMP proposal was to terminate the amortization and immediately to distribute titles to tillers. In addition, the KMP proposed free distribution of land improperly acquired by the deposed dictator and his cronies, idle or abandoned lands, lands foreclosed by the banks, and logged-over areas.

The KMP has always advocated free land distribution, arguing that the farmers have more than paid for the land they till through exorbitant land rent exacted by the landlords for so many years. Since May 1986, KMP barrio units have sequestered thousands of hectares of idle, abandoned, and crony-owned lands and have given them to the tillers.

In March 1987, when I visited the sugar-growing island of Negros, Bishop Antonio Fortich told the group of American human rights lawyers I was with, "It is high time our lady president is more serious about land reform. The blood is running. The peasants do not want a plastic solution to a real problem. Cory should make a decree about land reform before the Congress takes office in July and her decree-making powers are dissolved. There are too many landowners in Congress to make helpful laws for the landless."

In fact, Mrs. Aquino did prepare a decree called the Comprehensive Agrarian Reform Program (CARP) in June 1987, a few weeks before Congress convened. It is remarkably similar to the Marcos decree on land reform. The additional land beyond rice and corn fields and government lands it marks for use is the sequestered land of Marcos and his business cronies who fled the country after February 1986.

The KMP has taken over seventy thousand hectares of these crony lands since July 1986. However, Mrs. Aquino's decree disqualifies any "persons who illegally enter and occupy land covered by the program after January 1, 1986." So the 250,000 KMP peasants who moved onto the land and are already benefitting from their "homemade" land reform will be disqualified and forced to move.

The *Manila Chronicle,* a Manila-based daily newspaper, reported on July 4, 1986, that "in San Jose, Occidental Mindoro, Aquafil Corp., from which KMP members have taken over some 1000 hectares, destroyed the rice cultivated by KMP members by pumping sea water into the ricelands." The farmers viewed Aquino's Comprehensive Agrarian Reform Program as an endorsement of the harassment of its members who have taken over agricultural lands.

When Mrs. Aquino's decree was publicized and the large landowners began moving against the farmers, a KMP spokesperson warned, "If the peasants are ejected because of this agrarian reform decree, they will fight." Hungry people are desperate people. They will grow food where and how they can and they will work with those powers who have a genuine plan for security and livelihood.

The peasants are keenly aware of the duplicity of the native chieftains and *illustrado* allies throughout Philippine history, which only deepened the rural inequities. In the light of this history, it is only understandable that many farmers are saying, as KMP chairperson, Jaime Tadeo, said in February 1987, "We do not hold any illusion about the government being able to implement genuine land reform laws. We have become firmer in our belief that it is only through the peasants' own strength that genuine land reform can become a reality."

On June 7, 1988, the Philippine Congress passed a land reform bill, Republic Act 6657, which claims to grant land to the tiller but is riddled with enough loopholes, omissions, and contradictions as to render it meaningless. The bill allows for a lengthy period of implementation, exempts most lands from redistribution, allows landlords to avoid redistribution through incorporation and sale of stocks to tenants and workers, and allows multinational corporations to maintain control of key areas of agricultural production. Its provisions will likely lead to inflated landlord compensation agreements which could bankrupt the whole program.[17] Congressman Bonifacio Gillego, one of the sponsors of the original bill, ended up disowning the amended version which passed, calling it a "grand deception on the people."

News of the farmers' land reform initiatives, which are independent of the government's, reached the Manila and international press in 1986 and 1987. However, the reality of their

17. Based on an analysis by Dr. Walden Bello, "New Law Fosters Grand Illusion of Land Reform," *Philippine Monitor* (published by Philippine Resource Center), June 22, 1988.

agrarian reform started much earlier. In 1980, I visited a farmers' cooperative in a remote area of Davao del Norte in Mindanao. After supper, the farmers gathered around the flickering kerosene flame to talk with their American visitor. The glowing mosquito coil balanced precariously on a Pepsi bottle was a small sign of "affluence" in this outlying barrio.

During the introductions, I told the farmers that I had come to learn from them. They took my words seriously and plied me with questions about life in America. "Is it true that Americans don't know their neighbors? How can you organize? Here we must know everyone and we must know if we can trust them. A discontented neighbor can easily inform the military about our activity. That could mean our lives," said the president of the cooperative.

In the houses of co-op members I had visited I noticed gigantic barrels filled with rice, though it was almost harvest time. Usually by this time of year a farm family has depleted its supply and is waiting for the new crop. The farmers explained, "Since we don't have to pay the landlord, we aren't forced to sell to the middleman at harvest time when the price is so low."

"Oh, you own the land. How did you manage that?" I asked. "Well, we don't have Manila government titles," they grinned. "We just made our own agrarian reform."

Farmers who try to accomplish land reform through nonviolent direct action are shot at and killed in the streets of the capital city when they participate in an unarmed demonstration. Those farmers who quietly proceed as though they own the land they till are also in grave danger. Local farmers realize that they will need a power or authority beyond their barrio initiatives in order to succeed. The main power centers within the Philippines are the civilian government and its military; the National Democratic Front and its military, the New People's Army; and the church. The main power outside of the Philippines is the United States. Each of these power centers is faced with decisions about how to respond to the problem of land and livelihood for the majority of Filipinos.

The farmers, too, are faced with choices. They will choose what they conclude is the best option to help them secure their land, their economic livelihood, and their safety.

That reality struck me quite forcibly while I was guiding a tour group organized by the Center for Global Education, based at Augsburg College in Minnesota, in February 1986. Most of the participants came from the readership of *Seeds*, a hunger and development magazine based in a Southern Baptist church in Georgia, and from the readership of *The Other Side*, a justice magazine that has strong evangelical Christian roots. A few days after they arrived in the Philippines, the tour members met with tribal Filipinos who had been forced to flee from their mountainside homes because of military operations.

The evacuees were bunched together under makeshift shelters and in homes of relatives on the outskirts of Cagayan de Oro City in Mindanao. They had been there for several months with very little prospect of returning home and even less prospect of making a living in their new situation. Their faces and stories brought home the reality of their misery. One member of our group, a Minnesota farmer, told me early in the trip that he was in danger of losing his land because the bank was threatening to foreclose on his mortagage. Until the day we encountered the evacuated farmers, he resisted any information that he considered "political" or anti-American. Surrounded by the sad faces of men, women, and children, he blurted out, "This is terrible that you can't stay on your farms. I am going back to the States and I will tell Reagan not to send any more guns to the Philippine military." The farmer himself looked surprised at his strong "political" statement. He had seen his own future in their plight.

But the scene was not over. One of the young male refugees who had remained silent throughout most of the discussion suddenly responded with blazing eyes, "No, don't do that. If Reagan wants to send guns, tell him to send us the guns instead. If we had had guns, we could have defended our right to stay in our own houses and on our farms. Then we could have eaten what we planted. We wouldn't be here, dependent on others for food and housing."

The Minnesota farmer looked hurt; the rest of the tour participants looked stunned. There was a flurry of conversation among the evacuees in the tribal dialect. As I watched this encounter between sympathetic Americans who were hearing firsthand the stories of inequity and repression, perhaps for the first time, and the Filipino farmers who had lived these stories for generations, I felt the enormous gap between the two sides. Time was running out. The choices were narrowing.

4

Castle and Cooke

CASE STUDY OF A MULTINATIONAL
IN THE PHILIPPINES

Sixty-five per cent of children below six years of age in banana plantations are either mildly, moderately or severely malnourished.

>—Banana Export Industry Foundation study in Philippines, January 1979

Those who believe in capitalism must fight back. . . . We practice good business and good citizenship in every country. As a result, we are welcomed by the people and governments, wherever we are involved.

>—The late D. J. Kirchhof, former president of Castle and Cooke Inc. (Dole) in *Barron's National Business and Financial Weekly*, 19 February 1979

Dolefil is in the long run a national liability; the threat of violence will hang over the country so long as the multinationals operate plantations while many Filipinos remain poor, hungry and landless.

>—Fr. Loreto G. Viloria, Prelature of Marbel, Philippines, 26 May 1980

In contrast to the vision portrayed in stereotypical ads of beautiful grass-skirted Hawaiian maidens by the sea with luscious golden pineapple slices in their hand, the scene in Polomolok, southern Philippines, the site of Dolefil operations, is one of dusty roads circling acre upon acre of two-foot high "spiky"

49

plants. In the fields on either side of the road are groups of workers dressed in long sleeves, long pants, hats, and sometimes face coverings. They stoop low to weed or bob up and down as they follow the huge mechanical harvesters. Pineapple planting and harvesting is a year-round project with planters, plowers, weeders, harvesters, and canners working almost eleven months of the year.

The more than seven thousand islands of the Philippines were formed through volcanic eruptions millions of years ago. The result is fertile flatland in the coastal regions and between some of the inland mountain ranges. The hot, humid, tropical climate is conducive to plant growth. In some areas of the country, like southern and central Mindanao, a steady rainfall pattern and protection from typhoons present an ideal situation for farming year-round. Other islands like Samar and Leyte in central Philippines and portions of Luzon and northeastern Mindanao lie in the regular pathways of seasonal typhoons, putting them at a disadvantage in agricultural production.

It is no accident that the bulk of international agribusiness is located in southern and central Mindanao, while Filipino tenant farmers annually dig out of the wreckage of typhoons in Samar and Leyte in the Visayas, the Bicol region in southern Luzon, and the Surigao provinces on Mindanao.

Castle and Cooke, which markets bananas and pineapples under the Dole label, is one such international agribusiness that operates plantations and processing plants in the typhoon-free provinces of southern Mindanao.

In 1977 my husband, Gene, and I went to the provinces of South Cotabato and Davao del Norte on the island of Mindanao, southern Philippines, to make an on-site report for the United Church Board for World Ministries (UCBWM), the overseas arm of the United Church of Christ. This denomination originally sent Samuel Northrup Castle and Amos Starr Cooke as missionaries to Hawaii in 1836.

The UCBWM, which holds shares in Castle and Cooke, joined forces in 1977 with the United Christian Missionary Society (Disciples of Christ) and the Passionist Congregation of the Philippines, a Catholic religious order, to present a shareholder resolution requesting public disclosure of basic information about the company's labor policies and practice abroad. They asked for information about wages and working conditions, worker-management relations, and their U.S. employment patterns in order to compare them with practices in the Philippines. The church leaders had gathered the business data and held meetings ahead of time with the corporate executives, but needed on-site data to fill out their report for the upcoming shareholders meeting.

We soon realized there was much more to be studied than could possibly be done in time for the shareholders meeting in March 1978. We made a cursory report and then spent the next few years gathering more data in the Philippines and the U.S. and from Latin America.

xWhat emerged from our study was the picture of an American agribusiness—the board of directors, the stockholders, the president, and the general managers are American—with a cluster of foreign branches, plants, and affiliates in Latin America and Asia. It is American based and American controlled, using subsidiaries in Third World countries to increase profits because wages and operating costs are much lower there than in the United States.

In addition to the growing, processing, and marketing of bananas and pineapples, Castle and Cooke is in several other markets. They package tuna fish under the Bumble Bee label and sell Bud Antle lettuce; they market mushrooms grown on large American farms, many in Michigan, utilizing low-paid immigrant labor. In the last twenty years this American conglomerate has diversified into real estate in Hawaii and California.

From its beginnings with missionaries Castle and Cooke in Hawaii, the organization has had intimate relationships with government officials—both American and those of the native Hawaiian royal house.[1] The company has used its political connections and relationships with Third World military and government juntas to its own advantage. It floundered economically, trying to expand through acquiring already-existing industries, and thus overreaching itself. It weathered hostile takeover bids and finally, in 1985, went the way of many modern conglomerates—it merged with another company, Flexi-

---

1. Frank J. Taylor, Earl M. Welty, and David Eyre, *From Land and Sea: The Story of Castle and Cooke of Hawaii* (San Fransisco: Chronicle Books, 1976). This book was commissioned by the board of directors of Castle and Cooke because they said, "We believe every business organization that has played an important role in the life of its community and area for a long time should have its history recorded."

Van, to avoid bankruptcy. As the 1986 corporate annual report described the transaction, "the merger was accounted for as a purchase by Flexi-Van although Castle and Cooke is the surviving legal entity with a new basis of accounting. . . . As a result of this reevaluation, Castle and Cooke's net assets were written up approximately $116 million."

Castle and Cooke is the quintessential American company, but with its own particularities. Thus it can serve well as a case study of the effect of a relatively large American corporation in a poor Third World country whose government is either not willing or not able to pursue an independent economic development course.

Samuel Castle and Amos Cooke, the former Congregationalist missionaries to Hawaii, turned their missionary zeal into entrepreneurial efforts in 1852 after the mission board decided to withdraw all financial help in 1849. Castle and Cooke operated the depository for the missionary families and started their own import supply business on the islands. In 1858, the partnership branched out from the mercantile business with its first investment in Hawaii's infant sugar industry. In 1932, Castle and Cooke reorganized and took over Jim Dole's company, Hawaiian Pineapple, after the already distressed company took a further downward turn. In 1964, Castle and Cooke purchased 55 percent of stock in Standard Fruit, which grew and exported bananas from Latin America. By 1968, Castle and Cooke had 100 percent ownership of the company.

Castle and Cooke began their business firmly rooted in Hawaii. In 1963, however, in order to increase profits by lowering labor and land costs, the company shifted its pineapple growing focus from Hawaii to eighteen thousand acres around the town of Polomolok, southern Philippines. Thousands of agricultural workers in Hawaii were left jobless; ironically, many of them were Filipinos who had been brought to Hawaii to work in the pineapple fields. Although first headquartered in Honolulu and now in Los Angeles, this American company is actually "supranational," with a sense of responsibility to its stockholders rather than to a geographical community or nation.

Setting up Dole Philippines (Dolefil) was part of a long-range plan to develop low cost pineapple farms in the Third World. Less than ten years after the move to the Philippines, Dolefil surpassed the Hawaiian operation in product and profits. In 1967 Standard Fruit opened banana plantations in

South Cotabato and Davao del Norte, Mindanao, under the name Standard Philippine Fruit or Stanfilco.

In 1852 the missionaries' company had assets of $7,113. By 1972 when it was firmly ensconced in Mindanao, Castle and Cooke had become a diversified multinational corporation with $563 million in assets and landholdings and subsidiaries in various countries around the world. The classic joke in Honolulu is, "Castle and Cooke came to do good. They got out doing very well." The company's 1986 annual report lists $1,519,403,000 or one and a half billion dollars in assets as of January 1987.

However, in the late 1970s and early 1980s, the company fell on hard times, partly because it decided to take out short-term loans with higher interest in order to expand more rapidly at a time when the international market for fresh fruit was saturated. It floundered in the early 1980s. Throughout the lean years, however, the Philippine subsidiaries continued to make money for the parent company.

Dolefil grows, processes, and exports fresh and canned pineapples to the United States, Europe, and the Middle East. Stanfilco grows bananas for export, mainly to Japan. On May 17, 1980, Stanfilco dissolved its corporate existence in the Philippines and merged with its sister company Dolefil.

Castle and Cooke management has cited transfer of technology, capital, and jobs as contributions that a multinational like itself makes to an impoverished country like the Philippines. We examined these claims and balanced them against other realities through the study of Dolefil and Stanfilco's own documents, government documents, interviews with workers, local church and government officials, and the company executives over a three-year period from 1977 to 1980.

More than fifty thousand people in Mindanao, southern Philippines, are involved in the growing and processing of bananas and pineapples, basically controlled by the three fresh fruit giants—Del Monte (owned by Reynolds), United Fruit (Chiquita label) and Dole. Approximately twelve thousand people are directly employed at Dolefil and thousands of others are employed by the "independent growers" who are actually an integral part of the total enterprise.

We interviewed the independent growers and looked at their monthly balance sheets. Mrs. Salas's situation is typical of what we found among the growers. She owns eleven hectares of land near General Santos City, South Cotabato. In 1968 she signed a production contract with Standard Philippine Fruit Company, Stanfilco, the Dole banana grower and exporter.

She has had a good harvest every year, but after ten years she had a debt to the company of $15,500. We began to understand the enormity of the debt when we realized that an elementary school teacher in the Philippines (one measure of middle-class income) earns about $100 a month.

Sales from Mrs. Salas's bananas are not enough to cover the costs of aerial spraying, fertilizers, and chemicals, charged to her by the company, and give her a fair income. When her contract ends she thinks she will have to renew because she has no way to get out of debt to the company. Even if she takes the land back she will have no money to level the ditches, plant alternative crops, and repay her debt.

In 1979, Stanfilco paid Mrs. Salas approximately eighteen cents for one box of bananas. We calcluated this as 1.6 percent of the final retail price in Japan. Stanfilco canvassers told her in 1968 that if she would sign up with the company, "Life would be good." Mrs. Salas was promised enough money for the best education for her nine children, a new car, a new house, and electric appliances. "Where is the car? Where is the college education? Where is the new house?" she asked us rhetorically when we interviewed her. "We are like dirty tenants in our own land."

The company contracted with people like Mrs. Salas to acquire land. They also set up other independent companies like Checkered Farms to grow bananas. By using local companies, Dole does not have to deal directly with land and labor difficulties. Filipino workers have to deal with Filipino management, even though the company is American. The effect on local people is telling. One older woman who rents out her land to the company had a litany of complaints about the unjust treatment she received. She ended with, "But I'm sure it's not the American owners who are doing this; it's the Filipino managers who are at fault."

Checkered Farms has approached small growers like Mrs. Salas, offering to assume her debts in return for leasing her land. "Why can Checkered Farms make money while we small growers are going further into debt?" asked Gregorio Naval, another small grower who got out of debt after two years of planting and assumed from then on it would be sheer profit. Ten years later, he too was indebted. Seventy-five percent of the small growers were in debt to the company.

The small growers association appealed to Stanfilco to change the terms of the agreement of cost and profit sharing to 30 percent for the farmers, 70 percent for the company. The former arrangement was 22-78. Fertilizer and irrigation charges have risen. The Philippine government's own agriculture office agreed with the growers' complaints, noting that Stanfilco's costs per hectare for fertilizer, pesticides, and irrigation were much higher than comparable costs on independent plantations.

Company officials told us in 1979 that the smaller growers outproduce Checkered Farms because they have better land. Checkered Farms is managed by the House of Investment, which has 33 percent interest in Stanfilco. Castle and Cooke has 17 percent equity in House of Investments.

We asked Mr. Naval about going independent. "I can't do that. I am not big enough to deal with the Japanese importer and I can't sell these giant cavendish bananas on the local market. Filipinos prefer our smaller, sweeter native varieties of bananas."

In a 1979 publicity brochure entitled "The Lives We Touch: Castle and Cooke's Presence Around the World," two pages are devoted to those who contract with Castle and Cooke. It says: "Some 25% of all the land producing pineapple for Dole is owned by local farmers who have contracted with Dole." Agapito Mabilangan from the town of Tupi, Philippines, is pictured with his family and in his testimony he says, "The land here was not good. Farmers could not plow because of the stones. I urged my neighbors with small holdings of eight hectares or less to contract so the land could be developed for growing pineapples. . . . My neighbors thanked me for opening their eyes. They and their families are better off and so is the entire community."

I showed this brochure to a retired teacher from Tupi. She was aghast at Mabilangan's statement that farmers could not plow because of stones. "I have been here since the 1940s. This has always been a fertile area," she said, and she brought out a song composed in 1955 by another teacher, Mrs. Patrocinio Ma. Marbas, to prove her point. Part of the lyrics read, "Come to Tupi, land of luscious fruits, land of healthful cli-

mate and of water pure and fresh, cabbage and potatoes, on-
ions and tomatoes, Thrive abundantly for you, Come to Tupi,
you will not regret." This song was sung in the community
school almost a decade before Dole arrived.

Much of Dole pineapple land is secured from the National
Development Corporation, a government company set up to
help companies like Dole acquire large tracts of land. Since
1963, Dole has paid only eight dollars a year per hectare. The
contract is for a twenty-five-year period, renewable for another
twenty-five-year period. Technically, the company owns no
Philippine land; it only controls it. By law a landowner in the
Philippines can require 25 percent of the crop as payment from
the tenant. Most tenants pay twice that much. We concluded
that Dole must be one of the most favored tenants in all the
Philippines.

Through the help of the local labor union, the Protestant
pastor, the parish priest, and lay catechists, we were able to
interview workers in some depth. We also talked with workers
more informally in the fields or while they waited for their rides
to the fields in the morning.

Mario Balayon's story is typical of many workers in the
Dole pineapple fields. He came to Polomolok seeking work
after his family lost their land to another corporation. On an
income of $40 per month he tries to support his wife and two
children. When we interviewed Mr. Balayon, D. J. Kirchhof,
then president of Castle and Cooke, was earning $300,000 a
year, plus benefits that included the dividends from his 16,749
shares in the company. The 1986 company report listed the
cash compensation of board chairman and chief executive officer David H. Murdock as $1,204,261. Murdock also controls
13,544,721 shares.

One third of Mario's salary goes for rice, another third for
other food. A small tin of pineapple juice costs about thirty-
two cents in the Philippines. The same amount will buy one
kilo of rice, enough to feed Mario's family for a day. Mario has
to work more than two hours in the pineapple fields to purchase a tin of pineapple or enough rice for one day.

Mario's house has no electricity; it is built from old pineapple boxes and has a corrugated tin roof. His wife carries
water from a distant tap for the household needs. The majority of company-provided housing is for management.

Superintendent-level and above live in a mountain country club estate called "Kalsangi." Huge suburban ranch-style houses dot the carefully manicured lawns. Kalsangi has a nine-hole golf course, tennis courts, swimming pool, and a restaurant for its residents and their guests. At that time the residents paid about 130 pesos in monthly rent (in 1979, 130 pesos = $18), which included water and electricity. "It's subsidized by Dole," beamed a happy Filipino mother, whose husband is in upper-level management.

Down the mountain from Kalsangi where the air is not quite so cool and the streets are not paved live the lower- and middle-level management in what is known as "cannery housing." Rent is about ten dollars monthly. A small playground and recreation building are provided for the workers' children.

At the beginning of its operations Dole built some small houses for its rank-and-file employees. These houses accommodate less than 2 percent of the hourly wage earners. The rest must seek accommodation where they can, often at exorbitant prices charged by local residents. Families in one section of Polomolok called "Little Tondo" (after a well-known slum in Manila) pay up to five dollars a month for one room.

When we asked Dolefil general manager Richard Wolford about the disparity between executive and employee housing standards and rents, he commented that, "If the board meeting were held in Little Tondo, probably some of our stockholders would be shocked, but the Kalsangi housing is important to attract the best qualified people to run the most sophisticated plant in the Philippines."

Mario's daily work on the pineapple plantation begins at 4:30 in the morning when he lines up to be checked off by a foreman. At 5:00 A.M. he is transported by truck to a company site where assignments are made. At 5:30 he is transported to the field where work begins at 6:00 A.M. He is not paid for this waiting time; when it rains there is no protection on the open trucks. If there is no overtime, the day ends at 3:00 P.M. but he often has to walk or hitch a ride home, so he may not be home until 6:00 P.M.

In the banana fields the work day is similar to the pineapple field schedule, except that many workers are hired by company appointed labor contractors. Massive layoffs of these nonunion workers occur during slack periods. Contractors pay at their own convenience, sometimes failing to give legally prescribed benefits such as Medicare, mandated by the Philippine labor code. Workers told us that their payments are occasionally "forgotten" by the contractors for several weeks.

Most of the seventy or more laborers in each banana packing plant are women contract workers. A packing plant manager told us that 80 percent of his workers complain of rashes or sores from chemical infections. Bananas for export are heavily treated both while growing and in the packing plant. Another manager said that the company had supplied protective aprons and gloves but that such protection was largely discontinued to save costs.

Angie, a female contract worker, told us in the privacy of the Catholic chapel, miles from the packing plant, that the workers had complained about "forgotten wages" and about the lack of protective gear while working with chemicals. They were ignored. When they tried to organize, the foreman threatened them. "We got death threats from local bullies. One of our most active organizers had to go . . ." Angie made a dipping motion with her hand, palm down. It was the sign for "underground" or joining the New People's Army.

Aerial spraying of a chemical for use against leaf spotting disease is cause for concern by both workers and independent farmers. Some growers who live on their plantation showed us skin rashes caused by the spraying. A government agriculturalist who has worked in the area for over twenty years told us that dermal inflammation is common.

Workers are also concerned about the diazionon and benlate insecticide mixture used on the plastic bags that are placed over the banana bunches by nonmasked workers in the field. After taking blood samples from workers during the 1970s, the Banana Foundation, an organization funded by the Banana Growers' Association of Davao del Norte, discovered that the ability of the blood to absorb oxygen, which is needed to fight disease, is at a critical level in banana plantation workers. If these workers contract a disease like tuberculosis, it can be fatal. Practices did not change as a result of the study.

In addition to aerial spraying, chemicals are mixed in the rainbow irrigation. Rainbow irrigation sprays water through the air onto the banana plants. "It is so pungent my throat hurts after every spraying," a banker who lives near the plantations told us. Applying the chemicals directly to the soil would minimize these effects since the toxic effect comes from mixing the chemical with water and air. However, it is cheaper and easier to apply the chemicals through the irrigation system.

One local fertilizer dealer with agricultural training was concerned that Fumazone, also known as DBCP, used to kill round worm "nematodes" that attack the roots, is destroying the ecology. Fumazone is applied twice a year by injecting it directly into the soil. Dow Chemical manufactures it, but in 1979 the Environmental Protection Agency banned its use in the United States because there was substantial evidence that DBCP could cause cancer or sterility. The EPA allowed its use in the pineapple plantations in Hawaii, though, and it continues to be used in the Philippines as well.

A soil scientist in Mindanao told us that a proper soil balance in the Stanfilco banana plantations in Davao has been disturbed as a result of the intensive banana cultivation over the years. He estimated that it would cost a hundred dollars per hectare per year for three years to bring the soil back to normal production. Small farmers like Mrs. Salas were afraid that Stanfilco would abandon them rather than spend a great deal to build up the soil again. General manager Richard Wolford confirmed as early as 1978 that he would favor moving away from contracts with small farmers. That has been the general trend of company strategy.

After the national daily newspaper *Bulletin Today* published the results of some of our findings on chemical destruction, a representative of the Philippine government's Fertilizer and Pesticide Authority (FPA) came to see us. "Any evidence you can get for me would be very much appreciated," he said. "It is very hard for us in the government agencies to get any information from these multinational corporations." We have never been sure if the FPA representative was so cooperative and quick to respond because Gene was quoted in the paper as General Stoltzfus, a title that commands respect in martial law society.

Dolefil says that one of its contributions is that it generates jobs. Agribusiness is considered labor intensive and this has ostensibly been the reason that the World Bank has encouraged the Philippine government to move more deeply in this direction. We talked with a Filipino executive in a locally owned plantation that supplies bananas to Dole. He told us that with mechanization on his farm, he hopes to reduce the present average of one-and-a-half workers per hectare to one worker per hectare. A family farm would employ or give work to at least two workers per hectare.

In the early days of the company, sixty stevedores were required to load ships during the banana harvest. Now, due to mechanization, only eight are required. A surveyor, who worked for Stanfilco when bananas were first planted, estimated that as many as seven hundred tenants were driven from the land to make way for bananas. The industry's claim that it creates jobs is questionable.

Castle and Cooke, like most multinational corporations, says it brings capital to poor countries, but insiders told us that Stanfilco, which sells about $25 million in bananas each year from the Philippines, invested only one million dollars when it began in 1967. The remaining capital was borrowed from local banks such as the Rizal Commercial Banking Corporation. In 1978, Leonard Marks, Jr., Castle and Cooke vice president and former assistant secretary of the U.S. Air Force, told church workers that "one of the benefits to the Philippines is a responsible enterprise that uses local financial institutions." Meanwhile local farmers are forced to use informal borrowing arrangements where interests range far above government ceilings of 17 percent. Most farmers, especially tenants, cannot borrow from local banks. A University of the Philippines study of foreign investment found that for every dollar invested in the country by a foreign corporation, three dollars are taken out.

Fruit company spokespersons told us that managerial skill and technology is transferred to the Filipinos. But soon after this statement was made, a photographer who wanted to visit the Dolefil cannery was told that the company would not allow pictures. They said Filipino businesses had recently gone into pineapples too and Dolefil feared that they might steal designs and copy unpatented advanced technology.

Dole and Del Monte have a worldwide hold on pineapples. They do not take kindly to capitalist competition when it affects them directly, despite the fighting words that the Castle and Cooke president addressed to the Merchants and Manufacturers Association: "Those who believe in capitalism must fight back!"

In an average year, the Philippines earns $75 million from the sale of bananas. Dollars are also earned by selling coconut products, sugar, lumber, and pineapples. Dollars, this precious foreign currency, are used to buy oil and manufactured goods not available in the Philippines. The international corporations have worldwide marketing and shipping linkups that are almost impossible to break into.

Through its system of vertical integration, Castle and Cooke can keep the majority of profits within its company.

> Vertical integration is a key ingredient in Castle and Cooke's corporate strategy for profit, stability and long term growth. . . . The concept can be defined as having management control over as much of an operations activity as possible from growing the raw product through sale to the customer. The concept can be divided into four major components—source, processing, distribution and marketing.[2]

Thus, for example, Castle and Cooke's shipping line can charge Dolefil an enormous fee to transport the pineapples and bananas. It looks like Dolefil has lost money, but that money has simply gone to another part of the conglomerate.

A study commissioned by the Banana Export Industry Foundation examined the nutritional needs of children of the banana workers in the province. It found that 65 percent of the children in all the plantations and farms suffer from some degree of malnutrition. This general figure for the plantations is slightly higher than the national average. In some farms the degree of malnutrition was much higher than the national average. The study was immediately suppressed and was not published as planned. We managed to get a copy because the janitor at the foundation fished it out of the trash can and discreetly left it on our desk in an adjacent office.

The foundation did spring into action as a result of the findings and secured corn soya milk through the American government's Public Law 480 program. Staff were hired to administer the food and to provide medical care to the families of the workers. This gave employment to several trained middle-class Filipinos. The companies pointed out their quick response to a perceived need.

But this kind of charity bears closer examination. Workers in the plantation whose children are malnourished receive less than 2 percent of the final market value of the bananas of any of the American based corporations—whether it is Dole, Del Monte, or Chiquita. Bananas grown in the Philippines sold

2. Castle and Cooke Annual Report to Stockholders, 1974, p. 5.

for twelve dollars a box in Japan in 1979. Thirteen percent of that twelve dollars comes back to the Philippines for workers' pay, fertilizers, pesticides, local management costs, and other "middleman" company work within the Philippines. The remaining 87 percent stays in Japan or returns to the United States to cover costs and as profit for the company through the liberal capital remittance scheme the Marcos government set up and the Aquino government has continued.[3]

The charitable donation of nutritious soya milk is used in this case to subsidize the Japanese consumer and the agribusiness companies. "We earn about two dollars a day in the field. We don't need charity. We need a living wage," one labor union official told us emphatically.

Fr. Loreto Viloria of the Catholic Social Action Center in Marbel, the capital city of the province where Castle and Cooke is ensconced, pointed to the implications of further multinational control in the Philippines in a 1980 memo to the Passionist Religious Order, which holds shares in Castle and Cooke: "Dolefil in the long run is a national liability; the threat of violence will hang over the country as long as the multinationals operate plantations while many Filipinos remain poor, hungry and landless."

After our initial two-year investigation into Castle and Cooke in the Philippines, my husband and I traveled around the United States and Canada, presenting our findings in slideshow form to schools, churches, and community groups. At the end of a day of presentations at a private school in Pennsylvania, a high school senior approached me and declared, "Why don't we just take over these banana republics and give them good government!"

This self-assured high school student is not alone in his question. In subsequent years on the road, a somewhat more humble version of the same inquiry continued to surface. "Who is to blame for the inequities and malnutrition? The Philippine government? The corporations? The U.S. government? The Soviets?" For some it was an intellectual inquiry; for others it was a question of where to focus their efforts to relieve world hunger or confront human rights abuse.

3. We calculated the in-country costs and sales in Japan, based on 1979 figures. The actual numbers have changed in the interim, but the percentages for workers' pay, inputs, and other costs have remained the same.

5

Banks, Corporations, Governments

WHO CALLS THE SHOTS?

Our initial investigation into the structure and operation of foreign agribusiness was conducted during the Marcos era. The entrance of the Aquino administration made little difference to this basic structure. Why not? To answer that, we have to examine the relationships between foreign governments, foreign business, the multilateral lending institutions such as the International Monetary Fund, and the Filipino elite. A study of the interplay of power and mutual benefit among these four provides some clues. This examination can also help point to the players within the cast who can most appropriately lead the way to a remedy.

Advocates of corporate responsibility lament the lack of control that communities in the United States and Canada have over the behavior of multinational corporations that move in and out of a community at will, based on the bottom line of their balance sheet. While there is just cause for their complaint, it is also true that there is more protection for individual workers and communities in Canada and the United States than in a country like the Philippines. Why did neither the Marcos nor the Aquino government protect its natural resources and its population from foreign corporations?

In order to determine this, we must examine the basis of government in the Philippines and its neighbors—for example, Indonesia, Burma, and Thailand—all of which started out as liberal democracies after the Second World War and have now become authoritarian governments. Many Americans are confused about these shifts in government. A common notion we encountered during our North American speaking tour came either bluntly stated or circumspectly asked, "Isn't the Asian personality and society more inclined toward authoritarianism? Isn't it an imposition of our own standards to force them to have democracies?"

One cannot understand this shift from some sort of electoral process to a virtual dictatorship, with the military playing a prominent role, simply by looking at the surface events. A deeper analysis is necessary. Some Asian scholars have pointed to economic factors.

> The U.S. supported the formation of liberal democratic governments in Southeast Asia at the end of World War II primarily to facilitate the region's integration into the world economy. This economic integration in turn, has made the continuation of these liberal democratic forms impossible.[1]

What does this mean—"economic integration has made continuation of liberal democratic forms impossible"?

In the Philippines, a mestizo class, born of the intermixing of the Chinese merchant and native landowning groups, gradually developed into a national political elite. Over time, landownership, though important as a source of political and economic power, became less significant than control over the government's financial resources and "partnership" with foreign investors. America's grant of independence to the Philippines in 1946 was largely in name only, since the new elite remained dependent upon their foreign partners economically and thus politically as well.

The form of government in the Philippines was patterned after that of the United States—a Congress with House and Senate, a president electable for a maximum of two terms, and a system of checks and balances between the legislative, judicial, and administrative branches. This form sounded good, but the reason for its implementation in the Philippines was fundamentally different from the original purpose of the birth and development of liberal democracies.

For example, the development of a parliamentary democ-

1. Joel Rocamora, *Southeast Asian Chronicle*, November-December 1978, pp. 7-19.

racy in Europe was a reflection of the shift in economic control from the landed class to the merchants. The nobles surrounding the king no longer held the most economic power in the country. Thus new political institutions had to be created which expressed the new economic power of the merchants. In the Philippines, on the other hand, the people who control the political institutions have not achieved the independent economic dominance that their European counterparts had before they challenged the king and nobles.

Since the Filipino elite lack this economic power, the government becomes a tool for achieving it. Thus the goal of a member of the Filipino elite—like Marcos, for example—is to use government resources for personal economic ends. This has resulted in the channeling of huge amounts of government funds and other resources into private hands, a system sometimes referred to as "bureaucrat capitalism." This use of government also poses the great temptation, to which Marcos succumbed, of absolute and permanent rule through the elimination of electoral politics. Marcos thus achieved unchallenged access to the "goodies" from abroad, whether from other governments or through business contracts.

No new independent capitalist class has emerged under Marcos or Aquino. The economy of the country remains heavily dependent on large infusions of western investment, assistance, and loans. Despite the fact that various factions control large amounts of economic resources, their control is almost completely dependent upon the retention of political power. For example, the minister of energy under Marcos was also at one time president of the board of Dolefil. The minister of finance under Marcos was part of Dole's auditing firm.

Juan Ponce Enrile, a former Defense Minister, amassed his fortune mainly through his connections in the coconut industry. He also has considerable land and influence in rubber production on Basilan Island and in wood processing in Agusan province in Mindanao. Enrile gave legal help to Castle and Cooke when they first began in the Philippines in 1963. His fortunes, however, have not contributed to the economic self-reliance of the country's economy.

In 1985, I took a guided tour of a matchstick factory in Magallanes, Agusan del Sur province in Mindanao, which belonged to then Defense Minister Juan Ponce Enrile. The management proudly pointed out the fact that this was now a Filipino-owned factory. Enrile had purchased it from a Swedish company. The Philippines can produce its own matches. I looked at the brand names of the machines that cut the wood, that produced the chemical for the end of the matchstick, that packaged the matches—all of them were European. "What happens if a machine breaks down?" I asked. "Can you fix it? Do you have spare parts? Can you produce this machine in the Philippines?" "No," replied the guide, "we get help from the former owners."

Thus in spite of his tremendous wealth, Enrile has not improved the Philippines' state of economic dependence because he has not transferred his base of power from bureaucratic office to ownership of capital. He will not be of much use to his international business partners if he is unable to mobilize licenses, credit, contracts, and other concessions. That provides a powerful economic incentive for Enrile and other out-of-power politicians to get back into government.

Agriculture's share of total employment has been declining annually. This decline would not be a problem in itself if industry were growing at a comparable rate, but the manufacturing sector has stagnated, resulting in an economic gap that is not being filled. Filipino capitalists have not been able to start their own industries. The Philippine economy has not been able to absorb the landless farmers into the workforce.

In the past, village-level social structures helped to soften economic difficulties and to mediate direct repression of the peasants. Traditional feudal social structures began to crumble due to the penetration of capitalism into the countryside. The familial relationship between landlord and tenant shifted toward a contractual business relationship. The cushion of the landlord's economic help for the peasants in times of crisis was vanishing. Thus the psychological control of the peasants through the use of the traditional debt of gratitude (utang na loob) was weakened. Politicization of the peasants began to spread more rapidly and on a nationwide scale. The government and the elite had to employ more direct and dictatorial methods to stem the tide of this militant politicized peasantry.

By the early 1970s, the traditional instruments of control in the Philippines had so deteriorated that practically every politician had to have a private army to stay in power. Elections were the method by which the various factions within the elite took turns with the perquisites of political office on which their economic power depended. But this electoral schema became more and more expensive. Many Filipino citizens did not oppose Marcos's declaration of martial law in 1972 because he presented it as a way to stem the violence and chaos and to provide a firm basis for economic development in the country.

In spite of popular hopes, however, martial law was not as helpful to the citizens of the country as it was to the international business community. The first cable of support Ferdinand Marcos received after declaring martial law was from the American Chamber of Commerce in Manila. In 1978 Dolefil's general manager, Richard Wolford, told us that "the actions of the government are now more predictable because the policies are now made by technocrats instead of interest groups." He added that this predictability made the Philippines the best investment for Castle and Cooke in Asia at that time.

Marcos's political survival depended on U.S. military and economic assistance and on direct and multilateral development loans and commercial credit. When Reagan was finally forced to abandon Marcos at the eleventh—almost twelfth—hour, Marcos knew there was no use trying to stay on at Malacanang. All other support in the country, including his military, had withered. The American card was his last one.

The reality of the economic picture in the Philippines did not change when Mrs. Aquino assumed power in 1986. She inherited the problems of unemployment and landlessness that were the result of the fact that the expansion in industrial employment opportunities had not kept pace with the displacement of rural labor. The government policy that contributed to this problem—emphasis on export-oriented agricultural economy—was continued under the Aquino administration.

Aquino appointed a new minister of economic planning, Solita Monsod, to plan new economic development, increase production, and help business grow. The Philippines had to earn enough dollars to purchase oil and large-scale equipment not manufactured in the Philippines and to deal with the $28 billion foreign debt which Marcos left behind. To get these dollars, something had to be sold. Since the Philippines has few industrial products to sell as a result of the World Bank advice to focus on agriculture, the Aquino government was forced to depend on the export of agricultural products. Jaime Ongpin, Aquino's first minister of finance, presented an economic development plan to American bankers in 1986 that continued to emphasize agricultural exports, but suggested shifting from coconuts and sugar to cacao and coffee.

Ongpin represented the Philippine government in its discussions on loan-restructuring with the International Monetary Fund and the foreign banks. Critics insisted that he gave in too readily to the demands of the IMF in the 1987 round of negotiations. Mrs. Aquino herself complained bitterly about the harsh terms that the international finance community exacted from the Philippines. A Chase Manhattan Bank officer who was part of the talks reported that Ongpin and his associate Jose B. ("Jobo") Fernandez came to the United States, offering a shopping list of Filipino assets to U.S. banks and private investors.

Both Ongpin and Central Bank governor Fernandez, a holdover from the Marcos era, are dedicated to an international free enterprise system à la the design of the International Monetary Fund (IMF). Both are examples of Filipino capitalists who made their fortunes through depending on a financial base outside of the Philippines.

In 1974 Ongpin was made head of Benguet Mining Corporation in the Philippines by the owner, Charles Allen and Company, the private investment house of the late dope king, Meyer Lansky. The Allen Brothers played a major role as laundry men for Lansky. According to organized crime investigators, Benguet Mining was used as one of the corporate shells to launder money.[2]

Fernandez founded Far East Bank and Trust and is still associated with it. Far East was bought by Shaul Eisenberg, who coordinates a $2-3 billion a year trading corporation. He is notorious as an arms smuggler; his Far East Trading Corporation manufactures light weapons in China, some of which are ending up in the Philippines in nongovernment military hands, according to American intelligence sources.[3]

During one of the Cabinet shake-ups in 1987, Ongpin was replaced as minister of finance. An investigation was launched into his alleged financial misdealings. In November 1987, a few months after his dismissal, Ongpin was found dead in his office. The family said it was suicide.

The IMF, a multilateral institution based in Washington,

2. Al Douglas, "Dope, Inc.'s Bid to Wreck the Philippines," *EIR Journal*, July 26, 1986, pp. 37-39.
3. Ibid.

is a key player in the Philippines. Because of its significant influence in banking circles, this institution has a tremendous amount of power over Third World governments and their policies. Yet most Americans know little and care less about the IMF; it does not affect our lives so visibly or directly as it does those of urban squatters or rural peasants in a country like the Philippines.

In the first days after our arrival in Manila in 1977, an older resident of the squatter community known as Tondo handed us a mimeographed sheet summarizing the structure, function, and activity of the IMF. "This is important for you to understand. Your government controls that institution."

Why is the IMF perceived as such a monster in the Philippines? How is it connected with the behavior of a company like Castle and Cooke in a country like the Philippines?

The International Monetary Fund and the International Bank for Reconstruction and Development, the latter more popularly known as the World Bank, were established in 1944 at Bretton Woods, a year before the end of the Second World War, on American and Allied initiative. The stated reason for their establishment was to prevent more world wars by promoting international free trade. This was to be done by using a system of credits through centralized institutions to keep the nations around the world economically interdependent.

One of the best analyses of the actual function and purpose of the IMF is *The Debt Trap: The International Monetary Fund and the Third World*. Author Cheryl Payer writes the following in the introduction to her book of case studies in the Third World:

> The IMF must be seen as the keystone of a total system. Its power is made possible not only by the enormous resources which it controls . . . but more significantly as a result of its function as an international credit agency. All of the major sources of credit in the developed capitalist world, whether private lenders, governments or multilateral lending institutions such as the World Bank Group will refuse to lend to a country which persists in defying IMF "advice." The real importance of the IMF lies in the authority delegated to it by the governments and capital markets of the entire capitalist world.[4]

4. Cheryl Payer, *Debt Trap: The International Monetary Fund and the Third World* (New York: Monthly Review Press, 1974), pp. ix-x.

The IMF did not change its advice to the Philippines when the Aquino government came into power. It is the same advice Marcos heard: Keep wages down; let the peso float; tighten up the fiscal belt. This is a prescription for trouble for any head of state of a poor country. The hard-earned currency in the country goes to pay off foreign debts. Meanwhile, the poor feel the brunt of the fiscal conservatism because they pay more for basic commodities whose prices are not controlled. Their wages do not rise in tandem with the price hikes. The financial pinch results in their going without basic needs like shelter, food, clothing, or health care. In the Philippines, 80 percent of the population now lives below the poverty line. Such a large number of people in dire economic straits is dangerous to the stability of the rulers.

To enforce stability, any administration in the Philippines has two choices—improve the economic conditions to keep the people from revolting or build up the military to put down the peoples' revolts. However, improvement of economic conditions will mean that the government must disregard the IMF prescription of controlled wages and instead put its scarce resources into human needs. If the Philippine government does that, the IMF will not certify the government for a loan to help stabilize its balance of payments deficit. If the IMF says the debtor nation is not cooperating, the international bankers will not renegotiate their loans with the nation, either. The IMF acts almost like a guarantor for private (nongovernmental) money. Without the IMF stamp of approval, there is virtually no place for a government like that of the Philippines to get foreign currency.

As a result of historical developments, the Philippines is so enmeshed in the international economy through trade that there is virtually no way out. Foreign exchange is needed to buy oil, to pay for shipping, to purchase manufactured goods, and to buy the machinery and parts used in the few factories the Philippines does have. If the government defaults on its loans, even those left from the Marcos regime, it will also have difficulty selling its export products to those same nations to whom it owes money and has refused to pay.

It is a vicious cycle; "debt trap" is an apt description. The single largest expense in the Aquino budget for 1987 was debt repayment. The Aquino government chose to honor all debts incurred by the deposed government instead of selectively repudiating them; thus fully one quarter of the budget will be eaten up by debt repayment and interest.

The *Manila Chronicle*, a leading Philippine daily newspaper, reported on December 17, 1986, that the 32.6 percent increase in the government's debt payments for the year is largely due to its assumption of the National Power Corporation's liabilities from the mothballed Bataan Nuclear Plant. The nuclear power plant was set up through a contract with Westinghouse arranged by a Marcos relative and business crony, Herminio Disini. The reactor itself has not passed international safety standards. The plant was built at the foot of a still active volcano, near an earthquake fault, in an area subject to tidal waves. Despite tremendous opposition from a broad spectrum of society, Marcos went ahead with the construction.

When Mrs. Aquino became president, the plans for the nuclear plant to go on line were stopped. Nevertheless, the Aquino government assumed the debts and cost overruns, which total over a billion dollars, at least $35 million of which went into the pockets of Marcos's crony. The money to pay these debts is being squeezed out of an already overtaxed population.

Dr. Payer points to other players in this drama as well:

> The IMF has been the chosen instrument for imposing imperialist financial discipline upon poor countries under a facade of multilateralism and technical competence. . . . The IMF is not the real villain of the piece, though it is the agent of the villains. They are the multinational corporations and capitalist governments which are the natural enemies of Third World independence and can usually mobilize the resources to crush it.[5]

Filipino nationalists view the behavior of Castle and Cooke in Nicaragua after the revolution as an example of how a multinational is able to mobilize resources to try to crush a Third World country's attempt at economic independence. Filipinos have watched events there very closely since 1980 when Castle and Cooke decided to pull out.

The Nicaraguan government offered the Standard Fruit Company tremendous concessions—the same exclusive purchase rights as they had under deposed dictator Somoza, a

5. Ibid.

curb on labor unrest, a promise of no criticism in the press, suspension of a governmental nationalization decree, and assumption of the company's ten-million-dollar debt at a time when the government had only three million dollars in its treasury. Foreign Trade Minister Alejandro Martinez said the overriding reason for the concessions was that three thousand jobs were affected and "we couldn't eat all those bananas."[6]

Standard Fruit and the Nicaraguan government then signed a five-year agreement stipulating that Standard Fruit would be responsible for transportation, exportation, and marketing of bananas grown in Nicaragua. By 1985 the state would become the owner of the company's properties, valued at six million dollars.

According to Nicaraguan government sources, the government had already paid four of the six million dollars when on October 26, 1982, the company gave notice of suspension of its activities. Mr. Charles Bauman, senior vice-president in charge of fresh fruit operations, said Castle and Cooke was leaving behind $9.8 million in physical assets and loans to producers. Castle and Cooke claimed its withdrawal was due to the disappointing financial results for the fiscal year that ended June 19, 1982 and "had nothing to do with the political ideology of the Nicaraguan government." At that time, Castle and Cooke had not withdrawn or cut back its banana operations in any other country.

Before pulling out, company executives met with the U.S. Department of State. According to Hawaiian corporate researcher and activist, Ian Lind,

> the State Department wanted Castle and Cooke to stay in order to keep connections with and provide support for the Nicaraguan business class. . . . In deciding to withdraw, the company seemed to be following its own idealogical/political agenda, or perhaps took cues from higher in the U.S. government administration.[7]

6. *Honolulu Star Bulletin*, July 14, 1987, p. D-1.
7. Ian Lind, former director of the Insititute for Peace, Social Science Research Institute, University of Hawaii, has researched and produced materials on Castle and Cooke for over ten years. This interpretation of Castle and Cooke's pullout from Nicaragua and the State Department advice is based on background material obtained from the U.S. Department of State in response to a Freedom of Information Act request.

The Nicaraguan government, however, viewed the pullout in the context of the Reagan administration's anti-Sandinista campaign. The Nicaraguan newspaper, *Barricada*, quoted Dr. Sergio Ramirez Mercado, member of the government junta, as saying, "The goal [of the pullout] is to accentuate economic difficulties and thus bring about destabilization of the government." With fifteen banana plantations, Nicaragua accounts for about 5 percent of Standard Fruit's banana purchases. Eighty percent of the plantation lands are held by private owners while Standard Fruit held the rest. Banana exports represented 5 percent of Nicaragua's export sales, an annual revenue of twenty million dollars. *Barricada* commented that twenty million dollars is the precise amount of foreign exchange the government uses to import medicines.

Less than fifteen days after the Standard Fruit pullout, the Nicaraguan government chartered a ship and found smaller marketing companies on the U.S. West Coast to distribute the bananas. Sales of eighty thousand boxes of bananas were assured until December by Pandol Brothers, a Delano, California, company that distributes the bananas under the Three Brothers label. A price war immediately ensued on the West Coast, with Dole, Chiquita, and Del Monte lowering the price per box from $6.00 to $5.50 and $5.00. The three big companies also charged that Nicaraguan bananas were not good quality.

In July 1987, a suit brought by the Nicaraguan government against Castle and Cooke and its subsidiary, Standard Fruit, was heard in U.S. Federal District Court. The Nicaraguan government sued Castle and Cooke for breach of contract, charging that the country lost $35.5 million when Standard Fruit stopped buying bananas from seventeen thousand acres of plantations, despite signing a five-year memorandum of intent.

Leonard Marks, Jr., the former executive vice-president of Castle and Cooke, was asked in court about a line in their 1981 annual report that said the company had "reached agreement on a five year contract." He replied "It didn't say we *signed* a five year contract."[8]

This action against Nicaragua in the international marketplace raises questions about how a small country with a

8. Ibid.

nationalist government can organize itself to fulfill its primary task—to feed and protect its citizens. Filipinos are quick to see that the Nicaraguan situation has implications for the Philippines, where someday a nationalist government could come into power.

The problem of malnutrition among children of banana workers would not be solved immediately if a government with different priorities would come to power. A repressive Third World government is only one of the partners that keeps the peasants and workers from the full enjoyment of the fruits of their labors. The other partners—international governments, businesses, and banks—also play a key role.

I glimpsed the implications of this role in 1984 when I accompanied a group of Filipino leaders in Chicago to talk with Continental Bank about cutting back its support to the Marcos government. The Chicago dialogue was part of a concerted effort by human rights advocates in western countries to put economic pressure on the Marcos regime. Over two hundred banks in the United States were involved in business in the Philippines. Continental Bank had 30 percent equity or $117 million in Rizal Commercial Banking Corporation, which made the initial loans to Castle and Cooke for their operations in Mindanao. The Filipino leaders of the delegation argued that the money was going into the private pockets of Marcos's friends and that when a new government would take over, Continental might not be able to recoup its investment.

What interested me was the response of Continental spokespersons to the Filipino delegation. "Why are you picking on us? Why don't you contact the International Monetary Fund? They hold the power for deciding on these things." At that point the IMF and Marcos were negotiating a $650 million balance of payments loan. The consortium of American banks of which Continental was a member were dealing in billions of dollars in loans and investments. I reminded the Continental vice-president for Asia that in actual cash amounts, the consortium of banks were certainly bigger than the IMF. "Ah, yes," he said, "but the IMF makes the risk assessments." Continental did not seem worried that they might not be able to collect on their Philippine investment.

Only a few months later, Continental was saved from bankruptcy by a quick bailout from sixteen other major banks, the Federal Reserve Board, and the Federal Deposit Insurance

Corporation. Their precarious financial condition was attributed to the fact that some bank officers had made risky loans for oil ventures in the southern United States. In contrast, the government of Mrs. Aquino got no such bailout or reprieve for bad debts incurred by Marcos. The citizens of the Philippines, the majority of whom live under the poverty line, will be taxed for years to come to pay these debts.

The interplay of the major financial institutions—the banks, the IMF, and the multinational corporations—with the help of the Philippine elite, have created a structural impasse. The Philippines has a gigantic foreign debt and needs dollars to pay it. Since the country is hooked into an export economy, it must try to sell its raw agricultural products. But the costs of purchasing foreign goods far outreaches the earnings, and the country goes further into debt. Profit from the sale of pineapples and bananas, for example, pays only the interest on the debt.

Thus, the government has to borrow even more to pay the debt itself. This increases the debt and the cycle continues. But the tax base upon which the structure stands becomes increasingly unstable as more people are thrown off the land to make way for foreign agribusiness and the landless are not absorbed into the manufacturing sector. Many of the landless move into the cities but never become part of the formal economy. As the tax base decreases, more of the tax burden is loaded onto those who still earn a salary but who do not make enough to avail themselves of tax loopholes.

The multinationals are part of the cycle, too. The managers of Castle and Cooke are caught in the ever-expanding cycle of international financial competition that requires more control and more profits. They must grow, but they can't make money selling food to the poor.

Only by understanding the machinations of the corporate business and government world can one see clearly that no matter who sits in Malacanang, the result will inevitably be the same. Without significant changes in the relations between international business, banks, and the elite of the country, the only alternative is to use the military to control the people upon whose backs the principal economic burden is laid.

While understanding this structure is vital, coming to grips with the human cost of perpetuating it is equally important. The story of the IMF, Castle and Cooke, and the elite in the Philippines ultimately points back to the workers and farmers whose blood, sweat, and tears keep the system going. The plight of Mrs. Gonzaga, a Dole employee I met on a follow-up visit to Polomolok, illustrates the narrowing options for farmers and workers.

One evening I accompanied the local parish priest of Tupi, a town situated in the midst of the Dole pineapple plantation, to christen a baby of one of the Dole workers. We drove in his four-wheel jeep along narrow roads, almost paths, through the pineapple fields and stopped at a tiny house with walls made of Dole pineapple and banana crates.

Inside the tiny shack, eight small children slept in a row on the floor and on top of a bamboo bench along one side of the wall. Mrs. Gonzaga sat in the second room, her baby in her arms. After we were seated around her makeshift table, she began her story.

Two months earlier, a bulldozer arrived at the Gonzaga's two hectare farmlot, ready to flatten their corn crop. The land they rented bordered the Dole plantation. The company wanted to expand. The Philippine government's National Development Corporation arranged with the landowner to trade these few acres for land elsewhere. No one had informed the Gonzagas. Mr. Gonzaga pleaded with the driver and with an official from the Ministry of Agrarian Reform who accompanied the driver. The official explained that in order to plant the pineapples uniformly, this field needed to be prepared as soon as possible. Mr. Gonzaga left the field rather than watch the destruction of his crop. The Gonzagas had experienced a bulldozing before.

Late that night, Mr. Gonzaga returned to the house, woke his wife, apologized for any bad things he had done to her during the course of their marriage, and said good-bye. "The most painful thing was that the official from the Ministry of Agrarian Reform did not protect me. He was on the other side. There is no hope anywhere," he told his wife. He had swallowed poison. At that hour with no available public transportation, Mrs. Gonzaga, eight months pregnant, could not get her husband to a hospital. She was left with eight children and the ninth on the way.

She told the bare facts, with no intonation. Her eyes varied between stony and expressionless. She must still have been in shock, going through the motions of the living—working in the field, preparing food, having her baby baptized.

When the Catholic Social Action Center heard what happened to the Gonzagas, they pressured Dolefil. The company gave Mrs. Gonzaga two sacks of rice and the cardboard crates to build a house beside the pineapple fields where they also gave her a weeding job. The priest told me, "The Dolefil public relations officer said they did not legally have to do anything since they did not bulldoze her crop. It was the Philippine government through the National Development Corporation and the Ministry of Agrarian Reform who are responsible. He told us Dole was making a humanitarian gesture."

Mr. Gonzaga and Mr. Ongpin were on opposite ends of the economic transaction that handed over more power to the multinational banks and corporations in the Philippines. Mr. Gonzaga lost his crops and his land. Mr. Ongpin lost his job and his prestige. They both chose suicide.

I was struck by the uniform reaction of Filipino friends all over the country when I recounted the story of Mr. Gonzaga's suicide. "Oh, Mr. Gonzaga didn't have to lose hope just because the government ministry official didn't protect him. Doesn't he know there is a movement he could join?" The movement they referred to includes the militant labor and peasant unions many people in similar circumstances to the Gonzagas are joining. Mr. Ongpin could have joined the movement, too. Nationalist businesspersons have their own voluntary association. But for Jaime Ongpin it would have meant mind-boggling shifts in economic theory and practice.

Joining the movement may be an act of hope for an individual, but it is no guarantee of survival. Andrew Cortez, a lay official in the Philippine Independent Church, was a labor organizer who introduced us to many workers in Stanfilco when we were doing our research. Polite, helpful, and soft-spoken, Andrew never inserted himself or his ideas into our conversations with the workers. He had an infinite faith in the truth of the workers' story and in the justice of their demands.

Andrew rarely talked about himself, but his commitment to the welfare of the workers was very clear to everyone who knew him. Existing on a subsistence wage, he spent most of his time on the plantations—talking, encouraging, and organizing the workers into unions strong enough to bargain collectively with corporations like Castle and Cooke.

In 1983, as a result of his organizing work, Andrew was picked up by the Philippine military in Cotabato. For months, no one knew where he was or what had happened to him. A detainee who was held at the same place was later able to recount the story. Andrew was interrogated and tortured in much the same way as most male detainees are—water torture, beating, and electric shock treatment. However, he was killed in a way that I have not heard of before or since.

Andrew's captors cut slits all over his body. At night they stitched the cuts with coarse thread and a rusty needle. The next day, they ripped open the stitches and in the evening they sewed Andrew's cuts again. This procedure continued until he died of his infected, open wounds. What the military did to Andrew Cortez was clearly designed for its chilling effect on other organizers. However, the effect has been quite the opposite: since 1983 there has been even more determined union organizing in the pineapple and banana plantations of Mindanao.

The military's method of inflicting a slow, painful death on Andrew was unbelievably gruesome. For many of his friends, it seemed necessary to lengthen the grieving process in order to exorcise the way he died. Later, his death became a metaphor for me for the slow, painful death process the IMF inflicts on Third World peoples. Its policy of brutal austerity is a key factor in creating the conditions of discontent favorable for destabilization. First the loan is made; then restrictions become tighter; more money is loaned; the debt increases; so do the restrictions. The cycle continues until the country is sucked dry.

The International Monetary Fund is not the only actor, however, and its machinations do not complete the final act in the Philippine drama. Just as Andrew's death did not deter others from union organizing, so the IMF demands are not deterring voluntary associations like the Basic Christian Communities from following a different path.

6

Theology of Struggle

BASIC CHRISTIAN COMMUNITIES
IN THE PHILIPPINES

"What is now emerging as the most dangerous form of threat from the religious radicals is their creation of the so-called Basic Christian Communities (BCC) in both rural and urban areas. They are practically building an infrastructure of political power in the entire country," wrote Col. Galileo C. Kintanar in an article entitled "Contemporary Religous Radicalism in the Philippines," published in the *Philippine National Security Review* in 1979.

What are Basic Christian Communities? Why are they "the most dangerous form of threat"? Whom are they threatening?

Since Vatican II, the Catholic church in the Philippines, like the church in Latin America, has opened its windows for some fresh air. This includes encouraging lay people to read and reflect on the Bible for themselves. The Philippines has an 88 percent literacy rate and even in rural areas most people attend school for at least a few years. Thus the idea of people reading the Bible for themselves is indeed possible.

Because priests are scarce, some remote barrios see one only once a year on the fiesta day of their patron saint. The priest celebrates Mass, baptizes the babies, and performs any other needed ecclesial functions for the year. In the late 1960s and early 1970s, seminars abounded to train catechetical workers to conduct liturgies and Bible studies in *kapilyas* ("little chapels"—often just some rough-hewn benches under a roof supported by a few poles). This process brought a certain democratization, a sharing of power—the power emanating from the Book that before had been accessible only to the priests.

Ordinary people—farmers, fishermen, vendors, workers—gather together to read the Bible, to pray, and to discuss their social and economic conditions in the light of what they are reading. Like the *communidades de bases* in Latin America, these Philippine Basic Christian Communities (BCC) have taken off, especially in rural and urban poor communities.

Colonel Kintanar is not the only prominent figure in the Philippines who realizes that the Basic Christian Communities are important. Bishop Julio X. Labayen, the Carmelite bishop of Infanta Prelature in Luzon who has encouraged BCC building for over ten years, told his counterparts in Belgium,

> I predict that the Basic Christian Communities will prove to be the major powerful influence in the Church of the future. They will affect the whole church as deeply as the growth of the monastic orders, . . . or the evolution of the Protestant Churches over the recent centuries. I foresee that the Church will form a consensus to promote the growth of the Basic Christian Communities and this decision will be as important for the life of the church as the decision made by the Council of Jerusalem to open the church to the Gentiles on the Gentiles' terms.

Unlike Latin America, the Philippines has not produced a great liberation theologian to provide the framework for base community building or to explain the concept to the western world. "Listen to our songs, our poetry, our stories—that is how our theology is expressed," says Karl Gaspar, a prominent Catholic layman and former political detainee. Ed de la Torre, also a former political detainee, activist, and artist agrees, "The Philippine theology of struggle is initially oral and takes many literary forms—songs, poetry, images. If you think about it, that is how the Bible developed, too."

There is no shortened, condensed version of Philippine liberation theology. You have to be with the Christian communities in their daily routines and lives in order to understand the faith of the people.

The Bienvenida Farmers' Basic Christian Community is a good example of what Colonel Kintanar fears and Bishop Labayen promotes. I met this community in 1977, shortly after thirty-four of their people had been released from jail.

Vicente Adimos, the Bienvenida farmers' leader, migrated to Mindanao from his native island of Samar in 1952. Like most of the other Bienvenida farmers, he was looking for land—and in 1952, there was still lots of unclaimed land and few people to farm it. Mindanao was the last frontier. Vicente and his brothers and sisters found land and began farming in the province of Davao del Norte. The Basic Christian Community movement began in that province in the early 1970s and Vicente was soon an active participant.

Most peasants, even though they may have been on the same piece of land all their lives, do not go through the complex process to obtain a legal title. It entails coming to the city, getting a lawyer, and dealing with an unfamiliar setting.

The land which Vicente and his neighbors farm was titled in the 1960s to a wealthy family in Davao. Jorge Marquez, in whose name the land is held, was eleven years old at the time of the titling. The Marquez family made little use of the land and other landless farmers drifted onto unused portions as the years went by. The farmers, with the support and encouragement of the local parish, gradually formed themselves into a Basic Christian Community.

Meanwhile, a neighboring agribusiness corporation, Sarmiento, was looking for more land to fulfill its obligations under the Corporate Farming Act. This act required corporations to grow an amount of rice equivalent to what its employees could consume. The employees never really got the rice. Marcos constructed this plan to increase rice production in the 1970s after the government found itself in the awkward position of having to import rice. Sarmiento made arrangements to lease Jorge Marquez's land and remove the farmers. The Basic Christian Community of Bienvenida refused to leave to make way for the corporate farm. "Bienvenida, you know, means welcome," says Vicente.

Over a meal of *camote* (a root crop, like a sweet potato) and peanuts from their farms, Vicente Adimos and the Bienvenida farmers shared the dramatic story of their confrontation with the military and the owner's goons. Government troops moved in to clear the land. "On September 26, 1976, they burned my house," begins Vicente. "My sixteen-year-old child got burned. I lost about seven thousand pesos worth of property." (In 1976 the exchange rate was $1 = 7 pesos.) The men, women, and children of Bienvenida stood firm in front of their houses. One of their members was shot and killed. In the melee the bulldozer driver was killed.

The farmers have not forgotten those deaths. Vicente cautions, "We must love our enemies. We have nothing against Jorge Marquez as a person but we want to farm our land without being harrassed.

"I built another house of cogon grass. My wife and children had to sleep somewhere. It was bulldozed a month later. There went another 250 pesos. I built a third house," continues Vicente.

In September 1977, almost a year later, the Basic Christian Community was holding firm to its right to the land, based on having farmed there for more than ten years. By law in the Philippines, if tenants till the land for ten years they have "usership" rights and cannot be summarily evicted. They were offered a relocation area they had never seen. "We had to decide in twenty-four hours or go to jail," says Claudia Docsin, auditor for the farmer's cooperative and the only woman among the thirty-four imprisoned. "How could we accept such an offer without seeing the land?"

The experience of jail quickly turned these Christian farmers into prison reform advocates. "The food was terrible; the spirit among the prisoners was inhuman," says Vicente. Some prisoners had been in jail three years without their cases coming to trial. Political prisoners and common criminals were all together in the local jail.

"Well, the first thing we did was to organize Bible studies," explains Vicente. "We looked for all the people in the Bible who had been in prison to see what they did and how they handled their trials. We read about Paul's and Jesus' arrest, for example. Later on, we tried to study about the Roman Empire because we thought we might learn about the United States."

The other prisoners went on strike for better food. "We farmers were trusted by the prison officials, so we tried to talk to the guards about improving conditions," adds another farmer in the circle around the pot of camote. "We worked on the worn-out housing in the jail," says Vicente. "After all, by now we have a lot of experience putting up houses quickly."

The farmers were planning to build a chapel in the prison when they were released in November. "I guess they had enough of our prison reform," laughs one of the farmers. "Our best times were 'happy-happy hour' with skits, songs, stories, and jokes which we organized for ourselves and the other prisoners."

"We have had a lot of experience working and praying together, so we have enough patience and solidarity as a group to meet the trials coming our way," explains Vicente. "The rich and powerful cannot easily push us around if we are united."

The Bienvenida farmers were confident and flushed with success when I talked with them. After all, they had been released from jail and were still farming the land through their sheer persistence.

Three years later, I was witness to a much less successful struggle by a similiar Basic Christian Community in the same province of Davao del Norte. Many of the eighty-seven tenant families in that community had been tilling the same land since 1956. The landlord, a small Filipino businessman, strapped for cash, eagerly agreed to sell the land to the chief Marcos crony in the area, Antonio Floreindo. Not only did Floreindo represent Marcos's business interests in Mindanao, he was also the link to United Fruit, which markets bananas under the Chiquita label. As a condition of the sale, Floreindo insisted that all tenant farmers be removed and their crops ploughed under. The corn was within a week of being ready to harvest.

I agreed to accompany the Davao City emergency response crew—three sisters, a priest, and several lay catechists, who planned to support the farmers. "We need a witness, a photographer, someone to tell the story," said a nun in a white habit as we bounced along in the back of a Ford Fiera, a minibus of sorts, which is a common vehicle of wealthier rural Catholic parishes in the Philippines.

By the time we arrived, several houses had already been smashed. Thirty people were huddled in a group under a huge tree on the top of a small hill. Suddenly a young boy in the tree pointed and yelled. Everyone ran—the children, the women, the nuns. Another young boy, the only one with a bicycle, pedaled furiously down the hill toward an approaching bulldozer. The people surrounded the bulldozer and began to plead with the driver. "Think of our children. They will have nothing to eat if you bulldoze the crops," cried one mother. "You must have children, too." The driver eyed the people uneasily and slowly backed up his vehicle. The crop was safe, for the moment.

The farmers whose houses had already been destroyed set up kitchen under the trees. The group gathered around the huge pots of corn set on planks on an open fire. I joined them for boiled corn, a few greens, and some fish the Davao City delegation had brought. Almost everyone sat on the ground; the sisters and I were told to sit on the one available bench.

We were still eating when one of the nuns from Davao poked me and whispered, "Look there." A young Muslim woman with a haggard face, holding her stomach, walked slowly toward us. Her look of pain brought me to my feet. We stood face to face, wordless at first. Then the sister translated the woman's story. "The bulldozer came toward my house yesterday. I ran to stop it. I was three months pregnant, but I lost the baby last night. Now I have no baby and no house." The woman looked down at the ground. I was still wordless. No experience in America had prepared me for this encounter. I didn't finish the food on my plate. I hoped she could read tears.

Later in the afternoon, the bulldozer returned, this time accompanied by a convoy of army jeeps, the soldier's shiny guns reflecting the afternoon sun. The farmers were unarmed. They watched the corn plants fold in the wake of the huge, unrelenting machine. The small boys watched their fathers. If your father is your hero and he is unable to protect your house and your food . . . I could only guess what was in their minds. Everyone was silent.

The Davao City visitors drove the farm community's spokespersons to town to dialogue with the owner and the military. This is an important step in the process in the Philippines and is rarely missed. Although the outcome is sealed, the ritual is still followed. "I really am very sorry for you," said the small businessman, "but think of it from my point of view. I need money desperately for my own debts. Anyway, I let you stay on my land for many years."

The delegation moved on to the buyer's office. Mr. Floreindo was unavailable. A flunky entertained them. "I am very sorry to hear about your situation, but that is really not our business. It is between you and your landlord."

The delegation filed a complaint with the mayor's office and appealed to the governor's office, knowing full well that the civilian government is powerless. Marcos's military and business friends were the determinative powers here.

Each farmer was given a bag of rice. "This is crazy," said

one of the farmers. "They plow under our crops and then give us a bag of rice. Why don't they let us eat from the fruit of our own labor?"

Fr. Ben Montecastro, who worked with these farmers through the Mindanao Development Center, reflected on their efforts later. "What the farmers really need is land security. Each family will have to find a way to survive, which probably means moving in with relatives. Members of this BCC will be scattered everywhere."

The building of the Basic Christian Communities is interwoven with economic survival. I followed the progress of yet another such community that began with the premise of land security thanks to the efforts of the Philippine church development agency and wealthy donors in Japan.

K'TAM, a community farm, was established with forty-nine families in Davao del Norte in 1978. The majority of the farmers were originally from the Ilocos provinces in Luzon, home of Ferdinand Marcos. Most had migrated to Mindanao in search of land and a better life. All had been tenants. Some families were evacuees from war-torn Cotabato province in Mindanao. Some were migrants from the Visayan provinces, Central Philippines. Nine families were *lumads* or tribal Filipinos, natives of Mindanao.

Together these diverse families felled trees, plowed up the soil, and built their houses by hand, using only bolos (large curved knives, the mainstay of Filipino farmers' tools) and handsaws and the traditional carabaos (water buffalo). After months of backbreaking labor, they were ready to dedicate the land and begin the first planting.

While most Basic Christian Communities grow out of the Catholic tradition, K'TAM is a mixture of Roman Catholic, Seventh-Day Adventist, United Church of Christ in the Philippines (a union of Presbyterians, Disciples of Christ, Congregationalists, and other mainline denominations), and native religions. The Philippine population is 85 percent Roman Catholic, a legacy of the 350 years of Spanish colonialism, and 8 percent Protestant, a legacy of the 50 years of American colonialism. The 5 percent Muslim population is a result of the presence of foreign Muslim traders in southern Philippines as early as the thirteenth century and the work of Islamic missionaries in the fourteenth century. Native religions account for the remainder of the population.

Catholic farmers in the Philippines opening up new land traditionally invite the priest to bless it. Tribal Filipinos usually pour the blood of a pig or a chicken around the land to ensure its fertility. Some Filipinos do both: after the priest leaves, they might pour the animal blood just to make sure. Strict Protestants would do neither. Knowing this, I was eager to see how the farmers would handle the ceremony.

The big day arrived. Flora Loquellana, a layworker who had been guiding the community's reflection sessions, greeted me at the path leading to the farm and offered to give me a tour. The farm was buzzing with activity. Children were hauling water, stumbling along with plastic pails and gallon tins that advertised Minola Cooking Oil on the outside. Women were washing and cutting vegetables. Men were stirring the rice pots and poking at the pots of meat that bubbled over the open fires outside the main building, which Flora has named the "Poustinia." It is essentially one large room on stilts.

"*Poustinia* is a Russian word that means 'desert' or 'quiet lonely place that people can enter to find the God who dwells within them,'" Flora tells me. "I read a wonderful book about it. I hope this house will be a poustinia for the farmers—a place to come to gather courage to speak and do the truth."

"You won't believe this, but I just read the same book [*Poustinia: Christian Spirituality of the East for Western Man*, by Catherine de Hueck Doherty]," I tell Flora. "I found it in a bookstore in Singapore a few months ago. The title, connecting east and west, caught my eye because the Philippines seems like such a unique mixture." What I don't tell Flora is that the book was published at Notre Dame University in Indiana in 1974, while I was attending a Mennonite Seminary twenty miles away. I hadn't heard of the book then and even if I had, I probably would not have read it. My thirst for a deeper spiritual life was developing as the pain of the Filipino farmers and the gross unfairness of their lot in life threatened to overwhelm me.

Flora looked at me as though she heard what I didn't tell her and then simply said, "I hope you will be able to understand our ceremony this morning."

We gathered in a small clearing, trees surrounding us on three sides. A makeshift altar—a low table spread with a white cloth—is the focal point. The Seventh-Day Adventist, an old man with a wrinkled face, walked slowly to the gnarled tree beside the altar. He held up his tattered Bible and began to read slowly, firmly, loudly. He began in the Book of Exodus, chapters 23 and 24—with the instructions and rituals for Israel on their way to the Promised Land.

> I will send an angel ahead of you to protect you as you travel and to bring you to the place which I have prepared. . . . If you worship me, the Lord your God, I will bless you with food and water and take away all your sicknesses. In your land no woman will have a miscarriage or be without children. I will give you long lives. (Exod. 23:20, 25-26)
>
> Moses sent young men and they burned sacrifices to the Lord and sacrificed some cattle as fellowship offerings. Moses took half of the blood of the animals and put it in bowls and the other half he threw against the altar. Then he took the book of the covenant in which the Lord's commands were written and read it aloud to the people. They said, "We will obey the Lord and do everything that God has commanded." Then Moses took the blood in the bowls and threw it on the people. He said, "This is the blood that seals the covenant which the Lord made with you when God gave you all these comamnds." (Exod. 24:5-8)

This story was picked up in the New Testament Letter to the Hebrews (chs. 9 and 10) by another reader who took her place in front of the old tree.

> In the same way, Moses sprinkled the blood on the covenant tent and over all things used in worship. Indeed according to the law, almost everything is purified by blood and sins are forgiven only if blood is poured out. . . . In the same manner Christ was also offered in sacrifice once to take away the sins of many. (Heb. 9:21-22, 28)
>
> Because Jesus Christ did what God wanted him to do, we are all purified from sin by the offering that he made of his own body once and for all. . . . So let us come near to God with a sincere heart and a sure faith, with hearts that have been purified. . . . Let us be concerned for one another, to help one another, to show love and to do good. (Heb. 10:10, 22, 24)

Then Father Montecastro commented on salvation history—from Israel, to Jesus, and now to the K'TAM farmers—with the theme of sacrificing for each other to the point of death; this led to the celebration of the Eucharist.

The men in the group approached the altar and laid down their bolos. One by one, they declared what the day meant for them. "Like Israel, I feel like we are entering the Promised Land." "Our bolos symbolize our life and work and we lay them down together for the benefit of all." "We could never have this land if we worked alone. By working together, we will enter the Promised Land."

Then the women came forward and laid down pots and pans in front of the altar. "These represent our tools, our life, our work, and we share them for the benefit of all." "Just like Jesus sacrificed his life, we also will sacrifice our life for each other."

With this, the group was ready. The *lumad* men slit the throat of the pig and, as it squealed, carried their sacrificial animal solemnly around the clearing, leaving a trail of blood as they walked. Then they cut off a chicken's head and again walked around the clearing.

A deep seriousness set in on the farmers' faces as they watched this ritual. In addition to allaying the evil spirits and invoking the fertility goddess, the blood was the symbol of the awesome responsibility they were shouldering in this project of building a collective farm and a Basic Christian Community.

As I participated in this occasion, I saw in a new way what it means to "work out your own salvation with fear and trembling for God is at work in you" (Phil. 2:12). While in seminary we scrutinized this chapter in great detail; I sat through countless hours of lecture and discussion about this "foundational Christian confession of faith."

Have this mind among yourselves, which is yours in Christ Jesus, who, though he was in the form of God, did not count equality with God a thing to be grasped, but emptied himself, taking the form of a servant, being born in human likeness. And being found in human form he humbled himself and became obedient unto death, even death on a cross. (Phil. 2:5-8)

These farmers know the cost of being co-creators of their own salvation. They know the meaning of being humble and obedient, even to the point of death—death as a political subversive. Death by hanging on a cross was a punishment reserved for those who thwarted the imperial power of Rome.

Bishop Labayen predicts that the "church will form a consensus to promote the growth of Basic Christian Communities . . . as the Council of Jerusalem opened the church to the Gentiles on the Gentile's terms." The farmers at K'TAM will not be able to deliver august lectures at theological conferences in Europe and North America, but the truth they carry is vital for the life of the church. They can share their knowledge with those who are ready to listen and to understand the context of oppression in which this knowledge is forged.

The Basic Christian Community theologians of the Philippines face the same danger that Jesus did—an untimely end as a result of collusion between the religious establishment and the imperial rulers. As Bishop Labayen explains the process, "Because of the urgent and prior problem of underdevelopment, the BCCs focus their attention on ways and means to liberate themselves from the claws of induced poverty and to promote the common good. It is when they become militant in the project of liberation . . . that the machines of propoganda accuse the BCCs as subversive of the State."

Subversive (subersibo) is a word I often heard while living in Davao City. Basic Christian Communities are not only rural phenomena. Many urban poor neighborhoods in cities like Davao also have active BCCs. In fact, a large percentage of the people in the urban squatter areas are from the countryside. Like the BCC members of Bienvenida and elsewhere, they were threatened or chased off land they tilled. Thrown off the land to make way for multinational agribusiness, farmers come to the cities looking for work.

But factory jobs, if available, don't pay enough to cover expenses. Many become vendors—cigarettes, fish, vegetables, anything to make a few pesos. Faced with the option of spending their meager earnings for food or for housing, food is the obvious choice. So they beg, borrow, or scavenge material and build makeshift houses on any empty spot of land they can find. Sooner or later, a developer eyes the land for a supermarket complex or port expansion and, like the farmers, the urban squatters are forced to move.

Because I lived in a Davao City squatter community, I was witness to their resistance to demolition as well as to their community building. One Lenten season soon after having moved to Davao, I joined the squatter community's traditional Good Friday Stations of the Cross reenactment, relating the sufferings of Jesus to the sufferings they experience in their confrontation with the authorities. I followed the actors and the crowd as they slowly moved along the little alleyways of the Buhangin community, one of the more organized squatter neighborhoods. Every few yards they stopped to enact a scene from the Passion narrative. During the scene between Pilate and Jesus, my neighbor whispered to me, "You know, they are on their third Jesus. The first two quit."

"Why?" I asked.

"They were afraid the military might pick them up."

"That's crazy! Why should a teenager in a poor community fear being picked up by the police for playing Jesus in a street drama? He clearly has no powerful following, no access to arms. Who is threatened by that young skinny boy?"

"The military thinks that whoever plays the role of Jesus must be a key organizer in the resistance against demolition of our homes here," she replied. "Remember, Jesus didn't have an army, either."

Her answer set my mind spinning. What makes the Basic Christian Communities such a powerful force? A real-life drama enacted in another squatter community reinforced what I already suspected. The heroine of the drama is Karin Guantero, a former nun who left her religious order because she felt life in the convent was too comfortable and too protected. She is the first among a cloud of Filipino witnesses to point out to me, through her very body, the power of blood shed for others. (But countless heroes and heroines contributed to my conversion experience in the Philippines—conversion to the God of the poor, to the privilege of being a co-creator with the God of justice.)

When I first met Karin, she was living in Piapi, one of Davao's poorest slums. She was helping to organize neighborhood groups for fire protection since one favorite way to get rid of squatters is to light a fire and let it jump from one wooden shack to the next. Karin also worked to establish small backyard industry. With her encouragement, groups sprang up for legal aid, Bible study, and representation at the mayor's office.

Many of the members of the Bible study group were vendors at Bankerohan, the local market and jeepney depot. I often caught a jeepney ride at the market to visit a friend on the outskirts of town. One evening in June 1978, I caught my usual ride near the market. Everything looked normal. By the time I reached my destination, excited radio announcers were reporting a fire at Bankerohan market. In the midst of their on-site description, we heard a loud boom. "A grenade was just thrown!" gasped the announcer.

An hour later, a telephone call from the hospital brought the news closer to home. Karin's friend Olga was tearful. "Karin and I were downtown, when we heard that there was a fire at Bankerohan. Karin got worried because some of the women in her Bible study group are vendors there. She wanted to go help them rescue their belongings. She was running ahead of me when all of a sudden there was an explosion. She was thrown to the ground, bleeding. I held her and screamed for someone to get her to a hospital."

But it was too late. More than a hundred people were hurt in the explosion. Ten were killed; Karin was one of them.

This was the seventh such grenade-throwing incident in Mindanao in the space of a few months. Many of the bombings were traced back to the military. Some people suspected that the government was trying to foment fear among the general population in order to justify the moving in of more military troops.

In 1978 large demonstrations, marches, and strikes in Mindanao were illegal—and almost unheard of. Funerals, however, were common. The custom in the Philippines is to accompany the body from the church to the graveyard on foot. Thousands of people accompanied Karin's body—people whose lives she touched, people she loved.

Before proceeding to the graveyard, we gathered at the Ateneo de Davao chapel. During the funeral mass, the priest intoned the familiar words of Christ from the Last Supper. "This cup is the new covenant in my blood which will be poured out for you." As he spoke, I could not help but think that the communion cup is the fruit of Karin's response to her friends—and the fruit of Jesus' response to his friends, all the people of the world: "This is my blood poured out for you."

In the midst of the funeral service, an organizer of the march asked me in a last minute panic if I could find other foreigners to attend or take pictures in order to discourage more grenade throwing. But since my time and energy for the previous year had been focused on Filipinos, I was unable to contribute any names. Besides, any foreign missionary who was vaguely sympathetic was already in attendance.

After the mass, Karin's neighbors, squatters from other barrios, students, and church workers walked slowly out of the college gate into the streets. Cassocked seminarians flanked us on either side as a sort of security guard. Singing, we carried placards with the names of each person who had been killed by the grenades in Davao and elsewhere in Mindanao.

The air was tense, for clearly Karin's death had provided the occasion for an otherwise illegal march. The participants cast glances at the gathered crowds, wondering who among them were plainclothes military intelligence officers and who among them had another grenade to throw.

By the time the procession passed the San Pedro Cathedral, there seemed to be an easing of the tension, although I didn't know if the mood accurately reflected the reality. "It's as though Karin is not dead," said one of her neighbors as we marched. "We are exercising our human rights like she always wanted us to do. We were afraid before, but because Karin was killed, we knew we had to stand up ourselves. We really have no other choice."

I sensed a new spirit—a defiant spirit—among those squatters marching courageously down Davao's main street. There is indeed power in the blood. Jesus' power lay in his willingness to give up his life in the pursuit of "bringing good news to the poor, release to the captives and liberty to those who are oppressed." That willingness then inspires others and more people get involved and soon "they are practically building an infrastructure of political power in the entire country," as Colonel Kintanar said.

7

The Church Divided

TEMPORAL AND SPIRITUAL CONTRADICTIONS

While the Basic Christian Communities offer considerable life and vitality and Bishop Julio Labayen predicts a glorious historical future for them, the communities represent only one tendency within the Roman Catholic Church in the Philippines. The Philippine church, both Protestant and Catholic, is divided as it faces pressures from the military, from the United States, and from its own grass roots members.

Historically, the church has been ambivalent in standing with its poorest members. In describing the essential nature of the Catholic church in the Philippines, Col. Galileo Kintanar, a military intelligence officer who specializes in theology and the church, says that it

> has temporal interests that apparently fix it on the conservative or even reactionary side. It has tremendous assets in capital and land. It would not risk these in a violent revolution. The temporal interests of the church are derived from a long history of colonial domination and from being a close ally of the ruling elite in whichever social system has arisen in the Philippines. It is bound by countless social ties to the incumbent social elite in the urban and rural areas. *Considering the conservative interests of the church, the religious radicals . . . will have a hard time winning its unqualified support and assistance.*[1]

1. Col. Galileo Kintanar, "Roots of Religious Radicalism in the Philippines," mimeograph copy of article printed in *Philippine Military Intelligence Journal,* 1978.

93

Kintanar's historical summary is essentially correct. In 1521 when explorer Ferdinand Magellan landed on Mactan Island in the central Philippines, he was accompanied by both a chaplain and a Spanish military officer. This was only a few years after the Spanish had driven the "Moors" from Spain, and the Spanish thirst to stamp out the infidels' influence extended to the Philippines. Before the arrival of the Spanish, Filipino Muslim influence was extensive, stretching from Mindanao to Manila.

Magellan's combination of the cross and sword continued throughout the 350 years of Spanish colonialism. Permanent occupation of the islands began in 1565 with the arrival of the Legazpi expedition. King Philip II of Spain projected a peaceful occupation of the Philippines in which the religious orders would play an important role. The papacy transferred the administration of the new Church of the Indies to the Spanish crown, and the crown in turn entrusted the specific task of Christianizing the natives to the regular clergy.[2]

By 1565, the Augustinian order was dispatched to the Philippines as missionaries to the islands. Other orders participated in the conversion of the Filipinos as well: the discalced Fransiscans (1578), the Jesuits (1581), the Dominicans (1587), and the Augustinian Recollects (1606). These orders had the authority to administer the sacraments and perform the duties of the parish priest independently of the local bishop.

The religious orders in the Philippines enjoyed a generous amount of autonomy—they were never subject to episcopal supervision. In contrast, the secular clergy, priests who were not part of a religious order, were directly responsible to the bishop of the diocese. However, the secular clergy were in a minority in the Philippines, a situation that directly challenged the authority of the bishops. The regular orders were able to remain in control because they knew they were irreplaceable. Every responsible officer of the Spanish crown realized that the continuation of Spanish hegemony of the provinces largely depended upon the authority and prestige that the religious exercised over their parishioners.

Spain was the source of government in the Philippines;

2. John Leddy Phelan, *The Hispanization of the Philippines: Spanish Aims and Filipino Responses, 1565–1700* (Madison: University of Wisconsin Press, 1959).

Rome was the center of the imperial religion brought to the Philippines. Yet most of the material burden for supporting the religious establishment in the islands fell on the Filipinos. The crown only assumed the expense of transporting the clergy from Spain to the Philippines. The first Spanish missionaries viewed themselves as soldiers of Christ waging a war with spiritual weapons to overthrow the devil's tyranny over pagan peoples. As the missionaries became increasingly aware of the limits of the Spanish resources and the magnitude of the task, however, the zeal of the first generation gave way to a spirit of apathy, routine, and discouragement.

More often than not, the Roman Catholic Church in the Philippines came down on the side of protecting the Spanish crown's interests. Though the clergy were aware of the crushing impact of taxation and forced labor on the Filipinos, with few exceptions they seldom recommended the system's abolition. Enormous churches were built in the eighteenth and nineteenth centuries through the back-breaking physical labor of the natives. Some clergy did try to at least ameliorate the harsh conditions.

However, if the power of the religious orders or the bishops was challenged or threatened by the secular power, they unequivocally moved to protect their interest. During the 350-year period of Spanish colonialism, the rulers at times were ready to abandon the Philippines because they were not a lucrative colony. In fact, the silver and other booty from Mexico was subsidizing the Philippine colony. Proposals to abandon the Philippines were debated at the Spanish court at the suggestion of Spanish merchants and the textile industry. The missionary orders reminded the Spanish sovereigns of their solemn vow to convert the Filipinos and preserve the faith in the archipelago. More than any other single factor, religious and missionary influence kept the Spanish in the Philippines.[3] Throughout the Spanish colonial period, the religious orders were able to build up their land holdings and their buildings and institutions. Much of this continued into the American period.

Soon after the American takeover in 1898, Protestant mission boards geared up in the United States for the task of "civilizing and Christianizing" the Filipinos. Though Colonel Kin-

3. Ibid., pp. 11-14.

tanar was writing primarily about the Catholic church, his description of the church as "allied with ruling elite" has some indirect application to the American effort as well. Protestant missionaries appeared only after the American military invaded. The message to the Filipinos could not be clearer—a new colonial master, a new religion. The "open door" to evangelize the Philippines was created through military conquest.

Just as the pope had divided the world between Spain and Portugal during their imperial height, so the various American Protestant denominations divided the Philippines among themselves according to the Comity Agreement of 1903. Methodists went to north and central Luzon, Presbyterians to southern Luzon and eastern Visayas, Congregationalists to Mindanao, Baptists to Panay, Episcopalians to mountain provinces in the north, Disciples of Christ to northern Quezon province, Nueva Ecija, and Cavite. That agreement broke down after World War II.

The final blow to this arrangement came in the 1960s when fundamentalist denominations, nondenominational conservative churches, and parachurch organizations began streaming into all provinces of the Philippines. Mormon missionaries and Jehovah's Witnesses appeared in great numbers as well. The Marcos regime encouraged revival crusades led by visiting evangelists. Military intelligence officers like Galileo Kintanar have advised the government to encourage the conservative mainstream of the church as a way to undercut the social radicals in the church.

This strategy has been suggested elsewhere in the world. In 1969, the Rockefeller Commission studying Latin America concluded that the Catholic church was no longer a reliable ally for American interests. Despite its ambivalent history, the same conclusion could be drawn about the Catholic church in the Philippines. Kintanar may have accurately described the institutional hierarchy of the church as "having temporal interests which fix it on the conservative or even reactionary side"; however, the pressure from the bottom—from the base communities and activist nuns and priests—has made an impact on the pronouncements and positions of the hierarchy.

This present dissatisfaction from below has its genesis in the history of the Philippine church. For example, the "secularization movement" within the church during the 1800s asserted the right to equality of Filipino priests in a church dominated by foreign religious orders. This movement was led by Filipino fathers Gomez, Burgos, and Zamora. The three priests were hung on the gallows for subversion by the Spanish administration, but their endeavor raised critical questions about both the religious orders and colonial domination in the Philippines. The work of these priests and others like them inspired the educated Filipinos and eventually the entire people to develop a sense of national consciousness.

At the turn of the century, when the Filipinos revolted against Spanish rule and then resisted the American takeover, the Filipino clergy, led by Fr. Gregorio Aglipay, participated actively in the struggle. They put church influence and facilities in the service of the Philippine revolutionary government and acted as chaplains to the revolutionary army. Father Aglipay and several priests even went as far as forming and leading guerrilla units against the American forces at the turn of this century.

After the defeat of the Spanish in 1898, Aglipay founded a nationalist church that broke from the Spanish clergy–dominated Roman Catholic Church in the Philippines. Known as the Iglesia Filipina Independiente (Philippine Independent Church or Aglipayan Church), it exists to this day. Though it has lost much of its revolutionary fervor, its very existence is a reminder of the power of religion when put at the service of nationalist sentiment.

During the Marcos era, the archbishop of Manila, Jaime Cardinal Sin, took the lead in articulating the "critical collaboration" stance of the church toward the government (a phrase popularized in the Philippines by Cardinal Sin). The church should collaborate with the government when it works for the benefit of the citizens, but the church also has a responsibility to criticize the government when it makes mistakes. The pronouncements of the bishop of Manila and the Catholic Bishops' Conference of the Philippines as a whole have had an important effect on political life in the country. Although there was a diversity of opinion within the Bishops' Conference, by the end of the Marcos era the bishops united in supporting a process of clean elections. They issued a statement urging people to vote their conscience; in effect that meant to vote for Cory Aquino. Cardinal Sin also participated wholeheartedly in securing the election for Cory Aquino and in bringing out the people on the street to protect the Marcos defectors, Fidel Ramos and Juan Ponce Enrile.

A few diehard conservative bishops like the archbishop of Zamboanga City continued a measure of support for Marcos or some expression of conservative politics long after he was forced to flee.

I visited Archbishop Cruces in March 1987 at his palace overlooking the beautiful Zamboanga harbor. He received me somewhat grudgingly in the anteroom. An enormous sculpted pool table covered with a brocade quilt sat in the middle of this wood-paneled room with its elegant high ceiling. Lace wall hangings, provocative sculptures on the bookshelf, and other elegant pieces of furniture placed strategically around the room overwhelmed me with the impression of religious decadence.

I asked Archbishop Cruces, "How has life changed since Mrs. Aquino became President? Has the work of the church changed?" Nothing has changed, Cruces assured me, responding in single phrases to my questions. The archbishop remained stiff and refused to be cajoled, humored, or charmed into more openness. Finally I asked, "Perhaps I am asking the wrong questions. You may have something you want to share, but I haven't given you the opportunity through my line of questioning."

He brightened. "Yes, I have something to tell the American people. I go to America every year. Your problem is orthodoxy. Filipinos here believe what the church believes. People are disobedient there. You mix the elements. Mass wine must be pure grape wine. Nothing else. There is to be no mixing of the elements. Only the priest should have the wine." With a satisfied smile, he added, "But now you have found out AIDS can be transmitted by saliva on the communion cup, so people don't drink the wine anymore."

In the days previous to the interview I had traveled throughout the archdiocese. While the city itself is booming with the black market trade from Malaysia and Indonesia and smuggled U.S. goods, the rural areas immediately surrounding the city are unbelievably poor. My mind reeled as he continued his tirade against the mixing of the communion elements. Finally I asked, "What about the poor?" "We have programs," he said. "Livelihood programs like stuffed animals." His eyes glinted. "The people make stuffed animals, beautiful stuffed animals."

I could hardly breathe. I mumbled my thanks and let myself out.

In contrast to the archbishop's palace by the sea in Zamboanga, the bishop's office in Bacolod City in the province of Negros Occidental is plain, sparsely finished. The Minnesota Human Rights Lawyers Committee tour group met with Bishop Antonio Fortich in his Bacolod office in 1987. Only a few months earlier the bishop's house was burned in a mysterious fire; as a result, Fortich received us in his makeshift office.

As we waited outside his office to see the bishop, we could not help but notice a prominently displayed poster of Dom Helder Camara, archbishop of Recife, Brazil. Camara's poignant statement was printed in bold letters: "When I give food to the poor they call me a saint; when I ask why the poor have no food, they call me a communist."

This could as easily be Fortich's motto. The bishop of Negros is from a wealthy sugar baron family in the province of Negros Occidental. In this premier sugar-growing province of the Philippines, the disparity between rich and poor has been most glaring. Since sugar prices have dropped drastically in the international market, many sugar planters themselves are in economic trouble. Some cannot afford to plant anymore. The workers have been laid off. Children of workers are not sent to school and many of them suffer from severe malnutrition. Malnutrition wards in three hospitals in the province are filled with children who look like those pictured in Ethiopian famine ads. When the workers tried to plant crops on the idle sugar lands so they could feed their children, they were harassed. Some were arrested; some were killed.

Bishop Fortich began as a conservative bishop, but the stark poverty of his parishioners and the murders of sugar workers who tried to defy the sugar oligarchy pushed him as a pastor to stand with the workers. For years Fortich has warned that the island of Negros is a "social volcano" that could blow up at any time. He has urged the planters to share their wealth and has supported the sugar workers in their organizing. As a result of his strong support for land reform, the sugar hacenderos consider the bishop a traitor. On the way to visit him, our lawyers group noticed huge signs hung on the streets near the cathedral in Bacolod denouncing communist priests and sisters.

The bishop served the lawyers chocolate cake he said he had baked himself. After an exchange of pleasantries, Fortich launched into a discussion of what he considered to be the key question in Negros—land reform. Suddenly, in the midst of the discussion, the bishop leaned forward and plaintively asked the lawyers, "In America, are people called communists if they help the poor?"

On April 28, 1987, a few months after our visit, members of the El Tigre, an anticommunist vigilante movement, hurled a grenade into the bishop's compound. Fortich was unharmed though it exploded just outside his bedroom. Despite the threats on his life, Fortich says he will continue to speak.

Even after the attempt on Fortich's life by vigilantes, his peers in the Catholic Bishops' Conference of the Philippines (CBCP) have not been able to agree on a statement condemning the vigilantes. In fact, Cardinal Sin is on record backing armed vigilante groups organized "purely for self-defense." He said arming anticommunist groups may be necessary for their protection. Given the Catholic church's strong influence on public opinion and Philippine politics, an official CBCP statement on the vigilantes would have a significant effect on dousing or fanning the vigilante fever. Bishops like Antonio Fortich in Negros Occidental and Julio Labayen of Infanta Prelature, Luzon, have spoken out strongly against abuse of human rights and the action of vigilantes. However, these bishops are in the minority.

During the Marcos era I witnessed the struggle of the poor and marginalized within the church to claim the gospel message and the institution as their own. A good example of that struggle was the grand experiment of the Mindanao-Sulu Pastoral Conference Secretariat (MSPCS) in Davao City. Unlike the regional social action centers that were creations of the bishops and essentially controlled by them, MSPCS was a pioneering effort of clergy and laity. The board was composed of bishops, priests, sisters, and lay people with equal voices in decision making. My husband, Gene, and I were fortunate enough to have a desk in that office in 1978-79 and to experience the vitality of the agency.

We were there during Karl Gaspar's term as executive director. Energy and enthusiasm was high. Guitar music, ice cream, performance of skits, songs with actions, or jokes— anything could happen during the course of a day or evening.

The staff worked unbelievably hard, spending long hours on the road visiting the far-flung parishes of Mindanao, encouraging creative drama, community organizing, cooperatives, and Bible studies for Basic Christian Communities.

Through their work, the MSPCS staff and other Christians involved in action for and with the poor gained the grudging respect of a variety of people. In some dioceses the bishop and the pastoral team welcomed the MSPCS staff. In others they were shunned. As a result of their work, peoples' organizations grew or were strengthened. Serious discussion about democracy and what it looks like in the church was the result of the Mindanao-Sulu Pastoral Conference experiment. We could see that MSPCS, with its emphasis on democratizing the structures and enabling the participation of the poorest and most marginalized, was on a collision course with the leadership of one of the most undemocratic institutions in the world—the Roman Catholic Church. Colonel Kintanar confidently predicted that "the religious radicals . . . can never fix the entire official church structure on a course of radicalism while the incumbent social system still stands."

The conflict expressed itself in MSPCS board skirmishes over a period of years. The final denouement came when the bishops simply withdrew from the Mindanao-Sulu Pastoral Conference board and left the sisters and lay people by themselves with their democratic prototype. Without the bishops' protection, the programs were in danger from the government and the military. Without the bishops' presence, the programs were also in danger of losing funding from the bishops' counterparts in Europe and Canada.

Like the Catholic church, the Protestant churches are also divided within their membership over the issue of their participation in securing justice for the poor. However, the question of democracy within the church is not the explosive issue it is in the Roman Catholic Church, since the very existence of Protestantism is based on a democratic order. The leaders of the United Church of Christ in the Philippines (UCC-P), the largest Protestant denomination in the country, have tended to side more often with the aspirations of the poor than have the rank and file members of the church. This may reflect the relatively smaller economic clout of the Protestant leadership in comparison to its membership. Unlike that of the Roman Catholic Church, the sociological profile of the Protestant church is not pyramid-shaped with the bishops at the apex.

In November 1987, the military published a list of organizations, including the UCC-P, labeled as a "communist front" or as "communist infiltrated." Bishop Erme Camba, General Secretary of the UCC-P, called this charge a "calibrated harassment against the church." He challenged the military to prove its case in court or make a public apology to the entire church constituency. He reminded the military that among the 500,000 members of the UCC-P were such prominent people as Chief of Staff Gen. Fidel Ramos, Senate president Jovito Salonga, and Supreme Court Associate Justice Abraham Sarmiento.

The UCC-P was only one among twenty-five groups targeted by the Philippine military. Another religious group was the Episcopal Commission on Tribal Filipinos, which is directly under the Catholic Bishops' Conference of the Philippines. Christians for the Realization of a Sovereign Society, another targeted group, denied the charges and said that their "activities flow from a spirituality of discipleship, to be ready to follow Jesus on the way of the cross."

A struggle for the hearts and minds of the church people that was waged during the Marcos period has intensified. Kintanar's 1978 article formed the basis of a carrot and stick strategy to deal with the religious radicals. Colonel Kintanar recommended that "the government should adopt persuasive ways of encouraging the conservative mainstream of the Church hierarchy and clergy to stress the primordial spiritual mission of the church and at the same time to let its superior numbers overwhelm the radicals in policy making bodies and in social action projects."[4]

The Marcos government followed this advice somewhat, but it was really after Marcos that Kintanar's suggestions had more chance of success. Kintanar's "carrot" had included a proposal that the government and the church cooperate in social action. However, the Marcos administration was so discredited that few bishops were willing to engage in joint social action work with the government, especially in the last years of Marcos's rule. The "stick" incorporated arrest and detention as well as a more subtle program of regular surveillance

4. Kintanar, "Roots of Religious Radicalism in the Philippines," p. 8.

on groups the military labeled "subversive," and, where possible, provocation of internal debate among the religious radicals.

Even the most conservative prince of the church did not want to leave members of the flock vulnerable to the martial law regime. Though the bishops worried during the Marcos rule about the leftist influence in the church, they did not feel free to blow the whistle.

By the time Aquino became president, the intermeshing of religious commitment and armed struggle among individuals and barrios at the grass roots level had already taken place throughout the country. For example, in 1984 I talked at length with the peasant leader of a Basic Christian Community who was attending a month-long Bible study training course in the province of Zamboanga del Sur. During our first conversation, he described the Christian community in his barrio, his own involvement, his motivations, and the joy of being part of a Basic Christian Community. The next day I mentioned that I knew the New People's Army were active in his area. Without blinking an eye, he said, "Yes, they have been in our barrio since 1975. I would be proud if my son joined them."

It is precisely this intermingling or fusion at the grass roots that causes grave concern among the church leadership. Many bishops, evangelical leaders, and scholars fear that when the church engages in social action, it simply becomes a tool of the communists. Several Jesuit scholars have extended this worry and written on the dangers Marxism poses to Christianity. They warn against Marxist infiltration of the church and cite the problems of priests accepting Marxism.

One of the most incisive rejoinders to this concern came from a poet and activist in Mindanao named Sol, who was targeted as a "hard core" Communist Party member by the Philippine military. In response to a dissertation on Christianity and Marxism by a Jesuit scholar, Sol wrote,

Do you really think the answer to the Marxist challenge is to "greenhouse" Christianity? Real Christianity grew out of a struggle with seductive Greek and Roman philosophies. The crude Christians, by sheer faith, finally triumphed over sophisticated cosmopolites. Christianity has survived 2,000 years of persecution, suppression, schisms, revolutions and capitalist affluence, so I don't see why it won't survive what you call the strong dynamic in Marxism.

A challenge faces the Philippine church, both Protestant and Catholic: how to incarnate the gospel in a militarized and revolutionary situation. Added to this challenge is the Catholic attachment to an affluent and authoritarian structure and Protestantism's strong historical identification with the United States. The positions and decisions of the Philippine church, both Protestant and Roman Catholic, in the next few years will have an important impact on the future of the country. Whether the churches follow the old patterns or open new channels may well depend on their ability to reconcile the contradictions between their temporal attachments and their greater spiritual mission.

8

Teetering on the Brink of Peace

WHAT MIGHT HAVE BEEN—
THE FIRST YEAR OF PRESIDENT AQUINO

The dramatic overthrow of Ferdinand Marcos through the efforts of Filipino citizens massed on the street against tanks and guns ushered in new possibilities in Philippines society. The special gift of the People's Power Uprising was the hope it kindled in Filipinos that change was indeed possible through a concerted nonviolent effort.

Only one year later that hope for reconciliation and peace with justice within the society lay dashed. In March 1987, one year after she took office, President Aquino called for a string of honorable military victories against the very people with whom her government was negotiating only a few months earlier. The New People's Army, who in the early days of the Aquino administration had offered to protect her against a military coup, moved into an offensive military posture. Human rights advocates who had initially served on the Aquino human rights committee began to criticize the administration actively. The Armed Forces of the Philippines, which defected from Marcos in February 1986 and supported Mrs. Aquino for president, showed marked ambivalence toward civilian authority, and factions staged coup attempts regularly.

Immediately prior to the 1986 election, the legal opposition to Marcos—church peace and justice offices, human rights groups, and labor unions—were gearing up for a Marcos move against them. "We have heard from our sources," said one priest, "that as soon as Marcos 'wins' this election, he plans to order raids of offices and mass arrests. This election is designed to give him the mandate to clean up the legal opposition." People discussed who would take which documents home, who would go on "vacation," and who would remain in the office. By September 1987, after only a year and a half under the Aquino administration, the same organizations were making the same plans, because the rumors of a crackdown by the military were again rampant.

For almost a year, society seemed poised on the brink of peace. That balance point has been passed and the die is cast. What might have been can only be mourned—and, of course, examined for what clues it offers for the future. But it is important to clarify and to examine the elements of this drama because other people in other places will look to this period in Philippine history for stories to inspire their own struggles. Even without all of the data yet available (declassified U.S. government documents and the memoirs of such Aquino advisers as Joker Arroyo, etc.), we can make some preliminary observations. Heroic myths may be inspiring, but in the long run truthfulness will be more of a contribution.

I was in the Philippines for the presidential election in February 1986 and witnessed the fervor with which people participated in this event. I returned a year later to observe the effects of the new administration upon the life of the people. It was clear to me that the population as a whole was yearning for peace and that many individuals and groups were actively engaged in peace building.

However, even before the change in government in 1986, there were widely divergent views among the population of how peace could be won. During the election campaign, for example, it seemed like two streams of activity in the country were passing each other, sometimes quite literally, without connecting, oblivious to each other's strength and roots.

In late January 1986, an American religious tour group I was leading in the Philippines joined our Filipino hosts in a march advocating a boycott of the elections. The march participants were primarily farmers from Central Luzon, with some teachers and religious people sprinkled among them. The three thousand marchers traveled by foot for three days to congregate in San Fernando, Pampanga. On the way I talked with one farmer, a Methodist lay leader in his church, who told me he had only ten pesos when he left home two days earlier. He gave five pesos to his wife and took five for himself.

Once in a while he would buy one cigarette from a street vendor, carefully wrapping the remainder of his money in a handkerchief he kept in the front pocket of his tattered shirt.

The marchers, who occupied one half of the road, were walking north one morning when we heard horns honking and people shouting. Approaching us was a caravan of Aquino supporters. Cars with air conditioning, trucks, and jeepneys were colorfully outfitted in yellow, the Cory color. Huge yellow plastic hands fixed in the L sign, the symbol for Cory's campaign, were attached to the vehicles. As the two groups passed each other, Cory's crowd yelled "Co-ry, Co-ry," while the marchers responded, "Boy-cott, Boy-cott."

Two impressions struck me as the groups snaked past each other: the clear class difference between the two bands and the markedly stronger fervency of the Cory caravan. It was difficult to be fervent after walking for two days under the tropical sun on an empty stomach, but it was not just the physical handicaps that dampened the spirit. Boycott was essentially a negative stand—noncooperation with the evil Marcos system. Boycotting a Marcos election was just another way to point out that Marcos controlled the courts, the media, and the military, and that the U.S. government still considered him part of the solution.

There had been a plethora of referenda, plebiscites, and elections throughout the Marcos years that had no meaning in terms of sharing power. This election seemed like just one more staged event. There was a sense this time around that a boycott might not hasten Marcos's downfall nor prolong his rule—it was just the principled thing to do. But it is hard to whip up much fervor on principle. The boycotters were in the protracted struggle mode, not ready to expend added energy in what they perceived to be an intermediate point in the struggle. They were prepared for the long haul, so pacing was necessary.

The campaign for Cory, on the other hand, was filled with potential. Here was an actual immediate alternative to Marcos. The Cory Crusaders could see a change just around the corner, when their candidate won. They believed it was possible and they were in the homestretch. They were ready to make that extra effort to cross the finish line successfully.

During the campaign, one middle-class NAMFREL (National Movement for Free Elections) volunteer told me, "This is our last chance. If we cannot remove the dictator through elections, we will have to join the militants." She voiced the sentiments of many sincere, patriotic middle-class Filipinos. Church leaders like Cardinal Sin, archbishop of Manila, were also counting on the election and its aftermath to sweep away the dictator. It had been virtually impossible for Sin to discipline activist priests and sisters during the Marcos years because he would have been seen as siding with the dictatorship.

The election was held on February 7, 1986. The vehemence many Filipinos displayed in protecting their vote was astonishing. They stayed in the polling places to make sure the count was clean, accompanied the ballot boxes to the central counting station, and kept vigil as COMELEC (the Marcos-controlled Commission on Elections) took over with computerized counting. No one really expected people all across the country to focus so intensely on the winning of the election. Even many in the rural areas who may have advocated a boycott participated in some way in the election process.

In the weeks immediately following the election, life was tense. Marcos proclaimed himself the winner based on the COMELEC returns. Mrs. Aquino claimed victory on the basis of the NAMFREL figures. People were on the streets demanding Marcos's resignation. American government personalities shuttled in and out of Manila trying to bend the situation to a compromise that would satisfy the people and satisfy their ally, Ferdinand Marcos.

While Aquino called for the people to take their money out of Marcos banks and not to pay their utility bills in order to paralyze the government, the nationalist peace and justice groups made plans for militant demonstrations and a three-day national strike. The strike was something farmers and workers could participate in directly. Some of Cory's suggestions for action, like withdrawal of money from banks, were only an option for people wealthy enough to have money to put in a bank.

Much of the election day's fervor had arisen spontaneously through individual initiative or loosely organized volunteer groups. The next stage of actually getting Marcos to accept the results of the election required solid mobilization. The nationalist groups swung into action; this, after all, was their strength: disciplined organization. Over the years these groups had organized regional and national strikes aimed at halting business and commerce in order to bring down the government through sheer economic pressure. They had been building up experience in how to handle the logistics and how to coordinate actions around the country.

Leandro Alejandro, chairperson of Bayan, the coalition of nationalist organizations, told our Mennonite study tour in 1985 that the call for national strikes was like having choir practice. "No one expects perfect singing at a practice. A portion of the choir has practiced in Davao City, in Cebu, and elsewhere. The Sunday morning performance will come when the majority of Manilans join the national strike."

Bayan's organizing activity was building up when the surprise defection by Ramos and Enrile cut the momentum. On February 22, Marcos's defense minister, Juan Ponce Enrile, and Fidel V. Ramos, the head of the Philippine Constabulary, joined forces at Camp Aguinaldo in a rebellion against Marcos. Actually, Marcos claimed he had uncovered a plot by the two men to stage a coup and so they tried to surround themselves with troops they could rely on before he could move against them. The national and international focus shifted from the peoples' strikes to Camp Aguinaldo and Camp Crame, where these former Marcos men were holed up.

Cardinal Sin and the Catholic station, Radio Veritas, were focal players in the drama. Sin called for the people to come to the streets and protect Ramos and Enrile since they were ready to ally themselves with Aquino. The faithful flock appeared. Cory's Crusaders carried their fervency right into the streets for four days, standing in front of Camp Aguinaldo and Camp Crame on the Epifanio de los Santos highway. They ate, slept, prayed, and talked to the soldiers. They stood against the tanks and inspired the whole world by their courage and determination.

The nationalist organizations, however, did not take up their positions as identifiable groups on the street with the sororities and fraternities and university clubs and churches and religious congregations and families. Many of these people had suffered directly at the hands of troops under the command responsibility of Ramos and Enrile. They did not know what game these two men were playing. Why would they choose to protect Ramos and Enrile?

As a result of the peoples' display of support, Mrs. Aquino

was sworn in as president on February 25. Hope was in the air. All the major forces seemed stunned and in flux. The military, the left, the United States government, even Mrs. Aquino's advisers did not move quickly.

Although Cory's followers were ecstatic, the movement that had been gearing up to withstand further Marcos military repression was dubious. The first test for the direction of the Aquino government was the question of what to do with the political detainees. The military strenuously objected to the release of prisoners like Bernabe Buscayno (alias Kumander Dante), Horacio (Boy) Morales, alleged chief of the National Democratic Front, and Jose Maria Sison, alleged founder of the Communist Party of the Philippines. The human rights groups persistently appeared at the justice department, at the gates of the prison, and at Malacanang to plead for the release of all detainees, the famous and the unknown.

President Aquino is no stranger to human rights abuse. Her late husband Benigno spent eight years in Marcos's prisons until he was allowed to leave in 1980 to go to the United States for triple bypass heart surgery. When he returned to Manila in 1983 against Marcos's wishes, he was shot and killed as he was escorted down the steps of the airplane onto the tarmac at the Manila International Airport. During the years that Senator Aquino sat in prison, Mrs. Aquino kept in contact with the human rights groups and got to know the other prisoners and the prisoners' families.

The idea of a debt of gratitude (utang na loob) is a deeply held notion in the Philippines. If someone does something for you, especially at a time when you are in great need, you will be in their debt forever unless you can repay in equally dramatic fashion. Feudal and familial ties are also a consideration in larger social and political affairs. Through her husband and her own family, Mrs. Aquino was connected to some of the detainees. Bernabe Buscayno, for example, was from the Aquino's home province of Tarlac. In his youth, he had been a laborer on a sugar plantation there.

When martial law was declared in 1972, Senator Benigno Aquino was immediately arrested. He sat in prison for a long time while a case was prepared against him charging him with communist terrorist links. When Kumander Dante (Buscayno) was arrested years later, Marcos saw his opportunity. He tried to arrange a deal with Buscayno to testify against Aquino. But

Buscayno steadfastly refused, and without his testimony, the case against Aquino was weak. Aquino was released to go the U.S. in 1980 and Buscayno remained in prison.

In 1986, when Mrs. Aquino was in a position to return the favor, she did. Over the objections of the military and her chief of staff, Fidel Ramos, she ordered the majority of the political prisoners to be released. Since many of the detainees had been in the nationalist resistance over a long period of time and were well known, a new hope pervaded the opposition about the possibilities for social change in the country under the Aquino administration.

Less than a month after becoming president, Aquino created a Presidential Committee on Human Rights through Executive Order No. 8. Its function was to "investigate complaints . . . of violations of human rights, past or present, committed by officers or agents of the national government or persons acting in their place or stead or under their orders, express or implied." The committee was also to "report its findings to the President and make them public, suggesting such action or actions by the new government to compensate the victims and punish culprits as it may deem appropriate."

Aquino's appointees to the committee were also the source of great hope among the people. One of them, Sr. Mariani Dimaranan, an elderly Franciscan nun, founded the Task Force Detainees, an agency of the Association of Major Religious Superiors that documented human rights abuses by the military throughout the Marcos regime. Sister Mariani and the Task Force were nominated for the Nobel Peace prize in 1986. The diminutive, gray-habited nun has probably done more than any other single person in the area of human rights advocacy in the Philippines. Her appointment to the Presidential Committee virtually assured that the committee would have the confidence of the common people. Those who might be wary of giving testimony for fear the military would use it against them or their family later, trusted Sister Mariani to protect them.

The chairperson of the committee was former Senator Jose W. Diokno and vice chair was Justice Jose B. L. Reyes, a man of integrity who had served the nation for many years. Other members were progressive professionals such as attorney Haydee Yorac, William Claver, and Zenaida Quezon Avencena. General Soriano represented the Armed Forces' Judge Advocate General Office.

The committee's progress, despite its competent, committed members, was painfully slow. It had only investigative powers and authority to recommend cases to the court for trial. No military person was prosecuted in the courts as a result of the work of the committee. The reasons were mixed. The military, needless to say, did not want any of its own touched publicly and so found ways to block the work. The committee itself had internal administrative problems that contributed to the snail's pace, according to Abelardo Aportadera, an attorney who was a later addition to the committee. The government coffers were virtually empty when Mrs. Aquino took over, so the committee was operating on a minuscule budget, which also hampered its progress.

In addition to some new support for human rights work, a flowering of cultural democracy also took place almost immediately after Mrs. Aquino took office. I was astonished to see the change at the Cultural Center Complex of the Philippines, which in the past had been the exclusive purview of Imelda Marcos. In the mammoth buildings on Manila Bay, Mrs. Marcos had sponsored performances or displays only by internationally acclaimed elite artists or local artists of whom she approved. As I walked up the grand red carpeted staircase in February 1987 and looked up beyond the huge white shell chandeliers, I saw hanging from the elegant balcony murals and banners that during the Marcos era were seen only in street demonstrations. The displays included many pictures that in the past had been passed surreptitiously around human rights agencies. I saw paintings depicting the everyday life of poor Filipinos that had previously hung in tiny alternative galleries. "We think of the Cultural Center as a liberated space," said one artist.

New dailies sprang up overnight to supplement the opposition papers such as *Malaya* and the Catholic newspaper *Veritas*, which had been allowed to exist under Marcos. Circulation increased as people felt they could believe what they were reading in the papers. New talk shows on television hosted guests from the entire spectrum of opinion in the society. For the first time audiences heard land reform discussed by people who worked on land reform in the New People's Army, in the former Marcos government, and in the Aquino administration.

Culture and education administrators were busy planning radio dramas with a new message for the country. In the rural barrios, radio is the main form of mass communications. The national dailies are centered in Manila and though they are flown to major cities on other islands, they don't really reach many in the rural towns.

The democratic spaces were perceived not only in the area of culture and human rights, but in the political realm as well. In the early months of the Aquino administration, the National Democratic Front (NDF) and the government were sending feelers to each other about conducting formal peace talks.

"This seemed like a different government than the Marcos dictatorship. Mrs. Aquino's statement that the root of insurgency is massive poverty was a good beginning," Carolina Malay, chief of staff for the NDF negotiating panel, told me several weeks after the talks had broken down. "Besides, we saw the peace talks as a good opportunity to talk directly to the Filipino people."

Despite pressure from the military, President Aquino voiced determination to talk before shooting. She appointed nationalist statesman Jose W. Diokno as chief negotiator for the government panel. Senator Diokno, well known for his courageous anti-Marcos stance, served in the Philippine Senate before martial law. When Marcos declared martial law, Diokno was arrested and placed in the same detention cell as Benigno Aquino. When he was released in 1974, Diokno defended other political detainees in the courts and organized lawyers to do the same through the Free Legal Assistance Group.

By 1986, however, Diokno was quite ill. He had had several operations for cancer and his health was rapidly deteriorating. His daughter Maria Serena "Maris" Diokno took his place when he was too weak to attend the negotiations. Ramon Mitra, a former journalist, parliamentarian, and minister of agriculture, was also on the government team together with Bataan Export Processing chief, Jaime Guerrero, and another cabinet member, Teofista Guingona.

The NDF appointed two former journalists, Antonio Zumel and Satur Ocampo, to represent them. Carolina Malay, Satur's wife and the daughter of University of the Philippines dean Armando Malay, was chief of staff for the negotiating team. Because no one on the team was a lawyer, the NDF hired two lawyers to act as counsel for them—Romy Capulong, who founded the Philippine Center for Immigration Rights in New

York, and Arno Sanidad, who was in private practice with several other progressive lawyers in Manila.

The sessions must have felt like old home week. Government representative Ramon Mitra and NDF representatives Zumel and Ocampo had been journalists in the 1960s in Manila. Government representative Diokno was NDF representative Ocampo's lawyer when he was a political detainee in the 1970s. Since then, Ocampo had effected a "self-release" during a National Press Club election he was allowed to attend with his guards. He went to the bathroom at the National Press Club and somehow disappeared with waiting comrades to rejoin the underground.

"There were a few times," Arno Sanidad told a visiting American human rights lawyers group a few weeks after the breakdown of the cease-fire agreement, "when members of the NDF panel were voting with members of the opposing panel on some matters." Personal relations between panel members was cordial.

The talks to establish a cease-fire, however, were held against a backdrop of uncertainty in terms of what factions in the military or Marcos forces still active in the country might do. Marcos supporters staged a series of coup attempts, none of them very serious militarily. The military laconically watched the Marcos supporters while they overran the elegant Manila Hotel in July 1986. The instigators and participants within the military were made to swear allegiance to the government and asked to do fifty push-ups.

A potential member of the negotiating panel, Rodolfo Salas, was arrested and held without bail in late September. His driver had already been present at earlier negotiations. Despite safe conduct assurances for panel members and staff, the driver was also arrested. In November, Rolando Olalia, labor leader and head of a new progressive political party, and his driver were both brutally murdered. Evidence pointed to elements within the military, though no one has been prosecuted for these murders. They occurred as Mrs. Aquino returned from a trip to Japan. The NDF pressed Aquino to demonstrate that she had control of the military.

The negotiating panels represented the civilian authorities—the Aquino administration and the National Democratic Front. The armies did not appear at the negotiating table since the supposition was that the New Armed Forces of the Philippines (NAFP) and the New People's Army (NPA) would adhere to the decisions of the civilian authorities. However, based on the coup attempts and the extrajudicial slayings of leaders like Olalia, the NDF representatives were not convinced that everyone in the NAFP would obey civilian authority.

The NDF insisted that if a cease-fire was supposed to precede the substantive peace talks, certain conditions must be met. The Civilian Home Defense Force and other private armies were to be dismantled; the military should return to their barracks; civilian authority must be established over the police force. The police had been integrated into the military structure during the Marcos years and, as such, ignored local civilian government. Although none of these demands were met, in November 1986 the NDF did sign a preliminary cease-fire agreement with the Aquino government, effective December 10, for sixty days. The two sides agreed to hold substantive talks during the sixty days as a basis for a final settlement.

"Both sides knew a comprehensive settlement was not possible," declared Charito Planas, a political exile in the United States during the Marcos era who returned to the Philippines soon after Mrs. Aquino became president. "Each side used the cease-fire for their own purposes. The NDF was able to talk to people openly about their ideas on TV and radio and in the press. The military used the time for surveillance. Both armies probably used the time for training."

During the first month of the cease-fire, NDF spokespersons Antonio Zumel and Satur Ocampo appeared on talk shows and at cocktail parties and coffee houses. Tish Bautista, academic dean of the prestigous De La Salle College and daughter of Felix Bautista, Cardinal Sin's speechwriter, told me, "The NDF and the insurgency was very vague for me. Then I saw these people on television and they were articulate and intelligent. I had no idea that this is what the communists were like." Tish is typical of a whole segment of urban professionals who finally had some direct exposure to the NDF platform through the panel's public appearances. Neither Tish nor her contemporaries were persuaded to join the NDF by any means, but the idea of an alternative government in the country was made concrete for them.

Both Malacanang and the White House were probably worried about the positive National Democratic Front public relations impact in early December. One diplomat in Manila compared the NDF cocktail circuit and media blitz to the "situation in the United States in the late 1960s when the 'radical chic' such as antiwar demonstrators and militant Black Panther activists were regulars in certain social circles."

Those of us who monitored press coverage in the United States during the period between December 1986 and February 1987 noticed a marked change beginning in mid-January. Articles began appearing about the intransigence of the NDF panel. Charges of NPA cease-fire violations by the Philippine military were printed without confirmation by the designated cease-fire committees. It seemed the public was being prepared for the breakdown of the talks and for the blame to be placed on the National Democratic Front.

After the end of the cease-fire on February 7, 1987, reports in the international press pointed to the NDF as the unilateral destroyers of the peace. For example, the *Washington Post* reported two weeks after the end of the cease-fire, "With the communists walking out of the peace negotiations and the government repeatedly appealing for them to return and work within the framework of the newly approved constitution, it suddenly appeared as if the left, not the government, was the intransigent party, analysts say." The "analysts" are not identified in the article.

However, a somewhat different interpretation was agreed upon by both sides when they appeared together in a public panel discussion I attended in Manila just days before the cease-fire ended. Panel members from both the NDF and the government had received death threats, so on January 22 they mutually agreed to suspend the talks but to keep the lines of communication open. It was during that meeting that news came about the massacre of nineteen peasants by government troops at Mendiola Bridge leading to Malacanang. The Dioknos resigned their position as government negotiators in protest over the actions of the government troops.

Representing the government at the public forum in February was Jaime Guerrero. The NDF members of the panel had already gone into hiding, so they were represented by their lawyer, Romy Capulong. Maris Diokno joined the public panel, though by this time both she and her father Jose Diokno were viewed as a third party in the discussions.

Guerrero, speaking first, appeared defensive and apologetic that the peace talks had not met with success and tried to explain the issues on which the talks had faltered. He said the government wanted to limit the agenda to resolvable issues. Major issues such as land reform or industrialization could be talked about, but only within the framework of the new 1986 constitution. Guerrero argued that the constitution had been drawn up by Aquino appointees from various sectors of society and was ratified in a national referendum in early February by over 80 percent of the population. Therefore it was a legitimate demand on the part of the government to use the constitution as the basis for any agreements. Guerrero firmly rejected the NDF proposals for a coalition government or an integration of the New People's Army into the government military.

Romy Capulong, legal counsel for the NDF, pegged responsibility for the final breakdown of the talks to the government's insistence that the framework for the discussion be limited to the constitution. He said the NDF had entered the negotiations as a revolutionary group with their own program as the basis from which to discuss peace. When the two sides first sat down to talk, the government accepted the fact that the NDF represented 18.5 percent of the population, said Capulong.

*   *   *

Since the failure to agree on the constitution as the common framework within which to negotiate was a major stumbling block in the peace talks, it will be helpful to look more closely at the process surrounding the construction and national acceptance of this document.

Most of the Aquino appointees to the constitutional convention were national leaders or representative of an interest group within society. The NDF pointed to the bias toward the rich, the landed, and the managers within the membership of the constitutional convention. A convention numerically representative of the classes in society would have had stronger peasant, worker, urban poor, and youth input since these groups are the majority of the population.

Most Filipinos took the process of drawing up a new constitution seriously and tried to find ways to participate. Despite the fact that they were not formally included as constitutional commissioners, representative groups across the country submitted statements and provisions they thought should be incorporated. Farmers had their concerns about land reform. Workers carried their concerns about factory ownership and guarantee of labor and livelihood. "The country was like one big civics seminar with everyone discussing what should be included and how we wanted to run our country," said one school teacher.

Women presented one of the most creative additions to the constitutional discussion. Under the aegis of "Gabriela," a national coalition of women's groups, discussions were held nationwide on constitutional protections for women. Each group drew up provisions that were discussed regionally and nationally. The women then embroidered, sewed, painted, or sequined their demands onto squares of cloth. These were then publicly joined together to form a one-kilometer-long tapestry that was presented to the constitutional commissioners. Included in the demands was the equality of women in economic, political, cultural, and family life.

In the introduction to its Call for a Meaningful Constitution, Gabriela wrote,

> Drafting a constitution for a nation with newly regained morale and vigor is a critical and fundamental undertaking. . . . Each and every Filipino woman, man and youth should be involved. . . . Hence the Constitutional Commission must undertake careful and thorough consultation with the people. And the people must discuss the pertinent issues at hand, ascertain our own position and be vigilant in asserting our rightful demands and concerns.

It was not easy to translate "rightful demands" into the constitutional writing process. A whole generation has missed out on the practice of parliamentary procedures because of the declaration of martial law in 1972 and the suspension of an independent Congress. Training through the experience of running for office, managing a campaign, and learning parliamentary process in Congress was not an option. The older politicians who served in the pre–martial law Congress or even in Marcos's rubber stamp Assembly had the advantage in a parliamentary setting. During the Marcos era, the best and brightest of those under the age of forty were getting their experience in the "parliament of the streets" or in running clandestine organizations. Nevertheless, the people's enthusiasm for participating in shaping the next period of history in the Philippines was apparent across the nation.

Most independent observers agree that the strong "yes" vote for the constitution was a vote for stability and against the right-wing forces. In straw polls in mid-January, only 40 percent of the population supported the constitution in its final form. But after an attempted coup by the neo-Marcos forces, another straw poll indicated 80 percent support for the constitution.

Each force in society had its own agenda to work out through the constitution. The Aquino administration needed a strong ratification of the constitution to claim legitimacy as a government. (After all, Aquino ultimately came to power in an unorthodox manner.)

The left had its own revolutionary program as the basis for governing, but could not come out too publicly against the ratification of the constitution for fear of being lumped with Marcos supporters. In fact, handbills posted along the fences, walls, and public train pillars around Manila did indeed combine the Marcos followers and the left in a cartoon with the question, "Who are the people who don't support the constitution?"

The Marcos loyalists played an influential role by moving the entire spectrum of public discussion to the right and thus foiling the objections of particular groups like workers or farmers. By presenting themselves as a major threat to the stability of the Aquino government, they preempted any strong nationalist critique of the constitution. People's organizations did not have a defined acceptable space from within which to make their arguments to the public. They were continually associated with the far right troublemakers if they objected to anything proposed by the Aquino government.

The various legal nationalist organizations came down in different places on support for the constitution. The farmers union, the Kilusang Magbubukid ng Pilipinas (KMP), rejected the constitution. They felt it held no guarantees for the farmers, particularly in regard to substantial agrarian reform. Two weeks before the ratification vote, a KMP-sponsored march had been shot at by government troops, which probably helped to consolidate the peasant nonsupport. Television footage of the event, aired across the country, showed men in military uniforms riding in jeeps, their guns pointed at the fleeing farmers.

Although the majority of the armed forces voted for the constitution, their percentage of negative votes was much higher than that of the civilian population. The reasons behind this are myriad and are connected to complex internal dynamics. Each branch and each faction within the military had its own reasons for a negative vote.

Those in the Philippine Constabulary (PC) objected to the constitutional provisions that mandated the dissolving of the paramilitary and the separation of police and military functions and units. They saw this as meaning a change in the way the PC is structured. During the Marcos rule, the PC took on more and more military functions. Many of its members were afraid they might lose pensions and other benefits, licit or illicit, in the restructuring.

The officers from Marcos's home province of Ilocos, who had benefited greatly under his rule, were getting their wings clipped under Chief of Staff Ramos. In the Marcos era, loyal generals were allowed to stay beyond retirement years so they could continue their sideline graft and corporate businesses, which were somewhat dependent on their military position. Their immediate junior officers were given part of the action in exchange for their cooperation. When Mrs. Aquino took office, the overstaying generals were quickly retired, while others, more loyal to Ramos, were promoted.

One dissatisfied colonel explained his own internal logic for voting "no":

> Don't think the negative military vote on the constitution means we won't support it. We all took an oath to uphold the constitution when we entered the service. The issue for some of us was that Ramos campaigned for the constitution, so we voted against it. It was a vote against Ramos.

* * *

The peace negotiations were affected by all these agendas and maneuverings by various forces within the society. NDF legal counsel, Romy Capulong, insisted that both parties needed to agree on an analysis of the problems, agree on a common program, and then agree to work together on this program. In essence, he meant that they should form a coalition government and combine the two militaries. His argument was, "The NPA has the allegiance of 25 percent of the population if you use their figures, 18.5 percent if you use the NAFP figures. Secondly, the NPA is one of the most disciplined armies in the world and could be helpful to the NAFP, which even its own leaders admit lacks discipline."

This way of proceeding—insistence on common analysis and common program before doing any joint work—was a surefire formula for failure. Basically, it required the Aquino government to abandon its class base and its allies like the United States and to throw its lot in with the NDF's revolutionary program for the country. The NDF insistence on ideological agreement reflects their understanding of how change takes place. This confident insistence on acceptance of their platform contributed to their growth in the past. However, winning converts in the barrios and negotiating with an elite democracy are two different realms of work.

Setting up the requirement of a common analysis is setting up an impossible demand. Most other organizations, such as religious denominations, who have planned and executed voluntary mergers of two large entities emphasize the importance of doing some activity together. Working on a few joint projects builds relationship and trust. A coalition government between the NDF and the Aquino government may more aptly be compared to a potential merger in the business world. The more powerful company can dictate the terms. One company can be swallowed by another through a hostile takeover when the merger is not voluntary.

The government panel, knowing that it represented the most powerful entity in the discussions, also tried to dictate the terms. They, too, set up an impossible demand for an organization like the NDF: negotiations only within the framework of the constitution. It probably seemed reasonable to them since objectively the majority of the population had voted for the constitution, for whatever reason.

Arno Sanidad, NDF legal counsel, told a group of American human rights lawyers in late February, three weeks after the cease-fire had ended, "It became clear in the course of the talks that the government saw these talks as a way of having the NDF surrender. This was never the intention of the NDF when they came to the table. They stated that from the beginning, but maybe the government panel couldn't understand that they meant it."

By proceeding in the talks as though the NDF was an outlaw group and not another government with the support of a sizable minority of the population, the government panel also contributed to the eventual downfall of the talks.

The Aquino government's publicly stated analysis of the insurgency was that the majority of those fighting were people who had experienced the injustice of the Marcos regime and that they would come down from the hills and rejoin society if given the chance. The remainder, a few hard-core ideologues, would then be isolated and the military could go after them. This analysis proved faulty.

Despite the government plan to pay each guerrilla for the weapon he or she would turn in and promises of resettlement money, few availed themselves of the offer. Both the United States and Philippine intelligence expressed surprise that the NPA held their fighters and in some places actually gained recruits during the cease-fire.

Senator Jose W. Diokno, whose stature and presence as part of the government panel helped to keep the peace talks together as long as possible, suggested from his deathbed an agenda of "Food, freedom, jobs, and justice" to overcome the stalemate that had developed. The Dioknos behaved as though they were appointed by the nation itself to make peace. Until the very last hour, they tried to rescue the talks.

At the public panel discussion two days before the end of the cease-fire, Maris Diokno presented a proposal for renewed negotiation. She said,

> It is the government's responsibility to get the talks going again by recreating an atmosphere conducive to the resumption of talks. The government could take two steps immediately: (1) Enact a policy on land reform before the Congress convenes. Land is crucial economically and its equitable distribution is also crucial to end the violence. (2) Act to bring justice both to the Mendiola massacre of the farmers and to the generals involved in the recent coup. The people's perception is that the military can stage a coup and not get punished and they can shoot down unarmed civilians in the street and not get punished. The

government must show its sincerity and its control of the military at this point.

Maris went on to provide a much broader perspective in which to view the peace talks.

Acting on land reform is not a question of conceding to one group, but rather recognizing that agrarian reform is the desire of all people. It is important for the government to hear the criticism of the farmers and every group and not dismiss them as far left or troublemakers who aren't loyal. If we as the government want to represent the people, we must get citizen opinion so we can divorce the problem of land reform from the fact that the NDF were the first ones to raise it during the talks.

In addition to her suggestions concerning action the government should take, she also had some advice for the NDF.

It is not possible for the NDF and the government to agree on a common framework or a common analysis of the problems in our society. Even the nationalist groups who are on the same side of the political spectrum couldn't agree on if to participate in or boycott the 1986 elections. The groups on the same side couldn't agree on support or rejection of the constitution. How much less possible will it be for the Aquino government and the NDF to agree on a common analysis or program.

The final speaker on the panel, Fr. Ben Alforque, reechoed Maris Diokno's political sentiments from a religious perspective. He began his remarks with biblical quotations. According to the Gospel of Matthew, initiatives for peace come from the violated. Violators have no place in the society people are building. Alforque read from the Gospel to back up his contention. "If your brother sins against you, go and tell him his fault, between you and him alone. If he listens to you, you have gained your brother. But if he doesn't listen, take one or two others along with you, that every word may be confirmed by the evidence of two or three witnesses" (Matt. 18:15-16).

Turning to the NDF and government representatives, he said, "Do you think peace is in your hands? Must the people intervene to tell both the government and the NDF panel that peace is their issue and you have both violated the peace?" He added, "But the other player whom the people must confront as a violator is not visible. The farmers killed at Mendiola were ultimately killed by the anticommunist hysteria projected by the actor in Washington, D.C."

Father Alforque's testimony that the people wanted peace was borne out by activities around the country during that period. I discovered people working with a kind of tough hope in some parts of Mindanao that, under Marcos, had been war zones. The cease-fire provided an opportunity for positive interaction between the opposing armies and between the local population and the NPA in urban centers.

The church played a major role during the cease-fire. Bishop Antonio Fortich of Bacolod, Negros, was the chairperson of the National Cease-fire Committee. Even some of the NDF representatives on the regional cease-fire committees were priests, like Fr. Frank Navarro in Mindanao. Bishops like Miguel Cinches, SVD, in northern Surigao, Mindanao, who had not been deeply involved in social action work in the past, opened his cathedral and church facilities for the process. Streamers hung in the cathedral grounds welcoming the NPA. Sisters serving in the diocese became the "body guards" for the NDF participants in the local cease-fire committee.

In Agusan del Sur, Mindanao, where Bishop Morelos was an active supporter of the cease-fire, the local priests told stories of NPA who came down from the hills in groups of ten to fifteen each day. They wore hats with the words, "Give peace a chance" in front and "NPA" on the back. When the cease-fire ended, some of the government soldiers told their new-found friends among the NPA that it would be very difficult to shoot at them in the future.

Two local commanders in the province of Agusan—one NPA, the other NAFP (New Armed Forces of the Philippines) kept in touch after the end of the cease-fire through a two-way radio the NPA commander used regularly. The situation seemed so relaxed that one evening when the NPA commander radioed in, the NAFP commander cut the call short, saying, "Let's not talk long—I am in the middle of watching a movie on my Betamax."

I discovered other examples of civilians actively creating their own scenario out of the democratic space that presented itself. In Ipil, the capital town of Zamboanga del Sur, the fishermen's cooperative organized by the church began to send representatives to the provincial government's economic planning meetings. "We had to role-play before the fishermen went," Lito Yap, peace and justice coordinator for the Ipil Prelature said. "The fishermen's cooperative knows what it is doing and has something to contribute to the provincial planning, but they need practice in expressing themselves in the technocrats' meetings." Similar efforts were being made in Davao with former church-related development workers moving into advisory roles to local government agencies.

In Isabela, the capital city of Basilan, the predominantly Muslim island south of Mindanao, the new mayor was a former peace and justice worker in the diocese. "It's like night and day since Mrs. Aquino became president," he told me. "Before, I was on the hit list of the military, but look at me now." Accompanying him everywhere were his bodyguards—from the marines, from the army, and from the Philippine Constabulary—grinning from ear to ear as they followed him around.

Across the country, Filipinos were enthusiastically taking their own initiatives for peace. Churches sponsored peace forums and workshops to discuss possibilities in their own regions. Peace-building seminars were held in various provinces. Tremendous human energy was released in the process of waging peace.

In several provinces I discovered that local military commanders from both sides were arranging or observing de facto cease-fire agreements long after the national agreement had broken down. Most often these arrangements were made through the church. Some progressive people in Manila were critical of local cease-fires, which they feared would be used by the military to enable them to focus on one area at a time. Church people and activists in some rural areas seemed more open to trying even a limited cease-fire.

"Sooner or later, we will all have to work together," said Fr. Ben Montecastro, who helped to arrange a local cease-fire from his parish house in Bayog, Zamboanga del Sur. "Neither side is capable of defeating the other militarily here, so it's good if they can get experience in working with each other in little ways."

The local situation in Bayog, Zamboanga, is typical of areas in the country where a combination of factors made further peace negotiations possible—a church active in justice work; a civilian government official who felt secure enough to challenge the local military; a strong peoples' organization; and a reasonable military commander. Bayog provides a good grass roots study of what happened at the barrio level during the struggle for peace in the first year of Aquino government. I spent a week there in March 1987 talking to church leaders, local government officials, businesspeople, market vendors, schoolteachers, the town's political elite, and those working with the Basic Christian Communities.

Bayog is the end of the line for public transportation. From Pagadian, the closest coastal city, buses leave as early as 4 A.M. for Buug, a town at the halfway mark toward Bayog. The bus climbs up into the hills away from the port city of Pagadian. The houses along the route are tiny, the people catching the bus are poorly dressed. At almost every little settlement, fresh cheeked young soldiers jump on the bus.

From Buug public market, the next leg of the journey is by jeepney or Ford fiera, a truck-like vehicle with long narrow seats for twelve passengers in the back and at least as many passengers and their belongings on the roof of the vehicle. The jeepney to Bayog leaves whenever it has collected enough passengers to make the trip worthwhile. The paved road ends abruptly outside the environs of Buug and the jeepney bumps over dusty roads for an hour and a half before honking loudly to announce its arrival at the Bayog market.

I visited Bayog during fiesta time, so there was plenty of opportunity to talk at leisure with the people. "How do you think life has changed since Mrs. Aquino became president?" I asked. In the first breath was, "Nothing that I can think of," but this was usually followed by, "Well, we removed the 33d Infantry Battalion (IB)." The 33d IB was pulled out only a few weeks before the mid-March fiesta, over a year after Mrs. Aquino took office. "It took us that long to get them out," the townfolk admitted, "but just think how long it is taking Cory to get the same control of the military on the national level."

The 33d IB had a reputation for violence and abuse in the area. The parish priests, Fr. Ben Montecastro and an eighty-year-old American priest, Fr. Arthur Shea; the vice mayor, Frank Mabulay, an Aquino appointee; and Gloria Caray, the parish peace and justice coordinator, spearheaded the effort to get the 33d removed. Petitions, letters, and visits to the military with backup from the bishop of the prelature, Frederico Escaler, finally achieved their goal. But the removal of the 33d

IB did not mean the end of having a military unit in town; the 18th IB was assigned to Bayog to take their place, because the military views Zamboanga as a critical area.

However, the way in which the 18th Infantry Battalion moved in signaled a new era. The commander of the local unit, Lt. Perfecto, visited the two power centers in town—the civilian government and the church—to get acquainted before moving the troops in. He asked for advice. Frank Mabulay and Ben Montecastro did not mince words. "If you treat people decently, we can be friends. If you start to abuse people, we will ask for your removal as well." President Aquino's commitment to gaining civilian control of the military, a supportive bishop, and a militant peoples' organization within the church gave the men confidence that their strong words would not be in vain.

Norma Naces, a former teacher in Bayog, filled out the picture of change in the town. "We now have hope that if we try to stand up for truth and fight corruption, there might be a positive result. Before when we tried to stop the corruption, nothing happened." Several years ago, Norma had refused to pay the high school principal bribe money in order to get permanent employment. When Norma complained to the superintendent, she was fired, because he was part of the bribery chain. "I went back to my home in the Visayas to teach and discovered the same thing there. I just dropped out of teaching in disgust."

In 1986, the community rose up against the superintendent and he left. "We don't know if he was transferred or if he was fired, but at least he's gone," said Norma.

In the meantime the elementary school principal was also caught with her hand in the till. Students pay insurance premiums at the beginning of the year. The principal did not put the money into the insurance plan and so when one student had an accident and needed extensive medical care, there was no money. The parents were irate and confronted her. Teachers, who had their own complaints, joined the parents who planned to demonstrate at the school fiesta program if she didn't return the money and leave her post. Although he was an Aquino appointee, the mayor threatened to use the military against the parents, students, and teachers if they would make any trouble at the fiesta. "Be sure to come to the town parade and the school program. You will see Bayog defiance," Norma told me.

The next morning I stood at the side of the road, camera in hand. Through the streets they marched, smartly rounding Bayog's one and only intersection—the schoolchildren, the beauty queen, the school bands and baton twirlers. The parade was headed by the newly arrived contingent of the 18th Infantry Battalion, eager to ingratiate themselves with the town population. The procession ended in the schoolyard with eight hundred schoolchildren and twenty soldiers of the 18th IB in straight lines facing the podium where the notorious principal, the mayor, and other dignitaries were seated. The priests were conspicuously absent.

The usual welcoming remarks by dignitaries were followed by a song in English by the teachers. I may have been one of the few people in the entire town to understand the words. Though English is taught in the upper grades, no one in the town with the exception of the priests and a few of the parish workers use English. Then it was time for the principal's remarks. She got up, nodded at me and bustled importantly to the podium.

From somewhere a whistle sounded. Almost immediately the straight lines of children melted. Teachers and children slowly walked away in every direction except toward the stage. The 18th IB looked surprised. They watched the children leaving, shrugged their shoulders, lowered the Philippine flag, and wandered away too. Within a minute, the principal was facing an empty field, talking to no one but herself. My only regret was that I didn't have a movie camera.

I asked some teachers as they walked away, "Is this a demonstration against the principal?" "Oh no, the sun was getting hot, so the children needed to find some shade." The teachers didn't know who I was, so I didn't really expect a different answer.

Later that day, Lt. Col. Rudy Garcia, the commander of the 18th IB, and his men arrived at the parish house on their peace mission. "Brother Filipinos should not kill brother Filipinos. We can stop it here at least, in our area," said the Lieutenant Colonel. "But I am appealing for your help, Father." Father Monty, as Ben Montecastro is affectionately called in the parish, tried to guide the discussion away from surrender by the NPA to mutual negotiation.

After the formal meeting was over, Father Monty invited them for *merienda,* a delightful Philippine custom of a hearty snack in the morning and afternoon for those who can afford it. That afternoon, the snack was sticky rice, cooked in coconut milk. Father Shea took the opportunity to lecture the soldiers on the evil of the World Bank policies toward the Philippines. The stiff young Lieutenant Perfecto responded by telling Father Shea that he was once in seminary himself.

I asked Lieutenant Colonel Garcia the standard question, "How has life changed for you since Mrs. Aquino became president?" "Oh, it's changed a lot," he replied. "Before we never had human rights or the religious. Now we have human rights. Now we have the church sector to deal with. Think of it from my point of view, ma'am. When my men go on patrol, they can't just shoot if they see someone. What if we kill a civilian—then the human rights groups will take us to court. We just can't operate like we used to. And the enemy is very wily."

"When you talk about the 'enemy,' are these the same people you referred to as 'brother' when you talked to Father Monty about a cease-fire?" I asked. The Lieutenant Colonel laughed, "Well, you know," he leaned forward in a confidential manner, "when talking to the priests, you have to use certain language—language they understand."

As we talked, we all reached over to pick up the sweet sticky rice with our fingers from the steaming plate in the middle of the table. It was a communion of sorts—American, Filipino, priest, soldier—digging into the common plate, licking our fingers after each glob of rice was safely in our mouths. Here we were, celebrating the possibility of a mini–cease-fire while in most of the country the armies were gearing up for war.

The soldiers looked pleased with themselves. This was the first time they had eaten in the Bayog *convento* (parish priest's residence), which usually provided sanctuary to the victims of the military. Father Shea looked pleased—these soldiers were actually listening to his economic analysis of Philippine society. I looked around the table and remembered a very different scene three years ago when I visited Bayog with Edgar Baling, a native of the town and a church human rights worker.

When we arrived in Bayog in October 1984, the priest at that time, Father Dennis, an Australian, was hiding in the convento. His head was bandaged from cuts and wounds he had sustained at the military barracks while he was trying to get his lay catechists out of jail. One catechist was *salvaged* (a term that refers to extrajudicial murder) and buried in a grave behind the barracks. Father Dennis refused to leave the barracks until the military would let him see the other parish worker. In the morning, the worker was brought to him, his body a mass of cuts and welts from the torture.

At Father Dennis's suggestion, Gloria Caray, the parish worker, and I walked to the barracks in Bayog to talk to the commander about what happened. The commander, of course, was not there and instead his wife entertained us with stories about her difficult life as an army spouse. How different it is now in March 1987, I thought. The Lieutenant Colonel comes calling to ask help of the priest; before when the church went calling, the priest was hit and the foreign journalist ignored.

Mrs. Aquino's sounding of a human rights note has had an effect here in the hinterlands, though critics point to the fact that not one army officer has yet been brought to justice for human rights abuses committed during the Marcos regime. Lieutenant Colonel Garcia and his men were curbed. Father Monty and the parish were emboldened to push more strongly for decent behavior from the military.

"So you think it is Mrs. Aquino who has made the difference here?" mused Father Monty. "Perhaps, but what I saw was an arrogant military that overstepped its bounds by picking on the children of several of the wealthy merchants in Bayog. The mothers went crazy and so the Catholic Women's League was suddenly petitioning for the removal of the military. The military knew they had better rectify the relationships with the power centers in town, especially when they discovered during the cease-fire that the NPA had a lot more popular support than they expected."

Father Monty continued, "Don't misunderstand me. Mrs. Aquino's being in power instead of Marcos has helped, but please, give some credit to the day-to-day organizing and activity of the local people. They weren't just sitting around waiting for justice to come to Bayog. No matter what Mrs. Aquino decides to do—support an abusive military or discipline them, support measures to help the poor or side with the landlords—the Bayog residents, especially those active in the parish, will continue to work for justice here."

When I left Bayog in March 1987, I had a sense of a hopeful beginning. Five months later, I received a written plea from the Prelature of Ipil, which includes the Bayog parish. The bishop, priests, sisters, and leaders of the Basic Christian Communities documented the abuse of citizens by violent vigilante groups approved by the Aquino government as part of the counterinsurgency strategy. Parish workers were in danger. Several churchworkers had been killed. The parish began its work again with petitions and letters.

In light of these new developments, I recalled my discussion with Father Monty in Bayog: "No matter what Mrs. Aquino decides to do, the people are already deeply aware of their human rights and they will not abandon their journey toward attaining their full dignity. I only pray that Mrs. Aquino chooses to join them."

The initial signs across the country had been hopeful. Millions of people were engaged in making use of the democratic space. Filipinos expressed their yearning for peace in no uncertain terms and they translated these yearnings into concrete action. Their will was unmistakable. Throughout martial law, there was resistance to dictatorship and agitation for change from the bottom. When the possibility of a tightly supervised election presented itself, the people moved.

Mrs. Aquino may have been a candidate of the old family politicians; the U.S. may have encouraged the elections only to consolidate Marcos's position or to dump him; NAMFREL may have had its beginnings as a CIA creation in the 1950s; but people across the country, rich, middle class, and poor, both urban and rural, saw an opportunity through elections and election watchdogging to dump the dictatorship. They took the opportunity. Not only did they vote, but they took risks to protect their vote, even to the point of staging an uprising in Manila.

When the opportunity presented itself to establish a cease-fire and then negotiate a peace settlement, people joined in enthusiastically. When the opportunity to mold a new constitution came about, individuals and organized groups throughout the country suggested provisions and amendments during the actual writing and then they discussed the proposed constitution before its ratification. Throughout the Philippines, community leaders in towns like Bayog made attempts to clean up local abuses and corruption.

Millions of Filipinos expended tremendous psychic and physical energy as they tried to participate in the process toward peace and democratization. The failure of the process cannot be laid at their feet. Within their own spheres of influence, the majority of Filipinos went more than the second mile in the quest for peace.

Many believe that President Aquino also went the second mile in this quest. Her words, especially in the beginning of her administration, indicated that she believed the time was ripe for peace. She released the political detainees, set up a Presidential Committee on Human Rights to investigate military abuses, and sent feelers to the National Democratic Front and to the Muslim insurgents in the south to begin peace negotiations.

Most of her actions after that were aimed at appeasing her own military, who had opposed the release of the prisoners and bitterly resented the work of the human rights committee. Aquino backed away from strong human rights stands that would further antagonize the military. She let Chief of Staff Fidel Ramos protect the coup leaders from disciplinary proceedings appropriate to that act of treason. She also dragged her feet on establishing a strong agrarian reform program.

Though the cease-fire had broken down by early February, the level of fighting between the NPA and the NAFP had not reached the same level of intensity as under Marcos. Both sides were moving somewhat gingerly. An event in March, however, dramatically shifted President Aquino's public words and her orders to her military.

On March 22, 1987, Mrs. Aquino was scheduled to speak at the Philippine Military Academy graduation in Baguio City, 130 miles north of Manila. A few days before the graduation, the academy held a rehearsal with its graduates, using stand-ins for principals like Mrs. Aquino. A bomb exploded above the grandstand from which President Aquino would have spoken. Four people were killed and more than thirty were wounded.

I was in Armed Forces Southern Command headquarters in Zamboanga City on the day of the bombing. The first news the headquarters received that day indicated that the kind of bomb used and its placement clearly pointed to an inside military job. Nevertheless, the first public reports blamed the communists.

Mrs. Aquino appeared undaunted at the graduation exercises and delivered a brave speech, claiming she was prepared for death as were her soldiers. This speech, however, marked a strong departure from her previous statements about peace and seemed to indicate that the bombing did indeed affect her quite strongly. Ralph McGehee, a twenty-five-year veteran CIA officer, suggested to a Chicago audience he was addressing just after the event that a good bomb scare like the one at the Philippine Military Academy was the customary way for the CIA to bring a new foreign president into line with U.S. military thinking.

"God knows I have tried, but my offers of peace and reconciliation have been met with the most bloody and insolent rejections by the left and the right," declared Mrs. Aquino. "The answer to terrorism of the left and the right is not social and economic reform, but police and military action."

Mrs. Aquino's speech was a declaration of war on the left and a criticism of the slow delivery of military aid from the United States. The *New York Times* said on March 23 that it "appeared to mark an evolution of her approach from reconciliation to confrontation." It was a strange response to the actual circumstances of the bombing at the Philippine Military Academy since it was quite clear that the bomb was the work of right-wing elements in her own military. Aquino's prescription of military action was exactly what the right-wing elements wanted. In her speech, President Aquino in fact allied herself with the wishes of the "terrorists" who had planted the bomb. Perhaps the graduation was scheduled to be the occasion for announcing a policy shift that had already been planned and the bombing simply gave a sense of urgency to a get-tough policy.

Mrs. Aquino's conclusion was that the "forces of the extremes will not leave us in peace to achieve the recovery and progress we so badly need." The conclusion the NDF negotiators arrived at was that Aquino could not control the military and that the elite in the country would not brook a disturbance in their economic acquisitions. Based on that assessment, the NDF decided not to pursue further peace negotiations.

The assessment of the possibilities of peace with justice was made in the context of a whole history of betrayals within the revolutionary and nationalist movement as far back as the Spanish colonial era. Every time the *illustrados* (enlightened intellectual leaders) dominated the revolts against Spain or the United States and the upper strata of Filipino society were included, the peasants' interests were eventually forgotten.

The negotiations for peace in the first year of the Aquino administration were primarily between the rich and the poor. The rural and urban poor form the bulk of the core of NDF membership. The core support of the Aquino government, perhaps not in numbers but in economic terms, is made up of the middle and upper middle classes.

Cooperation between classes to make social changes has to rest on some kind of mutuality—a mutuality which, the NDF concluded, was not yet possible. The peasants, workers, urban poor, tribal Filipinos, students, and a section of the intellectuals and religious are not yet forged together strongly enough. While each group has its own organization, the majority of the population within each of these occupational or interest groups do not yet belong to these organizations.

While it is quite clear that the upper class is not united or tightly organized, the basis of its strength does not rest on organization but on wealth and access to media and the international world. Though there was considerable internal debate, the dominant perspective of the movement is that the time was not yet ripe for a peace with justice. The peasants and workers might again have been sold out in negotiations after having suffered the brunt of economic and military abuse throughout the years.

The stark realities of barrio life, where parents have been killed in front of children, children tortured in front of parents, houses ransacked or burned by the Philippine military, are firmly etched on the peasants' minds. "How can they keep negotiating with a government that cannot or will not control the military? There must be some guarantee of safety for us," said one peasant leader.

While there was considerable criticism of the NDF for not continuing some form of peace talks, in retrospect the NDF decision seems wise. Events since the end of the cease-fire in February 1987 have shown how fractured the military is and how little control Mrs. Aquino has. With each successive coup attempt, she yielded more of her power and her control of decision making.

Was it really possible for President Aquino to have chosen to throw her lot in with the poor or with reformers like the group in Bayog? During the public panel discussion, Fr. Ben Alforque expressed a sentiment, common among nationalist Filipinos, that the negotiations were not simply between the two visible civilian sides. The unseen guest at crucial points was the Philippines' closest military ally and largest trading partner. In a poignant moment during an interview, Carolina Malay, chief of staff for the NDF negotiating panel, curled in an almost fetal position in her chair, held her head in her hands and sighed, "It's so hard to fight the CIA."

An understanding of why the peace and democratization process veered off course so quickly in spite of the efforts of Filipino citizens nationwide would not be complete without looking at official American foreign policy and the role and interest of the American and Philippine right wing—whether government or private—and their connections with the Philippine military and paramilitary.

9

U.S. Government Links to the Philippine Dilemma

■■■■■■■■■■

THE DOTTED LINE

The United States' fateful entanglement in Vietnam began in Manila in the early 1950s, not in Saigon in the early sixties. The CIA's operation that made Ramon Magsaysay president of the Philippines in 1953 established a pattern of paramilitary, psychological, and political action mistakenly imagined to be workable anywhere, anytime.

—CIA agent, Joseph Burkholder Smith, 1976

President Reagan recently signed another secret "finding"—the first since the Iran arms deal became public—to authorize a multimillion dollar CIA operation against communist insurgents in the Philippines.

—*Newsweek*, 23 March 1987

The CIA role in advising, organizing, arming, financing or otherwise supporting vigilante violence in the Philippines is nothing less than a massive campaign of murder, deceit and manipulation.... The victims of vigilante violence are overwhelmingly poor farmers, workers, slum dwellers.

—Ramsey Clark Fact-Finding Mission, 20-30 May 1987

Our first year of living in the Philippines was a trial of confusion, joy, and pain. On one level, we were warmly greeted, welcomed, and given information, but on another we were under suspicion, being tested, and held at arms length.

After a few months of visiting and sharing in intimate moments of barrio life and development agencies planning, we were confronted by a National Council of Churches staff person one day over lunch. "Some people say that you are really with the CIA," he began. "Some people say" is a common way of delivering a message. We decided that there was really nothing to do about that kind of suspicion or charge, but to continue our work and hope that the "right" person would let people know we are "OK." For someone convinced that we were CIA agents, a denial would only be rhetorical. For anyone else, a denial would not be necessary.

Filipinos are not paranoid. There is good reason for their suspicion about the United States government's intervention in their country, although CIA activity is only one among many American avenues for influencing events in the Philippines. Historically, some of the most successful CIA counterinsurgency work ever done was in the Philippines.

This became clearer to me in March 1987 during a press conference given by then Chief of Staff Fidel Ramos in Davao City. General Ramos explained the "total strategy" of counterinsurgency warfare, which included military, civilian vigilantes, and economic reform. I asked Ramos whether he thought his total strategy seemed like the American strategy in Vietnam, notably the Phoenix Program. He blew up, "This is not American. This is not from Vietnam. This is not foreign. This is a home-grown Philippine invention. You may not know that even before Vietnam, we had our own President Magsaysay!" With those words, Ramos strode out of the room, leaving the media and his own staff to ponder the significance of his remarks.

My first guess was that Ramos was angry because he had been confronted directly and publicly about U.S. involvement in his work. Upon further reflection, it seemed conceivable that Ramos was genuinely hurt that Filipinos were not being given credit for developing a counterinsurgency strategy that was emulated elsewhere. As I stood in the middle of the room, watching Ramos' retreating figure, I thought of the thousands of civilians, members of legal organizations, who were systematically killed in the anti-insurgency Phoenix Program in the 1960s in Vietnam.

CIA agent Joseph Burkholder Smith, who was assigned to covert operations in southeast Asia in the 1950s, wrote in 1976,

> The United States' fateful entanglement in Vietnam began in Manila in the early 1950s, not in Saigon in the early sixties. The CIA's operation that made Ramon Magsaysay president of the Philippines in 1953 established a pattern of paramilitary, psychological and political action mistakenly imagined to be workable anywhere, anytime. The same Americans and Filipinos who created the Magsaysay administration in Manila created the Diem government in Saigon—Ed Lansdale and his team.[1]

The Lansdale strategy was forged through trial and error in the day-to-day conflict with the Huks. With a combination of dirty tricks, coddling of the press, clever use of the media, psychological warfare, suspension of the writ of habeas corpus, and a propaganda economic development and resettlement project called EDCOR, Magsaysay was projected as winning the war against the Huks.

Indeed, Edward Lansdale's partnership with Philippine president Ramon Magsaysay to defeat the Huk insurgency was, by the CIA's own accounts, one of the first major attempts at secret warfare by the agency's covert operations department established in 1948. From 1898 to 1946, American control was exerted through acts of the U.S. Congress and through direct colonial rule. After 1946, when the Philippines became "independent," the work of agencies like the CIA became more important in terms of influencing events in the Philippines.

In the 1950s, the various departments of American government converged with Philippine elite interests to insure the crushing of the Huk peasant insurgency. After World War II, the original Communist Party of the Philippines (PKP), the Huks (the armed component), and the peasant masses of Central Luzon had initially tried to achieve their goals through legal and parliamentary struggle. The candidates they supported, called the Democratic Alliance (DA), won at the polls. However, members of this loosely affiliated group were unseated through parliamentary maneuvers.

---

1. Joseph Burkholder Smith, *Portrait of a Cold Warrior* (New York: G. P. Putnam's Sons, 1976), p. 101.

As a result of the parliamentary defeat and the increased government military pressure on them, the Huks shifted to defensive armed struggle for survival. As time went on, they placed even more emphasis on armed struggle. The DA leadership who rejected armed struggle parted ways at this point with the PKP. As economic conditions in the countryside continued to deteriorate, the DA disintegrated because the bulk of its mass base was in active rebellion.

President Truman sent a new Bell Mission to the Philippines in 1950. They recommended $250 million in economic aid, which was disbursed over a sixteen-year period from 1951 to 1967. To secure this, however, the Philippine government had to sign the Quirino-Foster Agreement (November 14, 1950) and the U.S.-Philippine Economic and Technical Cooperation Agreement (April 27, 1951). The choice of economic and technical projects and allocation would be in American hands and the Philippine government was to appropriate counterpart funds. American "advisers" would be in all key departments, especially in military, economic, and educational matters. A large amount of this money went for roads and rural projects in Central Luzon in order to deal with the growing peasant rebellion.

JUSMAG (Joint U.S. Military Advisory Group) became the agency that actually directed the reorganization of the anti-Huk campaign. It was responsible for the complete revamp of the intelligence agencies of the Philippine government.

The U.S. National Security Council stated that the "security interests of the United States require that the Philippines become and remain stable, anti-communist and pro-American." They projected that with reorganization under JUSMAG, the Huk threat could be eliminated within one year. One American propaganda official said the solution for Asia was to "present American ideas dressed in Asian clothes, coming from Asian mouths." The need in the Philippines was to build up a leader who could recapture the Philippine confidence, but accept American direction. Ramon Magsaysay was the American choice to present American ideas.

Ramon Magsaysay rose from branch manager of a bus line to congressman to defense secretary and finally to president under American sponsorship. According to CIA agent Joseph B. Smith, "Long before the presidential election of 1953 in the Philippines, the CIA launched a program that would make Magsaysay a national hero and Lansdale an authority on combating insurgency."[2]

The drive for clean elections was a milestone in the build-up of Magsaysay. A citizens' organization for clean elections called NAMFREL (National Movement for Free Elections) was formally inaugurated in August 1951. Jaime Ferrer, national commander of the Philippine Veterans Legion, was chosen NAMFREL director. NAMFREL was active in the congressional elections in 1951 and in the presidential elections in 1953. Though NAMFREL was projected as a spontaneous coming together of many civic and business groups, it was actually run and funded by the CIA.[3]

Lansdale personally coordinated American participation in the drive for clean elections. In Washington, Secretary of State Dean Acheson made a speech stressing American concern that the upcoming Philippine election be a real exercise in democracy. All prominent publishers sent foreign correspondents to monitor the elections.

The Civil Affairs Office of the Philippine military worked with NAMFREL. American military officers were sent around the country, supposedly for inspection of Philippine military units stationed in provinces where the opposition party might cause trouble. Several days before the presidential election, some U.S. navy ships paid a visit to Manila Bay. Their appearance seemed to confirm the Magsaysay camp's rumors of a U.S. backed coup should elections be marred by large-scale fraud and coercion of voters.

Magsaysay won by a landslide. He became Man of the Year and *Time* magazine carried his picture on their cover. Eisenhower extended congratulations to the CIA station in Manila after the election, to whom he had given prior approval for an election operation. Clean elections restored popular hope that change could be effected peacefully, thus undermining support for the Huk struggle.

With Magsaysay as president, a much publicized but ineffectual land reform program was instituted, together with rural community development programs designed to undercut the Huk insurgency and build up future political leaders upon whom the U.S. could count. Jaime Ferrer, who had ini-

2. Ibid., pp. 104-5.
3. Ibid., p. 108.

tially headed the NAMFREL program, began actively organizing community centers in 1953 for this purpose.

After President Magsaysay was killed in a plane accident in 1957, his vice-president, Carlos Garcia, took over. Of particular concern to the United States was the growing support in the Philippines for a nationalist Filipino First program, of which President Garcia was an articulate exponent. In response, the CIA station in Manila received its order to "find another Magsaysay" to defeat Garcia and his Senate supporters at the polls. "Jimmy Ferrer was at the moment considered to be an asset on ice," said Smith.[4] He was taken off ice to assist CIA operative Joseph Smith in the 1958 senatorial elections.

The story of Philippine elections after the country was granted independence in 1946 reads like a CIA chronicle in those years for which information is available. The list of Filipino politicians, some of whom are still active in the Philippines, who were in touch or had an even stronger connection with the CIA in the 1950s reads like a Filipino *Who's Who*.[5]

During our stay in the Philippines in the late 1970s, we saw no visible evidence of CIA involvement at the local level, despite the suspicions of our Filipino friends. We knew only one American missionary who saw it as his patriotic duty to report in at the American Embassy when he went to Manila from his post in Mindanao. I remained skeptical of the "a CIA agent under every bush" mentality that punctuated many conversations in Mindanao in the late 1970s and early 1980s.

This skepticism, however, was tempered during a visit to the Philippines in 1987, one year after Mrs. Aquino took office. I was astonished to note the many elements of a sophisticated pattern of counterinsurgency well in place. Based on an already established historical precedent of American interference, it seems important to examine more closely recent U.S. administration actions, Philippine military activities like the various coups, and American right-wing visitors to the Philippines.

A general similarity appears in the focus and style of the CIA under Allen Dulles in the 1950s and under William Casey in the 1980s. Under Eisenhower, increasing emphasis was

---

4. Ibid., p. 268.

5. Renato Constantino and Letizia Constantino, *Philippines: The Continuing Past* (Manila: Foundation for Nationalist Studies, 1978), pp. 226-68. Also see Smith, *Portrait of a Cold Warrior,* pp. 109ff. and 265ff.

laid on psychological operations. John Foster Dulles, Secretary of State at that time, declared during the presidential campaign that the United States should use psychological and political offensives to accomplish its goals. The thrust of the CIA during the 1950s was not so different from the priorities of the late William Casey. Casey was the CIA director at the time of the 1986 change of government in the Philippines and the build-up of armed vigilantes in the year following. Casey was impatient with timidity and took bold risks, engaging in "extracurricular" activities to challenge and thwart the growth of communism. This general milieu must be kept in mind as other events are examined.

In March 1987, it was announced that President Ronald Reagan signed a secret "finding" approving a $10 million dollar, two-year plan for increased CIA involvement in the Philippine government's anti-insurgency campaign. *Finding* is the term used for the notice the president gives Congress that allows an agency to undertake actions that might otherwise be prohibited. By law, the president is also required to inform Congress within a "reasonable" period of time after the authorization. The Philippine directive was the first such finding Reagan authorized since the Iran arms deal became public knowledge in November 1986.

The finding calls for CIA operatives to gather intelligence with overflights (the flight of U.S. intelligence planes through Philippine airspace), if necessary, and to launch undercover political activities. The agency will increase the number of its agents from 115 to 130 at its secret station in Manila. The finding lists "eight to ten specific types of programs each with its own budget and also opens the door for use of CIA field advisers and is general enough to allow for the implementation of political dirty tricks." One source familiar with the plan voiced concern about a principle of the plan that could cover political action such as "planting of news stories and the creation of new political groups to publicize alleged human right abuses committed by the insurgents."[6]

Richard Kessler, of the Carnegie Endowment for International Peace, said, "This is the first symbol of direct U.S. in-

6. Phil Bronstein, "CIA Activity Increased in RP," *San Fransisco Examiner,* 23 March 1987; and "Covert Help for Cory Aquino," *Newsweek,* 23 March 1987, p. 7.

volvement in the counter-insurgency campaign. . . . It may be like the imperceptible steps you could see on Vietnam during the Eisenhower administration."

What are the elements within the Philippines that might be linked to U.S. government interest and involvement? The pieces of the pattern include:

1. The presence and activity of Maj. Gen. John K. Singlaub in the Philippines;
2. The splurge of public anticommunist conferences sponsored by CAUSA, an affiliate of the Unification Church;
3. A sudden jump in sophistication of the anticommunist materials used with the church and other media efforts;
4. The phenomenal growth of armed vigilantes, blessed by both the military and the civilian government;
5. The replacement of Aquilino Pimentel, minister of local governments, with Jaime Ferrer, one of the CIA "boys" from the 1950s.

Maj. Gen. John K. Singlaub (ret.) figured prominently in the Iran-Contra hearings as part of the privatization of American foreign policy. Singlaub has been active in destabilization efforts in Nicaragua and in training of anticommunist troops in Central America. His last government post was chief of U.S. forces in South Korea. He retired after disagreeing with President Jimmy Carter over a decision to reduce the number of U.S. troops in South Korea. Singlaub, sixty-four, worked with U.S. intelligence in World War II and the Vietnam War and was a close associate of the former CIA director, the late William J. Casey.

Singlaub has played a crucial role in the World Anti-Communist League. As head of the new American League chapter in 1981, Singlaub was an outspoken advocate of unconventional warfare, which he defined as "low intensity actions, such as sabotage, terrorism, assassination and guerrilla warfare."[7]

According to Robert Healy, associate editor of the *Boston Globe,* "The League was a collection of South African racists, anti-Semites, fascists, Nazi collaborators and fugitive terrorists when Singlaub's Council for World Freedom (an American chapter of the League) took over the effort to redefine it

7. Scott Anderson and Jon Lee Anderson, *Inside the League* (New York: Dodd, Mead, 1986), p. 120.

at a 1984 meeting in San Diego."[8] Singlaub is quoted as saying, in his address to that conference,

> I am convinced that our struggle with communism is not a spectator sport. As a result of that view, we have opted for the course of action which calls for the provision of support and assistance to those who are actively resisting the Soviet supported intrusion into Africa, Asia and North America.[9]

Maj. Gen. John K. Singlaub's presence in the Philippines was publicly noticed in the fall of 1986. Reputable Philippine newspapers, including *Business Day*, reported that Singlaub met with businesspeople across the country, advising them to put together their own armed bodyguard to protect themselves and their properties and investments. The previous Philippines chapter of the World Anti-Communist League had been filled with "cronies of dictator Ferdinand Marcos and those drawn from his rubber stamp National Assembly";[10] in the Aquino period a renewed effort was made to start WACL chapters nationwide. Philippine columnist Hilarion Henares reported Singlaub's meetings with Marcos's defense minister Juan Ponce Enrile, U.S. Embassy officials, the CIA station chief in Manila, as well as several members of the Aquino government.

By mid-February, reports appeared in the U.S. papers about Singlaub's recruiting of thirty-seven Vietnam War veterans to train Philippine soldiers in counterinsurgency. Singlaub claimed that he was only searching for treasures allegedly left behind in the Philippines by Japanese commander Yamashita during the Second World War. However, nine months later, in November 1987, Armed Forces Chief Fidel Ramos admitted that Singlaub had tried to persuade him to allow American advisers and trainers into the country to help in the counterinsurgency effort.

Singlaub was not the only international right-wing visitor on the scene in the Philippines. The *Philippine Daily Inquirer* reported on November 29, 1986, that other visitors included former CIA deputy director Ray Cline; (Heinie) Aderholt of Air Commandos Association; Edgar Chamorro, former director of

8. Robert Healy, "Did Singlaub play a role in Aquino Coup Attempt?" *Boston Globe,* 4 September 1987.

9. Ibid.

10. Anderson, *Inside the League,* p. 59.

the FDN (contras); and Col. Alexander M. S. McColl, military affairs editor for *Soldier of Fortune*.

Australian John Whitehall of the World Christian Anti-Communist Crusade of Australia has visited and written extensively on communism in the Philippines. In the summer and fall of 1986, anticommunist seminars suddenly flourished in Manila and other cities across the archipelago. CAUSA (Confederation of Associations for the Unity of Societies of America), the political arm of Sun Myung Moon's Unification Church, is also active in the Philippines. The president of the Philippine chapter is Celia Diaz Laurel, the wife of Mrs. Aquino's running mate and vice president, Salvador Laurel. CAUSA is one way in which the Unification Church continues its involvement in the World Anti-Communist League.[11]

By October 1987, Philippine national dailies were reporting that "American conservatives are setting up private aid projects to help the Philippines fight the Communist insurgency."[12] Mentioned were the Americares and the Knights of Malta, which have a Philippine counterpart called Sovereign Military Order of Malta. These projects were set up after analysts from conservative American think tanks visited the Philippines and concluded that the Aquino government and the armed forces are incapable of stemming the insurgency's continued growth. The rationale is that, given the current U.S. budgetary restrictions, a rise in government aid to fight the insurgency is not feasible. That is where private aid comes in. This assistance takes the form of logistical support for soldiers as well as relief and development aid designed to address local grievances in order to undermine popular support for the insurgents.

The *Manila Chronicle* commented in a front page story that "such aid parallels private efforts by U.S. conservative groups in Central America where humanitarian aid was also used to provide relief to communities ravaged by anti-insurgency operations. In Central America, humanitarian aid was occasionally used as a front for covert operations."[13]

Aid from right-wing groups in the United States must be given to some "humanitarian" organization in the Philippines. Philippine foundations are being set up in Manila to meet this

11. Ibid., p. 125.

12. Sheila Coronel, "U.S. Rightists Mount Aid to Fight Rebels," *Manila Chronicle*, 26 October 1987, p. 1.

13. Ibid., p. 1.

need. For example, the Philippine American Philanthropic Association and the Gen. Douglas MacArthur Foundation were established by retired Filipino military officers and former American servicemen associated with Star of the Sea.

The Star of the Sea is a treasure-hunting company whose chief executive officer until early 1987 was none other than retired U.S. Gen. John K. Singlaub. The chairperson of the philanthropic association, retired Lt. Col. Medrano Justinianao, worked closely with CIA operative Edward Lansdale in anti-Huk operations in the fifties and later in covert anticommunist operations in Vietnam. Justinianao was a founding member of the World Anti-Communist League and its local chapter, the Philippine Anti-Communist Movement.

A striking feature of Lansdale's Philippine anticommunist campaign in the 1950s was the emphasis on public relations and manipulation of public opinion. When I visited the Philippines in 1987, I noticed a sudden jump in the sophistication of the anticommunist materials used. The usual propaganda for peasants, which emanates from the Armed Forces, depicts communists as devils preying on innocent farmers. In contrast, in my travels around the country I discovered that selected activist priests had received a rather sophisticated packet of material from the New Armed Forces of the Philippines. Enclosed was a warm, enthusiastic letter from Col. Honesto Isleta of the Armed Forces Civil Relations Service.

Isleta wrote, "In this post-Marcos era, we in the New Armed Forces of the Philippines feel that we can openly solicit the support of the various sectors in our society in our efforts to check and contain the insurgency problem." The letter, signed, "Your servant in Christ," accompanied a packet of materials that included Joseph Cardinal Ratzinger's "Instruction on Certain Aspects of the Theology of Liberation," World Anti-Communist League materials, an article about the Philippine New People's Army entitled "The New Khmer Rouge," and materials on Vietnam and Nicaragua.

Isleta invited these selected priests who received the materials to join the New Armed Forces of the Philippines in their anticommunist fight because

> the February revolution and the events that followed have proven to one and all that truly the armed forces is on the side of God, democracy and the people . . . what has happened in Cambodia and to the boat people of Vietnam may

befall our own countrymen if we do not put our act together, so to speak, and join hands in preserving our rich
Catholic heritage and freedom under a democratic way of
life.

These anticommunist materials, which bear a certain
sophistication in their preparation and distribution, are aimed
at church leaders and middle-class professionals. A disinformation campaign was also aimed at foreign correspondants
and the international press. I experienced the way in which
disinformation can be passed along while I was waiting for a
press conference to begin in Davao City in March 1987.

A friendly representative of the official government news
agency, Philippine News Agency (PNA) handed me his card and
began chatting. He had been with PNA during the Marcos era
and had an office in Camp Aguinaldo. He began with questions, "Did you know that the Communist Party of the Philippines (CPP) since its inception was supported by the Soviets?"
When it became clear that I knew that the CPP was established in 1968 with the platform of Marxist–Leninist–Mao-Tse-
Tung Thought and in its early days had a history of bitter en-
mity with the old pro-Soviet party in the Philippines, he
changed tack.

"Did you know that Russian arms shipments meant for
the insurgents have been intercepted?" he continued. I quoted
a Philippine military source who claimed that it is actually
businessmen who are illegally importing arms for their own
version of death squads. He shifted gears again. "Did you know
that Russians have been sighted around the island of Mindanao?" Some Dutch visitors told me the day before that someone thought they were Russians because they did not speak
English with an American accent. I shared that observation
and he left. In a matter of moments I heard him engage a Japanese journalist in the same conversation.

In contrast to the use of fabricated information for the
press and sophisticated materials for the urban middle class,
the strategy in poor rural and urban communities has been
the use of armed vigilantes. In the space of a year, there has
been a remarkable proliferation of armed civilian vigilantes.
Although there have always been paramilitary groups, the new
phenomenon is the growth of these vigilante groups that use
specifically anticommunist names or religious names and
operate in the cities as well as in towns and rural areas.

As early as May 1987, former U.S. Attorney General Ramsey Clark led a fact-finding delegation to the Philippines that raised the question of improper American involvement in Philippine internal affairs, especially in relation to the vigilante groups. The team was composed of Ralph McGehee, a former CIA officer with twenty-five years of experience in southeast Asia, particularly Indochina; Leonard Weinglas, chair of the International Affairs Committee of the National Lawyers Guild; Dr. Gerald Horne, past president of the National Conference of Black Lawyers and professor at Sarah Lawrence College; Leonard Ruiz of the *World Policy Journal;* and Sr. Catherine Pinkerton, CSJ, of NETWORK, the Catholic social justice lobby in Washington, D.C.

The Clark delegation visited several areas of the country since the vigilante groups stretch from Cagayan Valley in the north to Zamboanga del Sur in the south. While the vigilante groups seem to multiply daily, researchers have counted at least 125 various groups with names like Anti-NPA Guerrilla Unit, Special Anti-Terrorist Group, Guerrilla Defenders of the Masses, People's Vigilantes, Philippine Divine Missionaries for Christ, Teachers against Communist Harassment, Rock Christ Jesus, Remnants of God, and Universal Family Central of Yahweh.

In a statement to the press in Manila after the investigation, former CIA officer Ralph McGehee said he saw "direct parallels" between the counterinsurgency operations involving vigilante groups that are being launched by the military in the Philippines and those conducted by the U.S. during the Vietnam War. The Vietnam counterparts were called "provincial reconnaissance units," actually assassination teams sent to "purify" villages of alleged communists. The other parallels McGehee mentioned included the ways the military and the vigilante groups have launched "search and destroy operations, created free fire zones and forced people from rural areas into population centers to deny the insurgents a recruiting base."

Lt. Col. Franco Calida in Davao City is the acknowledged founder of the Alsa Masa, one of the first vigilante groups in the country. Calida has trained vigilante leaders in other provinces as well. McGehee, who participated himself in the Phoenix Program in Vietnam, identified Calida as one of the Philippine officers who had received counterinsurgency training by special forces at Fort Bragg, North Carolina, in 1971 and

1972. The Clark Report also noted the frequent visits of United States Information Service official William Parker to the office of Lieutenant Colonel Calida in Davao City.[14]

Researcher Sara Miles, who has written extensively on low-intensity conflict strategy in Central America, also visited the Philippines in mid-1987. She pointed to the parallels between the death squads of El Salvador, the civil patrols of Guatemala, and the growing vigilante movement in the Philippines. She noted that in contrast to the Central American population, Filipinos were more knowledgeable about the low-intensity conflict strategy in their country at an earlier point in its implementation. This may be due to the higher number of literate people in the Philippines and to the greater degree of international penetration, even in rural barrios.

Given the relatively sophisticated Philippine population, it is essential for the Philippine government to gain civilian support in order for the low-intensity warfare to proceed unimpeded. The Ministry of Local Governments is key to this effort, but Aquilino Pimentel, Mrs. Aquino's first appointee to that ministry, was a liberal politician and could not be relied on to be an active supporter of the vigilante movement. In addition, Pimentel angered local politicians and their supporters by removing many of the pro-Marcos mayors and governors and naming pro-Aquino officers-in-charge to serve until local elections could be called. After a clamor for the ouster of Pimentel, Mrs. Aquino appointed Jaime Ferrer, the "CIA's asset on ice," to this extremely sensitive post.

Concurrent with Aquino's removal of Pimentel and progressive Labor Minister Augusto "Bobbit" Sanchez, was the removal of Juan Ponce Enrile because of his suspected role in the coup attempts. Most progressive people and organizations mourned Sanchez's departure, applauded Enrile's dismissal, but did not pay much attention to Pimentel's ouster.

In the long-term counterinsurgency plan, bringing Jaime Ferrer into the cabinet may have been a more important step than removing Sanchez or Enrile. CIA agent Joseph Smith, who took Lansdale's place in the Philippines, writes highly of "Jimmy" Ferrer in his *Portrait of a Cold Warrior.*

Ferrer became minister of local government at a time when

14. Ramsey Clark, "Report of a U.S.-Philippine Fact-Finding Mission to the Philippines, May 20-30, 1987," p. 17.

the vigilante movement needed the strong backing of civilian governments in order to survive. Journalists were writing exposés of the abuses of the vigilantes, especially in Davao City. Some of the new mayors and governors appointed by former minister Pimentel were working to bring the various branches of the military and paramilitary under civilian control. This was perceived as hampering the counterinsurgency drive.

In contrast to Pimentel, Jaime Ferrer used his position to commend the vigilante groups for their anticommunist work and ordered all mayors and governors to establish similar groups or risk losing their offices. He even went so far as to question the integrity of the bishop and the governor of Surigao, Mindanao, when they did not comply with his orders. Ferrer understood the necessity of a strong grass roots network from his work with local community organizing in connection with CIA activities in the 1950s. In preparation for congressional elections in May 1987 and local elections scheduled for 1988, it was important to control the town and barrio centers—both with loyal mayors and with paramilitary troops.

Until his murder by unknown gunmen in front of his own home in August 1987, Ferrer played a key role in sanctioning the vigilante groups across the country. The vigilantes helped to discourage any support for alternative candidates in the elections. Their operations also helped to further confuse civilian and military functions. The blur between military and civilian functions is a crucial component of the low-intensity conflict strategy, a theory now in vogue in American military circles. Ferrer's past history of cooperation with the CIA and the results of his work as minister of local government does raise the question of whether he was again cooperating with the CIA design.

Other points of American connection which should be investigated are the many coup attempts that started soon after Mrs. Aquino came to power. A plethora of cartoons on the coup phenomenon have appeared, making light of these attempts to topple Aquino. In one cartoon, various right-wing figures sit in a waiting room at Malacanang Palace while a receptionist says to the latest arrival, Ferdinand Marcos, "Just take a number and wait your turn." Despite the fact that no one got hurt in the early coups and the soldiers involved were punished with doing push-ups, there is a deadly serious side to these "unsuccessful" coup attempts.

The series of coups against the Aquino government began in July 1986 and served at least two important functions. They helped to distract public attention from civilian initiatives for social and economic justice, and they also provided the necessary pressure to push the Aquino administration to adopt economic and military policies more in line with the views of the American administration. The undercutting of the citizens' social agenda and the expansion of military influence on the Aquino administration policy bears further examination.

Bayan, a national coalition of citizen organizations, has pointed out the link between the attempted coups and various mass actions such as strikes and demonstrations. For example, on November 13, 1986, Rolando Olalia, president of the nationalist political party, Partido ng Bayan, was brutally murdered. Within one week a coup against Aquino was staged.

On January 22, 1987, the farmers from the National Peasants Union marched toward the presidential palace after numerous frustrated attempts to negotiate with the minister of agrarian reform, Heherson Alvarez. They were gathered at Mendiola Bridge, which leads to Malacanang Palace, when the police shot at them, killing nineteen and wounding many others. On January 27, five days later, there was another coup attempt.

In August 1987, the nationalist groups were preparing a mass rally and national strike to focus on rising prices, especially the price of oil. Manila was soon filled with coup rumors and on August 28 the most serious coup occurred. Thirty-nine people, mostly civilians, were killed. Two hundred and ten civilians and seventy-seven soldiers were wounded. Mrs. Aquino's son, Nonoy, was wounded and several of his bodyguards were killed.

The coups were well timed to distract public attention from economic issues. "People's desperation with their severe economic plight was always lost in the news about the coups," said one Bayan member.

It is also instructive to note the benefits that accrued to the military and the changes in policy that occurred after each coup attempt.

Five days after the July 6, 1986, coup attempt involving Marcos supporters and three hundred military men, Aquino authorized a 10 percent salary increase for military personnel and police. Three months later nine colonels and one navy captain were promoted on the recommendation of then Defense Minister Juan Ponce Enrile and Chief of Staff Fidel Ramos.

In the second week of November 1986 the government foiled yet another coup attempt staged by Marcos loyalists and a military faction loyal to Enrile. A few weeks later, in December, executive orders to boost the morale of the armed forces provided for restoration of military personnel buying privileges for tax-free consumer goods and combat clothing to officers. The "left leaning" Cabinet members were replaced in December as well at the specific request of military officers believed to be behind the coup attempts.

The third coup attempt, on January 27, 1987, was followed by a dialogue between Mrs. Aquino and twenty junior officers. Among the issues discussed were allegations about suspected "leftists" in the Cabinet, the low pay of soldiers, and the perception that the military is ignored and not considered part of the government. Two months later, on March 22, 1987, President Aquino ordered the Armed Forces to resume operations against the NPA.

After the fourth coup attempt, on April 18, 1987, 141 AFP personnel were promoted and 250,000 soldiers and 60,000 police were given a 15 percent across-the-board salary increase. This increase was announced only one day after the president in her May Day speech turned down the workers' demand for an increase in wages.

The fifth coup attempt, on August 28, 1987, was by far the bloodiest. On September 2, nine senators in the Philippine Congress filed a bill seeking an immediate lump-sum payment of thirteen months of pay to all government personnel, including the Armed Forces, plus a 1,000 peso yearly bonus to those receiving 3,000 pesos a month or less ($1 = 20 pesos). Two days later, Aquino announced three new housing projects for the AFP, scholarships for children of soldiers killed in action, and a 16 million peso allotment from the calamity fund for the renovation of the Camp Aguinaldo officers' clubhouse, which serves as temporary headquarters of the AFP. The headquarters had been bombed during the coup. To augment the 9.7 billion peso budget of the AFP, Aquino proposed a 200 million peso public works bill.[15]

15. "Concessions Given to Military after Series of Coups," *Philippine Agenda*, 12-18 October 1987, p. 5.

Any military person studying the results of the coups in terms of concessions and financial allotments for the Armed Forces could conclude that unsuccessful coups are a lucrative enterprise and might be encouraged to stage more. From its inception, the Philippine military was modeled on the American military. It is the institution in Philippine society most clearly connected to the United States. Many of its officers train in the United States and much of its equipment and financing comes from the United States.

But the Philippine military is not the only beneficiary of the coups. Other interest groups and forces inside and outside the country have their own agenda as well. How do the interests of the rebel soldiers intersect with the interests of U.S. right-wing elements, the U.S. military and business community, some in the Philippine business community, and even some members of Cory Aquino's Cabinet?

President Aquino's executive secretary, Joker Arroyo, became the symbol for the promotion of human rights, nationalist economics, and political independence—all of which was offensive to various sectors in the Philippines. The coup attempt of August 28, 1987, was the final straw in tipping the balance against Arroyo.

The International Monetary Fund, transnational corporations, Filipino landowners, and government technocrats had reason to worry about developments that took place before this fifth coup. In the July 27 opening of Congress, Mrs. Aquino's State of the Nation speech, which was presumed to have been written by Joker Arroyo and Teodoro Locsin, addressed the national debt question. Based on that speech, the Senate began discussing selective repudiation of the debt and limiting the service payments to 10-15 percent rather than the 40 percent Finance Minister Jaime Ongpin had previously negotiated with the banks. Both Fernandez of the Central Bank and Ongpin were under fire in Congress for the unduly harsh deal they agreed to in seeking repayment of the debt with the International Monetary Fund.[16]

Meanwhile, on August 26, in the parliament of the streets, the national people's strike, Welga ng Bayan, attracted broad popular support throughout the country from gas station

---

16. Ongpin was removed from office and a few months later, in December 1987, committed suicide, according to his family.

operators and local oil dealers in addition to laborers and drivers. It was the biggest protest since Mrs. Aquino came to power. Because of this mass action, Aquino was forced to roll back the oil prices by 50 percent. Her popularity was eroding and both sides perceived her as weak.

The government technocrats, many of whom were trained in American universities and institutes, saw the strike and the moves in Congress as possible deterrents to gaining more foreign investments they felt were desperately needed for repayment of the debts. Immediately after the coup attempt, the business community clamored for Cabinet reorganization. They declared Arroyo "inefficient" and demanded his removal.

The fifth coup attempt, the first that was aimed directly at Mrs. Aquino in Malacanang, helped to persuade her to situate her economic recovery program within an International Monetary Fund perspective. Until that point, the presence of nationalist Cabinet members like Arroyo stood in the way of that goal. The threat from the unsuccessful coup provided enough pressure for Aquino to dismiss Arroyo.

Vice President Salvador Laurel also played a role in the destabilizing drama. His aspiration to the presidency is well known. In 1986, however, after a great deal of pressure from his political colleagues, he reluctantly submerged his ambitions and temporarily stepped aside for Cory Aquino. Immediately after the coup of August 28, 1987, that threatened the president directly, Laurel interviewed soldiers and acted publicly as an advocate for their complaints. At the time of this inappropriate vice-presidential behavior, rumors were rampant in Manila about Laurel's forming a political alliance with former Defense Minister Juan Ponce Enrile as opposition to Aquino.

Several weeks after the coup, Laurel presented a list to the Senate that named one hundred "known" communists in the Aquino government, whom he said should not only be fired but should also be criminally prosecuted. (Laurel's wife, Celia Diaz Laurel, is the president of the Philippine chapter of CAUSA, the political arm of the Rev. Moon's Unification Church.) He viewed Arroyo as the protector of these "known" communists. Many in the Philippine Congress and in the press derided Laurel for this McCarthy tactic. But Laurel's audience extends beyond the borders of the Philippines.

Judging from his remarks in a 1987 interview, Ronald Reagan would be proud of Laurel. "Remember," said the president, there was once a Congress in which they had a committee that would investigate even one of their own members if it was believed that that person had communist involvement or communist leanings. Well, they've done away with those committees. That shows the success of what the Soviets were able to do in this country with making it unfashionable to be anticommunist.[17]

Another group of Philippine players in this drama, whose agenda overlaps but is not identical to American government interests, includes the Filipino business people and the landlords in Congress. They were threatened by Aquino's Comprehensive Agrarian Reform Program (CARP), viewing it as a possible danger to their lucrative part in transnational corporation holdings in agribusiness plantations. The landlords in Congress sponsored a bill to water down CARP. At the same time, even the World Bank, sister institution to the IMF, was pushing for a stronger land reform program. Without some land redistribution, they felt that the insurgency could not be undercut.

Thus, all of these various individuals and groups—business executives, Vice President Laurel, the military, and the technocrats—had their own reasons for wanting Arroyo to be removed from office. In addition, some members of Congress, a number of whom are Cory Aquino's relatives, also objected to Joker Arroyo's influence on her. Thus immediately after the coup they all coalesced to push for Arroyo's ouster. He was the last of the human rights lawyers in the Aquino administration. With his ouster, attention was shifted away from the danger to democracy that the coup symbolized. Ironically, though Arroyo has been portrayed as a radical nationalist, a human rights zealot, and even a communist by his opponents, very few activist groups even counted him in the inner circle of human rights advocates.

Arroyo's biggest "sin" was his pointing out the connections between business, military, and old-style government technocrats. Before he was dismissed from the Cabinet, Arroyo visited the Philippine House of Representatives to discuss the military coup. At the House he named three businessmen, Buenaventura, Navarro, and Concepcion, as enemies of the

17. Interview with Arnaud de Borchgrave, *Washington Times*, October 1987.

state and called them "guilty of treason." He said that they were involved in the process of sowing intrigue to divide the civilian government from the military. These businessmen have responsibilities within government bodies that linked them to such government technocrats as former Finance Minister Jaime Ongpin and Central Bank governor Jose B. Fernandez. Ongpin, Fernandez, and these businessmen were in contact with the International Monetary Fund and World Bank, which in turn are linked with the large transnational corporation banking institutions with whom the Philippine government has many outstanding debts.

While the interests of the technocrats, the landed and business elite, and the military in the Philippines are varied, the American government's agenda in the Philippines focuses most pointedly on the military bases. If the United States' bases are to stay in the Philippines, Aquino will have to support their retention. The people whom the Philippine military points to as "leftists" in the Aquino government are actually those who are against the renewal of the United States–Philippine base agreement.

At the time of the unsuccessful August 29, 1987, coup there were two bills in the Senate that would implement the antinuclear provision of the 1986 constitution. These bills were delayed until May 1988 as a result. Subic Naval Base services the U.S. Seventh Fleet, including maintenance for its ninety nuclear-capable fighters and fighter bombers. Clark houses the nuclear-capable Third tactical Fighter Wing.

Some within the American administration are convinced that if unhampered access to the bases is to be guaranteed, the communist insurgency must be crushed. They believe that Mrs. Aquino was not projecting a clear hard line against progressive and militant groups in 1986 and early 1987 because of the "leftist" influence in her administration. The U.S. government and the American right-wing are unsure about both Aquino's stand on the bases and her ability to stamp out the insurgency. This gives added impetus to interfere in the internal Philippine affairs.

Gringo Honasan, leader of the rebel soldiers who spearheaded the coup attempt, and the Reform the Armed Forces Movement (RAM) have their own agenda—as do the other Filipino actors on the political scene. Honasan's interests are not unconnected to the Pentagon or to transnational corporations or Filipino elite business interests in the country, but these interests do not always run parallel and can sometimes be contradictory.

When Enrile was ousted from the Cabinet, Honasan and his supporters were pushed to the periphery, although they still held key positions within the military machinery. They were interested in seizing power to guarantee their privileged position in the Philippine society, which they had enjoyed during martial law. With Arroyo, a former human rights lawyer, in the position of executive secretary, they saw themselves as being out of favor with Cory Aquino. Some were also worried that the Presidential Committee on Human Rights would move for an investigation of their past abuses. They viewed the committee as being under Arroyo's protection.

Another segment within the military was still loyal to Marcos and simply waiting for another chance to join a coup. Most Philippine military officers have had some kind of American training. Thus it is not surprising that many, whether Marcos or Honasan supporters, view Philippine society from the perspective of their U.S. military allies. Thus the coup leaders' consistently stated criticism was that the Aquino government was not strongly anticommunist.

Most analysts agree that lower-level officers like Gringo Honasan could not have organized the coup and moved toward the seizure of state power without the help of powerful individuals and groups. Elements within the U.S. government may have wanted to push Aquino to become more supportive of the bases and of the counterinsurgency drive, but they probably did not want to topple her. Honasan and the military officers have their own agenda, which Washington cannot necessarily control.

Evidence suggests that American government and private right-wing individuals were involved in one way or another. For example, retired four-star general Richard Stillwell, seventy, visited the Philippines for ten days in August, leaving the country shortly before the coup attempt on August 28, 1987. He denied that he was a U.S. agent but freely acknowledged that he was "a spook in the 1950s."[18] Part of his trip was coordinated by Amelia Benitez Reyes, whose brother worked closely

18. C. S. Manegold and Tim Weiner, "Some Say U.S. Has Lost Faith in Aquino," *Philadelphia Inquirer,* 16 September 1987.

with Imelda Marcos and whose deceased uncle Col. Napoleon Valeriano was a close associate of Col. Edward Lansdale.[19]

Upon his return to the United States, Stillwell circulated a report in the U.S. military and intelligence community and also testified in a Senate Foreign Relations Committee hearing in October 1987. His contention was that unless Aquino acted decisively to embrace the right-of-center leaders in the private and public sector, there could be a political breakdown resulting in a coalition government with the communists within the next two years.[20]

Another example that points to direct American government interest in the unsuccessful August 28 coup is provided by Felix Bautista, Jr., close friend and adviser to Cardinal Sin. Bautista told reporters that "someone from the Embassy called me and said, 'You know I think the only solution is a military junta. Could you tell Cardinal Sin to try to convince Cory to accept a seat on the junta?'"[21]

According to Philippine military sources, U.S. army attaché Lt. Col. Victor Raphael was at Camp Aguinaldo during the attempted coup and intervened on behalf of Honasan's troops. Raphael had maintained close contact with Honasan and other rebel officers before and during the coup. A Philippine congressional investigation studied these allegations. Philippine House Speaker Ramon Mitra charged that Raphael and two other U.S. attachés were "spies who quarterbacked the failed military coup." Philippine Foreign Minister Raul Manglapus and Defense Secretary Rafael Ileto lodged a strong informal complaint with U.S. Ambassador Nicholas Platt in October 1987.

The U.S. Department of State denied any improper involvement in the coup. Charles Redman, State Department spokesperson in Washington, said, "We reject any suggestion that we have interfered in a way that would support anti-democratic elements opposed to President Aquino."[22] Though the U.S. Embassy denied the charges, two months after the coup they sent Lt. Col. Victor Rafael back to the United States—eight

19. Sheila Coronel, *Manila Chronicle*, 25 October 1987, p. 1.

20. Manegold and Weiner, "Some Say U.S. Has Lost Faith in Aquino."

21. Ibid.

22. Marites Sison, Malou Mangahas, and Wilson Bailon, "U.S. Attache in Meddling to Be Recalled," *Manila Chronicle*, 29 October 1987, p. 1.

months before his tour of duty in the Philippines was officially to end.

Redman's statement came after the Iran-Contra hearings had demonstrated that the Reagan administration was involved in a two-track policy in Central America—a public governmental stance and a simultaneous private destabilization. The Tower Commission, which made the initial investigation into the alleged misconduct of supplying arms illegally to the Contras as well as illegal arm sales to Iran, pointed to the danger of privatizing U.S. foreign policy. It is not inconceivable that a two-track policy is also being followed in the Philippines.

Viewed piece by piece, the evidence pointing to inappropriate U.S. involvement within the Philippines could be attributed to coincidence or the natural outworking of the pro-American stance of many of the political leaders and general population in the Philippines. Taken altogether, these pieces point to a systematic attempt to move President Aquino to the right and disabuse her of any notion of including the militant nationalists in the national consensus. The evidence provides a reasonable suggestion of external influence—"a prima facie case of U.S. involvement which merits Congressional investigation," according to Lester Ruiz, a member of the Ramsey Clark fact-finding mission to the Philippines.[23]

The first track of the U.S. government's policy toward the Aquino government is strong public support. However, the second track of the administration policy toward Manila is to establish ties with right-wing military and vigilante networks in order to nudge the Philippine government to the right, or even to topple it, should it adopt a strong nationalist stance. A campaign of anticommunist hysteria and a series of coup attempts are like a gun pointed at the Aquino government, threatening it with destruction unless it capitulates.

---

23. Lester Ruiz, "Right Wing Vigilanteeism and the Betrayal of Democracy: Notes on a Fact Finding Mission" (Manila: National Council of Churches in the Philippines, 1987), p. 4.

10

U.S. Military Presence
in the Philippines

BASES OF INSECURITY

> Q: *Mr. President, are the two U.S. bases in the Philippines of paramount importance when you consider U.S. policy for the Philippines? Or would you put the future of those bases at risk if it meant standing up for democracy?*
>
> RONALD REAGAN: *One cannot minimize the importance of those bases.*
>
> —Presidential Press Conference, February 11, 1986

> *I would say right off that in the event that we were forced to vacate the Philippine bases that the United States would continue to carry out its primary military function in the Pacific. We would continue to have a presence there and we would continue to carry out those things which are necessary to protect our interests.*
>
> —Admiral Robert Long, Commander in Chief, Pacific, 1983

Philippine nationalism, troubled as it has been with co-option by foreign interests and politics, has never died. A consistent thread stretching back into Spanish colonial times is stained with bloodshed on behalf of "Mother Filipinas." Despite the honeyed words of American textbooks about the liberation of the Philippines from Spain, the facts show that the United States invaded the Philippines at a point when the Filipinos had almost driven the Spanish out of their country and declared themselves an independent republic. Half a million Filipinos died resisting that American conquest at the turn of this century.

Four hundred and fifty years of Philippine life and consciousness is bound up in colonialism, but Filipino historian Renato Constantino says it is precisely the Filipino resistance to colonial oppression that provides the unifying thread of Philippine history and the emergence of Filipino identity.

The greatest challenge to Philippine nationalism in this historical time is the continuing presence of U.S. military bases on Philippine soil. The two largest U.S. military installations in the Philippines are Subic Bay Naval Station in the province of Zambales and Clark Air Base in Pampanga province, both on the island of Luzon. Subic Bay, which services the U.S. Seventh Fleet, covers 450 square miles of land and ocean in one of the world's great natural harbors. Clark Air Base, which houses the Third Tactical Fighter Wing, has a 150,000-acre target range that is unmatched in any overseas installation. Another major base in the Philippines, the San Miguel Naval Communications Station, is the communications center for the Seventh Fleet and controls U.S. submarine movement in the Indian Ocean.

The military bases are the American government's bottom-line interest in the Philippines. According to annual Pentagon testimony at U.S. congressional hearings, the bases constitute a vital link in the U.S. Pacific strategy.

To understand what role the U.S. bases play in the Philippines and in Filipino life and consciousness, we must look briefly at the history of the bases, the bases' effects in the immediate area, the security concerns of Filipinos, and their attempts to dismantle the bases.

The Philippines has endured a foreign military presence on her soil since Ferdinand Magellan landed on Mactan Island in the Visayas in 1521 and emerged from his ship accompanied by by his chaplain and his army commander. On his second voyage to these Pacific islands, which he hoped were the "Indies," Magellan was killed by Datu Lapu-Lapu, a local tribal chieftain. "Datu" means leader or chief. Lapu-Lapu is celebrated in nationalist circles as the first Filipino to stand against foreign aggression.

However, no other chieftains joined Lapu-Lapu's attempt to repel the invaders, so in 1565 when Miguel Lopez de Legazpi began the official Spanish colonization of the islands, it took only seven years to establish 143 *encomiendas* and assign them to his men. An encomienda was an administrative unit formed for the purpose of extracting tribute from the natives.[1]

The Spanish retained control of the Philippines continuously from 1565 to 1898 except for two years (1762-64) when the British East India Company invaded and occupied the islands. American soldiers have been in the Philippines since 1898 with the exception of a few years during the Pacific War when the Japanese drove them out (1941-45). No country in all of Asia has had a longer continuous colonial heritage in the modern period. No country in Asia has had its identity so distorted or its great patriots so frustrated as they set about the task of fashioning an independent vision for its people and life.

The Pacific War, as Filipinos refer to their part of World War II, left the country in shambles. The Japanese had controlled economic life directly for their own benefit. All production was used for the war effort. Trade was virtually at a standstill. Many Filipinos were living off the land as guerrillas or guerrilla supporters. In the closing days of the war, American planes carpet bombed large areas of Luzon, destroying the old walled city of Manila. The country was in desperate economic shape at the end of the war.

The Filipinos were looking forward to national independence, the timetable for which had been interrupted by the war. Before granting its former colony independence or rehabilitation aid, however, the United States Congress passed legislation that had a long and profound effect on the economic health and direction of the country. The Bell Trade Act of 1945 provided for continuation of a form of free trade between the two countries, heavily favoring the United States. It also contained a parity amendment that obliged the Philippines to grant U.S. citizens and corporations the same rights as Filipinos in the exploitation of Philippine natural resources. A provision was then tacked onto the Philippine Rehabilitation Act prohibiting payments above $500 for war damage compensation pending Philippine acceptance of the Bell Trade Act. Since the country needed material help so desperately, the Philip-

1. Renato Constantino, *The Philippines: A Past Revisited* (Manila: Tala Publishing Services, 1975), pp. 40ff.; and John Leddy Phelan, *The Hispanization of the Philippines: Spanish Aims and Filipino Responses, 1565–1700* (Madison: University of Wisconsin Press, 1959), chap. 7.

pine Congress had to go along with the Bell Trade Act in order to get its war reparations, which were slated as $120 million for the reconstruction of highways, ports, and harbor facilities, $100 million worth of surplus military property, and $400 million for the compensation of property losses and damage suffered by Filipinos, Americans, citizens of friendly nations, and religious and private organizations.[2]

As soon as the Filipinos agreed to conditions set by the U.S. Congress for the economic rehabilitation, a military bases agreement was signed with the United States, giving the U.S. free use of twenty-three base sites for ninety-nine years. A week later, a Military Assistance Pact was signed under which the United States furnished arms, ammunition, and supplies, trained Philippine military personnel, and sent officers to U.S. military schools. A Joint U.S. Military Advisory Group (JUSMAG) was set up to "advise" the Philippine Army, Constabulary, Air Force, Navy, and Intelligence Services. This was paid for by the Philippine government.[3]

During the Vietnam War, Clark and Subic were key logistical centers for the U.S. military. Also during the war, Olongapo, the dilapidated entertainment city just outside Subic Bay Naval Station, grew to a civilian population of 190,000 from its post–World War II size of 5,000. Its estimated population is now 250,000. The city boasts no industry except for the base, where 22,000 Filipinos are directly employed and another 20,000 have jobs periodically through contractors. Columban College, a Catholic institution with 5,000 students, trains a new generation of base workers. An estimated 15,000 "entertainment" women ply their trade in the city, while 700 families on the outskirts of Olongapo make their living illegally scavenging the base garbage dumping area. Angeles City, the rest and recreation city outside Clark Air Base, located some two and a half hours from Subic, has a similar profile.

One of the most noticeable outgrowths of the bases is the thriving prostitution in the rest and recreation towns adjacent to the military installations. Young women are recruited from the poverty-ridden barrios of islands like Samar and Leyte, in

2. Renato Constantino and Letizia Constantino, *Philippines: The Continuing Past* (Manila: Foundation for Nationalist Studies, 1978), pp. 198ff.

3. John F. Cady, *The History of Post War Southeast Asia: Independence Problems* (Athens: Ohio University Press, 1971).

the central Philippines, to work in the bars of Olongapo. Buklod, a women's drop-in center for hostesses in Olongapo, estimates that the majority of the 15,000 women are between the ages of eighteen and thirty. The women cite poverty as the major reason for coming to Olongapo, but other reasons given are broken homes, troubled marriages, a sense of adventure, and hope of marriage. Prostitution is technically illegal in the Philippines, so officially there are no prostitutes—only hostesses, waitresses, cashiers, entertainers, or "ago-go dancers," as they are called in the Philippines.

It is difficult as an American woman to walk down the main nightstrip of Olongapo City and see the bars and massage parlors with young women, sometimes children, heavily made up and dressed in scanty uniforms. It is especially difficult to contrast this scene with the quiet modest life in the rural barrios from which many of these women come and to which they probably cannot return. I have always felt an internal resistance to accompanying travel seminar groups to this place because of the shame of knowing as a North American that this strip is here only because the American bases are here.

In 1985, Leonora, my friend from Davao City, helped me guide a visiting group of North American Mennonites to Olongapo. During our experience, Leonora made it abundantly clear through her tears that she too felt shame, though its source was different from mine. As we walked the strip with its flashing neon lights, provocative pictures, and displays of obscene T-shirts, Leonora kept her head down. "These women are Filipinas; I am Filipina. The men view everyone in this country as a prostitute—people for sale."

Through the help of Jan Lugibihl and Brenda Stoltzfus, two Mennonite women who work with the hostesses, the Mennonite visitors were able to spend an afternoon and evening in conversation with three of the women. This human interaction was in direct contrast to the garish tinsel of the nightstrip.

There was not a dry eye in the house after April, an obviously bright young woman who looked about fifteen but said she was twenty, shared her story with twenty somber Mennonites, sitting on their straight-backed chairs. Wriggling, giggling, hiding behind her hair, her hand, her friends, she shifted her small lithe body around on the chair in perpetual motion as she talked. April exemplified the Filipino gift for oral tradition. Though the life she described was fraught with disappointments, cruelty, and embarrassing choices, she plunged ahead with colorful detail.

Her desperately poor parents in Samar, in exchange for some money, agreed to let April go with a recruiter who came to her village on behalf of a Manila-based businessman. She worked hard as a clerk and as a maid, put in long hours, and came to the attention of the businessman—who was interested in her body as well as her work. She refused his advances, tried to run away, was caught and chained to her bed. Finally a relative found her and helped her escape. Unwilling to go back to the grinding poverty of the barrio and determined to send her family money, April moved on to Olongapo.

"I thought I could just work in the bar, serving drinks or cashiering. I was sure I wouldn't have to do anything else if I didn't want," she said. Women working in the bars are paid a pittance. The real money is made through their percentage on drinks and, of course, through the relationship with the customer. If the man pays a bar fine, he can take the waitress out of the bar. The bar owner receives the bulk of the fine; the woman gets less than half. Theoretically, April is correct. The women can refuse to leave the bar with someone; however, if they refuse night after night, they will be under pressure from the bar owner. That is, after all, how the owner makes money.

April succumbed to the pressure and joined the 15,000 other prostitutes in the city. The fear of pregnancy, VD, and AIDS plagues her. Feelings of weariness, worthlessness, and being taken advantage of intermix with feelings of love for some of the sailors. The ever-present hope of marrying an American, going to the States, and sending a lot of money home to her family spiced her narrative.

April and the other women who talked to us about their life described their American boyfriends and the pain they feel when the men desert them. I wondered as I listened if the men realize how much genuine emotion is showered on them. April and her friends do not talk about a business contract, but a relationship. So much heartbreak must eventually produce cynicism, but I am astounded at the tough hope it also evokes. "Loved much, forgiven much" is the phrase that passed through my mind simultaneously with April's narrative. The women's stories displayed a determined humanity, which must have some effect on their customers.

"Humanity? They are being taken advantage of—pure and

simple," scoffed a nationalist male friend later when I ventured my comments about tough love. "Just like our entire country. We smile as we hand over all our resources. You call that humanity?"

Added to the psychological damage is the physical danger of sexually transmitted diseases. The more common diseases in Olongapo and Angeles City are gonorrhea and infectious hepatitis. The American military sponsors and pays for a weekly clinic for women to be checked for venereal disease. Any woman working in the clubs must have a weekly bill of health from the clinic.

In 1987, at least thirty-four hospitality workers were tested as AIDS positive, which means they are carriers of the disease and may or may not suffer from its symptoms in the next three to five years. The exact number is difficult to determine. Philippine women's groups charged that the navy and the Philippine Health Department were under-reporting the figures.

The response of the navy seems to be denial and cover-up. In 1987, the U.S. Navy filed court martial charges against Lt. Commander Thomas O'Rourke, a navy physician who was researching the spread of AIDS. O'Rourke was charged with falsification of documents, illegal distribution of controlled drugs, theft of drugs, and unauthorized absence from his unit. According to Dr. O'Rourke's lawyer, Richard Walden, the navy instituted the court martial to harrass O'Rourke because his research blamed U.S. sailors for the spread of AIDS in the Philippines. Walden told the Associated Press in August 1987, "The figures go up and up and the Navy is getting more and more embarrassed because it is getting more and more obvious AIDS was introduced by the Navy to the Philippines. Dr. O'Rourke brought this out."[4]

Gabriela, the umbrella organization for women's groups in the Philippines, is urging the U.S. Navy to test its service members and not allow those with AIDS onto Philippine soil. The women's groups are also demanding that the U.S. Navy take financial responsibility for those hospitality women who have AIDS and can no longer work.

"The women have no other source of income. Many are supporting their families back in the barrio. If the women are

4. Associated Press, "Navy Charges Doctor Who Hid AIDS Data," *Chicago Tribune*, 22 August 1987.

not given economic help and they are still physically able to work, they will. That will be dangerous for everyone," say the women.

Concerned women in the United States who wrote to their congressional representatives about the AIDS problem among Filipina hostesses received a dismally similar letter from the Office of the Assistant Secretary of Defense:

> The Department of Defense and Military Services have taken aggressive action to test Service members for HIV infection. . . . HIV infection is clearly a worldwide problem, one which has no special or unique association with the presence of American Service members. We will therefore continue to take every reasonable measure and to co-operate with host nation authorities to prevent infection of our Service members and their close contacts.

"Not so," say the women working in Olongapo and Angeles. "Aggressive action has not been taken to test the Service members after they are in the service." A thorough physical examination is given when persons enter the service, so if there are many infected service members they must have acquired the HIV infection while in the service. This could possibly point to much heavier drug use within the armed services than the Navy or Air Force is ready to admit.

Another immediate, local implication of the bases is the question of land use. Miguel Caliwag, affectionately known as "Mang Mike," is a leading official in the National Peasants Union (Kilusang Magbubukid ng Pilipinas; KMP). He points to the 49,000 hectares Clark Air Base occupies (1 ha. = 2.2 acres). "They want to expand their facilities even further onto some prime farmland," Mang Mike told our visiting lawyers human rights group in February 1987. "Members of our peasant union who live there want that land to be included in the official government agrarian reform."

The prospects for a comprehensive land reform program seemed bleak, so we asked Mang Mike what the farmers would do if the land around the bases were not included. With a twinkle in his eye, he replied, "Well, the farmers in the area will 'reform' the land no matter what and we only hope the government will join us." As early as 1975, U.S. Senator Mike Mansfield observed in a report to the Senate Foreign Relations Committee that Clark Air Base "covers such a vast area that squatters operating surreptitiously are said to have raised an estimated $10 million worth of sugar cane on base lands last year."[5]

Designated as a military reservation by President Theodore Roosevelt in 1901, Subic Bay Naval Station has a land area of 70,000 acres. The base occupies two-thirds of the land area of the incorporated city of Olongapo. The 250,000 inhabitants of Olongapo live on 850 hectares, according to former Olongapo mayor Teddy Macapagal.

The original inhabitants of the base land are "Negritos," a tribal group, small in stature with negroid features, whose ancestors were perhaps among the earliest settlers in Southeast Asia. The Negritos were pushed further into the hills as the Americans took control of base lands and lowland Filipinos occupied the perimeters. Crow Valley Bombing and Gunnery Range, fourteen miles northwest of Clark, serves as a training ground for the entire U.S. Pacific Air Force. The Negritos along the perimeter have long specialized in gathering brass and other metals from bombs and bullets expended for target practice. A resident of Angeles told us, "The Negritos have gained great expertise in darting in and out between the falling bombs to mark their finds."

In the 1970s a trigger-happy GI sent to guard the target area killed a young Negrito. The case developed into a major confrontation between the base and the Negritos, whose communal value system demanded full compensation for everything the boy might have produced for his people in a normal lifetime. The confrontation was not settled until a major pow-wow was scheduled where a public apology was made and several cases of beef, vienna sausage, sardines, rice, and whiskey were turned over to the Negrito chief by the base commander, Colonel Hill. The ceremony was capped by presenting captain's bars and base privileges for life to the Negrito chief. The chief used his base privileges to purchase four-inch nails from the base exchange, which were promptly turned into spear points by his people and sold back to the GIs as souvenir weapons they could treasure from their days in the Philippines.

---

5. "Winds of Change: Evolving Relations and Interests in Southeast Asia," a report to the United States Senate Foreign Relations Committee, Washington, D.C., 1975, p. 14.

Along Zigzag Road over the Zambales mountains outside of Olongapo are barren hillsides with huts, makeshift shacks, and cardboard houses—homes of the scavenger community. In 1977, Subic Bay changed its dumping policy and these people were cut out of collecting junk. However, they continued to steal past watch dogs, heavily armed marines, and other security personnel in order to scavenge—their main means of livelihood.

When confrontations at the base perimeter between American soldiers and Filipino scavengers flared up, the servicemen involved would simply be transferred out of the country. These periodic confrontations built up Filipino resentment against the bases more than any logically argued treatise on national sovereignty.

In January 1979, when the United States and Philippine governments renegotiated the bases agreements, the Philippine Armed Forces were given responsibility for perimeter security, with authority to shoot to kill any intruder. Frances T. Underhill, former American Embassy official in the Philippines, stated the result of this measure succinctly in testifying before Congress: "We have in effect hired the Philippine Armed Forces to provide perimeter security and this may reduce for a time a source of major friction where American affluence on one side of the fence meets Philippine poverty on the other side." In effect, Filipinos now shoot Filipinos in defense of the riches of the American military base.

The late Filipino Senator Jose W. Diokno, an ardent nationalist, regarded the bases as the single most pressing issue in Filipino political and cultural life. He argued that "until the bases are removed, the country cannot move to more rational economic development that genuinely gives local needs priority."[6] He felt that the bases assure an open door and too many special privileges to transnational corporations. The bases also introduce expensive unsupportable tastes, alien culture, and consumerism that eats up precious foreign exchange.

Part of what Senator Diokno was referring to was the black market trade, especially active in Angeles City. The Dau and Napa markets in Angeles are notorious for selling PX items

6. Mimeograph of a speech by Jose W. Diokno, printed by Philippine Civil Liberties Union, June 1978.

and pilfered goods from the bases. Almost every conceivable American consumer item is available. Several base chaplains told us that 5 percent pilferage from the bases around the world is considered normal, but at Clark the rate is 23 percent, much of it attributable to American service members themselves. "Anything moveable is stolen—tires, radios, equipment, even cars. The only time this pilfering comes out in the courts is when someone doesn't get paid off. You know, there is a syndicate for everything," said attorney Anthony Aquino, who has done legal work for the U.S. base.

Basic survival for Filipinos is jeopardized by the presence of the bases. A real fear, though somewhat removed from the daily struggle for economic survival, is that the nuclear warheads stored at Subic Bay will be a magnet for attack from America's enemies, notably the Soviet Union. These bases pose a threat to the Soviet Union because they are important for U.S. first-strike capability and thus are likely to be an early target for attack during a U.S.-U.S.S.R. conflict. In keeping with their policy, the U.S. government neither confirms nor denies the existence of nuclear weapons at the bases. However, Subic Bay services the U.S. Seventh Fleet—including maintenance for its ninety nuclear-capable fighters and fighter bombers. Clark houses the nuclear-capable Third Tactical Fighter Wing. It is extremely unlikely that nuclear-capable submarines and planes would not carry nuclear weapons. James Kelly, Deputy Assistant Secretary of Defense for East Asia and Pacific Affairs, told a U.S. congressional committee in March 1986, "Conventional and nuclear deterrence are not separable in U.S. forces and the nature of U.S. deterrence responsibilities requires that they not be separated."[7]

It is no surprise that Filipinos who have researched the possibile implications of the bases are frightened. "The basis of the presence of the bases is a mutual defense pact. The Americans tell us the bases are for our protection—protection from whom? We have no external enemies. The bases make us sitting ducks for attack by America's enemy," said one antinuclear organizer in Manila.

The Anti-Bases Coalition, a broad group of Filipino nationalists, church people, national political figures, and attorneys,

7. Walden Bello, Peter Hayes, and Lyuba Zarsky, *American Lake: Nuclear Peril in the Pacific* (New York: Viking-Penguin, 1986).

formed in 1983 to "demand the immediate and unconditional removal of all US bases and military installations in the Philippines" and to "support the call for the removal of all foreign military bases and troops from, and the denuclearization of, Asia and the Pacific and of the world as a whole." The opening paragraphs of their Declaration of Principles state their concern:

> Never before has the right to live been so gravely imperilled.
>
> Every day, the big nuclear powers intensify their mad race for military superiority and political domination. Everyday they bring humanity closer to the final holocaust.
>
> Machines of war and destruction roll off their assembly lines in ever increasing numbers. Newer deadlier weapons take shape on their drawing boards. Sooner or later, these machines will be used to engulf the world in flames.
>
> The big powers ensnare less powerful nations in their webs of disaster, condemning them to become the first casualties in wars not of their choosing, by establishing military bases and facilities in them, especially by storing or deploying nuclear weapons in such bases.
>
> In the last two world wars, the smaller, weaker nations were sacrificial victims. In the coming nuclear war, no nation will survive.[8]

This fear of destruction is not unfounded. A 1982 Brookings Institution study said that the Far Eastern Rocket Army of the Soviet Union has targeted "nuclear ammunition sites and air force and naval bases in Guam, the Philippines, and Hawaii."[9]

In the early 1980s, Filipino research chemical engineer Jorge Emmanuel studied the consequences for the Philippines of a nuclear attack on the American military installations there. He wrote,

> If an attack [of one-megaton bombs] were to occur simultaneously at Clark, Subic, San Miguel and the JUSMAG

---

8. "Declaration of Principles of the Anti-Bases Coalition," Quezon City, 6 January 1983.

9. Robert P. Berman and John C. Baker, *Soviet Strategic Forces: Requirements and Responses* (Washington, DC: Brookings Institution, 1982).

[Joint U.S. Military Advisory Group] office in Metro Manila, the aggregate casualty figures would be 2.5 million deaths due to blast, 1.2 million deaths due to burns, 1.3 million deaths due to radiation sickness and 250,000 delayed deaths due to cancer. . . . Nothing will remain standing within a radius of ground zero. . . . For many years as much as 17,000 square miles of land and waterways will remain dangerously radioactive. Electric power, communications, transportation, sanitation and other facilities will be damaged. The operations of government and other social organizations will be severely disrupted.[10]

U.S. officials and Filipino proponents of the bases in the Philippines point to the bases' annual $200 million contribution to the national economy. Employment for 44,000 workers and millions of dollars—in contracts for local companies, in purchase of local supplies, and in off-base house rentals—would be lost if the bases left. The largest dollar contribution to the economy is in the form of money spent by service members on leave, since Olongapo is the rest and recreation area for troops from all over southeast Asia, not only those stationed at Subic.

"What can we do?" asked Olongapo acting mayor Teddy Macapagal in February 1987, during a discussion with a human rights lawyers group I brought to the Philippines. "I don't like the prostitution, but we have to live with it as long as our country is poor and the base is here." Macapagal, a former human rights lawyer during the Marcos era, admitted, "It is politically impossible to be against the bases in this area. I am pro-base for economic reasons only. My father worked in the base for twenty-five years and I was able to go to college because of the base."

Maria Socorro I. Diokno, Secretary General of the Anti-Bases Coalition and sister of Maria Serena Diokno, views the economic contribution of the bases differently. In a speech given at the Asian Institute of Management in 1986, she said,

U.S. bases actually employ less than 1 percent of the total Philippine non-agricultural force. . . . Furthermore the US pays Filipino base workers one half of what it pays Korean

10. Jorge Emmanuel, "The Immediate and Long Term Consequences of Nuclear War in the Philippines," *Southeast Asia Chronicle* (Berkeley), 1982.

workers; one fourth of what it pays Japanese workers; and one eighth of what it pays American workers doing the same kind of work with the same productivity. . . .

If we look closely at the contribution figures, we find that 35 percent of total contributions come from "navymen on leave." This is a euphemism for entertainment and recreation services—the so-called base related/base dependent industries—such as prostitution, drug trafficking, smuggling, racketeering. This is not the kind of economic development we Filipinos need nor want.[11]

What are the options for the Philippines if the bases are removed? Jeffrey Dumas, a University of Texas professor who specializes in economic conversion, visited the country in August 1986. He described the Philippines as "a country with just about everything going for it; ideal location, educated and skilled people and rich natural resources." He suggested that Subic Bay Naval Station could be reconverted for ship repair, a port for commerical trading, and a series of small industries. This possibility is more realistic if the U.S. navy personnel do not dismantle the facilities before they leave. Dumas recommended a "phased geographic conversion" beginning with the air facility at Cubi Point at Subic and then moving across the base over time.

The positive aftermath of base conversion is affirmed by the U.S. experience. A U.S. Department of Defense survey entitled "1961–1981: 20 Years of Civilian Re-use: Summary of Completed Military Base Economic Adjustment Projects" cites strong evidence based on ninety-four U.S. military bases in various states "that closing a military base need not be and often is not the local catastrophe that most people expect."

Teddy Macapagal, who resigned as mayor of Olongapo in May 1987 to run for the Philippine Congress, has visited American towns that converted a base or military site into an industrial park. He was impressed with what he saw. "Unfortunately," he says sadly,

that conversion isn't possible here because we are not an industrialized country, so we don't have the same econom-

11. Maria Soccoro I. Diokno, "The Economic Dimension of the Military Bases Question," mimeograph copy of speech sponsored by Nationalist Alliance for Justice, Freedom, and Democracy at the Asian Institute of Management, Manila, 9 September 1986.

ic opportunities for successfully putting up an industrial park. We have limited possibilities to accomplish anything in Olongapo by ourselves. Visit the environs around any U.S. base around the world. You will see bars and prostitution. It is only worse here because so many Filipinos have no other economic options, because of our lack of industrialization. What you see here in Olongapo is the result of a national problem.

A concerted effort to educate Filipinos across the country about the effects of the bases and the alternatives to them has been going on for several years. Under the Marcos regime, those efforts were made without access to the major newspapers, television, or radio, all of which were government controlled. The Military Bases Agreement between the Philippines and the U.S., signed on March 14, 1947, gave the United States full control over the bases for ninety-nine years, rent free. On September 16, 1966, the term of the agreement was reduced to twenty-five years. A 1979 review of the agreement provided for a review every five years until 1991, the date the agreement is to expire. After 1991, either nation is able to end the agreement on one year's notice.

Any official objection to the bases during the Marcos era was no more than a means of getting a better deal at the negotiating table. Before the 1979 agreement, we noticed a much greater emphasis in the Marcos controlled newspapers on friendship with the Soviet Union. Russian flags flew proudly at the five-star hotels and Russian cuisine and culture were touted by First Lady Imelda Marcos. In 1978, Imee Marcos, the Princeton-educated daughter of Ferdinand and Imelda, led the government sponsored national youth organization, the Kabataang Barangay, in a protest campaign to get rid of the bases. She signed a letter that said, "The bases are clear evidence of our being American stooges because they represent U.S. interests."

One Angeles City clergyman said at the time, "If the President's daughter protests the bases, she is a hero, but when anyone else does it, they are regarded as subversives." After the agreements were signed on January 7, 1979, nothing more was heard from Imee Marcos or the Kabataang Barangay about removal of the bases. President Marcos and his military and technocratic circle recognized the American presence as a key element in the continuation of his rule.

Much of American foreign policy toward the Philippines has been predicated on retention of the military bases. Jimmy Carter's human rights policy in the 1970s, for example, foundered because of the government's fear that Marcos would no longer go along with the bases arrangement if he were pressed too hard to correct the human rights abuses of his military.

In early 1985, a secret memo prepared by the National Security Council, the State Department, and the Pentagon summarizing U.S. policy toward the Philippines was leaked to the press. It said,

> Strategically, continued unhampered access to our bases at Subic and Clark is of prime importance. . . . Political and economic developments in the Philippines threaten those interests. . . . While President Marcos at this stage is part of the problem, he is also necessarily part of the solution. We need to be able to work with him and try to influence him through a well orchestrated policy of incentives and disincentives to set the stage for peaceful and eventual transition to a successor government whenever that takes place.

In other words, the U.S. concern was that Marcos could no longer guarantee a "stable" country for the U.S. bases and for economic investments. He needed to be strengthened or replaced with someone who could.

The American "incentives and disincentives" helped to spur the snap elections in February 1986, which would either consolidate Marcos's power or find a suitable replacement for him. Within the U.S. government, there were differing perceptions of the elections between White House hardliners favoring Marcos and what was left under the Reagan administration of the State Department "liberals." The evidence suggests that Cory Aquino's decisive victory and her support by many nationalists did not form the scenario the White House would have chosen as the best way to protect U.S. interests. Reagan only withdrew support from Marcos and acknowledged Aquino as the winner of the presidential election in an eleventh-hour turnabout.

Senator Jovito Salonga, a close ally of President Aquino, stated categorically in 1984, during his stay in the United States, that he was convinced that the bottom-line concern of the United States government was the military bases. It was a dramatic moment that I remember well since Salonga had focused much of his time during the era of martial law collecting evidence of the business misdeeds of Marcos and his cronies, for use at a later date. Salonga made the pronouncement at a meeting in Chicago sponsored by Eddie Monteclaro, editor of the prestigious *Manila Chronicle*, who was in exile at the time. "The American economic investment and banking interest in the Philippines is not as big as their interest in maintaining the bases," he said and then turned and looked directly at me and added, "Wouldn't you agree, Dorothy?" I would not presume to argue with someone who does such careful research.

A meticulous legalist, Salonga said the bases must stay until 1991 when the agreement officially ends, but he advocated that the bases be removed in 1991 in respect for Philippine sovereignty. Since he became Philippine Senate president in July 1987, he has had to deal with the question head on.

The first months of the Aquino administration proved to be a time for open discussion. The bases question was aired in the electronic and print media. By September 1986, three provinces and six major cities had declared themselves nuclear weapons free and foreign military bases free. A seminar focusing on Philippine-American relations in August 1986, which included representatives from the New Armed Forces of the Philippines, civil government officials, and major business people, reached a consensus "on the eventual removal of the U.S. bases as a prerequisite for Philippine independence." They differed only on how and when the bases should be removed.

One test of the strength of Filipino nationalism in regard to the bases came during the drafting of the new constitution in 1986. After a great deal of debate, the constitutional commissioners appointed by President Aquino wrote a statement that basically precluded the retention of the bases. "The Philippines, consistent with the national interest, adopts and pursues a policy of freedom from nuclear weapons in its territory." A nuclear free provision in the constitution, in the words of former defense minister Juan Ponce Enrile, would "render the bases useless." Many worry that the phrase "consistent with the national interest" helps to soften the strong antinuclear statement and could provide the loophole for retaining the bases.

In May 1988, the Philippine Senate acted on the Constitution's "Freedom from Nuclear Weapons" provision by passing a strong antinuclear bill which bans the development, acquisition, testing, and storage of nuclear weapons and components in the Philippines. The bill requires inspection of commercial aircraft for possible nuclear loads and the empowerment of the nuclear weapons monitoring commission to inspect and monitor facilities containing nuclear weapons. That such a strong bill was passed by the Philippine Senate encouraged the nationalist activists. However, the bill does not take effect until the more conservative House of Representatives passes its own version and the two versions are reconciled.

Our human rights lawyers group toured Subic Bay and visited with their counterpart, an attorney from the judge advocate general's office. Toward the end of the interview, after the pleasantries and anecdotes and facts had been exchanged, the lawyers asked the JAG representative if he thought Filipinos would vote for the removal of the bases. "Well, I don't know," he said, but he then leaned toward us confidentially and said, "But it doesn't really matter. You know as well as I do that the U.S. would never give up these bases."

I watched Rose, our Filipina guide, recoil in horror as she stood behind the group, and I could almost read her thoughts in her eyes. Later she said, "We went through all the democratic processes—elected a president, wrote and ratified a constitution, reinstituted a congressional system. But if we come up with a conclusion that the United States government does not like, our process will be ignored."

A few months after this exchange, Filipinos read in their daily newspapers that Gaston Sigur, assistant secretary of state for East Asian and Pacific affairs, told a U.S. congressional committee, "No one should underestimate our resolve to maintain our defense and security arrangements with the Philippines and to preserve our access to our facilities at Subic and Clark through 1991 and beyond."

Numerous bills based on the nuclear free constitutional provision were sponsored in the Philippine Congress after it convened in July 1987. The constitution calls for the Senate to decide whether to retain the bases; the Senate then has the option of opening the decision to the public by calling for a referendum on the issue. At that time, opponents of the bases were not confident that a majority of Filipinos would vote for the removal of the bases.

The U.S. government has been able to work its will through Filipino leaders in the past and there is no reason to doubt that it is capable of doing the same thing again. For example, in 1947 when the U.S. Congress passed the parity amendment and insisted that the Philippines accept that condition before the U.S. would grant rehabilitation funds, the U.S. also had to contend with the Philippine constitution, which provided that Filipinos should own 60 percent share in all corporations. To accommodate parity, the Philippine constitution had to be amended. This required a three-fourths vote of Congress and a national plebiscite. President Roxas, certain that the Philippines could not progress without the American rehabilitation money, used personal persuasion, patronage, and pork barrel funds in exchange for an affirmative vote in the Congress. He also charged election fraud against his opponents, members of the Democratic Alliance who were supported by the peasants of Central Luzon. Roxas successfully had the seven Democratic Alliance representatives unseated. The House then passed the amendment by one vote.

There is a disquieting sense of déjà vu when one considers the scuttled candidacies of many of the hopefuls of the nationalist political party, Partido ng Bayan (PnB), in the 1987 congressional elections. One of the PnB commitments was the removal of the U.S. military bases.

PnB organizers in Bacolod City on the island of Negros informed our human rights lawyers group in March 1987 that four of their organizers were arrested a few days before a scheduled regional PnB Congress. A teacher at the PnB office in Bacolod told us,

> The democratic space is getting smaller for those of us who believe in electoral struggles. We want to participate, but the military taps our office and harasses us. People get scared and drop out of the political process. Cynicism and indifference is the result.

Rolando Olalia, a supporter of Cory Aquino and head of the Partido ng Bayan, was found brutally murdered in November 1986—just two weeks before the PnB national founding Congress. Romy Capulong, a PnB candidate for the Senate, told me after the elections that one of his organizers in an urban poor community had been killed during the campaign; others had been threatened. Leandro Alejandro, an extremely popular young nationalist leader who ran for the House of Representatives on the PnB platform, was outspent and his supporters were harassed by goons. He lost to Tessie Aquino

Oreta, the late Senator Benigno Aquino's sister. Four months later, Alejandro was shot in the face and killed shortly after giving a press conference to denounce growing militarism. These harassments and deaths can be traced to right-wing military or paramilitary sources.

"Unless some of the elite politicians change their minds and vote against the bases, there are not enough votes in the Congress to dismantle the bases," was the conclusion of the PnB after the May congressional election results.

A strong stand against the bases by President Aquino would influence the Philippine Congress. However, Aquino's shift in attitude toward the bases does not bode well for Filipino nationalist hopes.

A year before the presidential elections in the Philippines, a Convenor's Group made up of prominent opposition politicians agreed on a common platform and then looked for a common candidate. They decided to support Cory Aquino against Marcos in the presidential elections. One of the planks in their platform was an abrogation of the bases treaty in 1991. Mrs. Aquino agreed with the platform.

During her first year in office, Aquino altered that commitment slightly and phrased her new position as "keeping her options open." However, her right-wing opponents released a controversial set of tapes which they said contained a conversation between Executive Secretary Joker Arroyo and President Aquino while she was on her American tour in 1986. Her concern in that conversation was that an antinuclear provision in the constitution would make her job of getting aid from the United States Congress very difficult.

By December 1987, Aquino was inching toward retention of the bases. In an address to the Association of Southeast Asian Nations in Manila, she stressed the importance of the bases for the region. In a published interview several weeks later, Aquino said the presence of the bases "in effect . . . provides for the security of the region." She added, "Where the Philippines is concerned, we have enough problems with the economy that definitely it is necessary that we have stability in so far as the security of the region is concerned."

The dilemma of the relationship of a small impoverished nation to a world military power continues no matter who the president is in either country. The words of the late Senator Jose W. Diokno, written in 1979, bear a warning that is as applicable to the Aquino administration as to its predecessor:

> The greatest threat that the regime faces is not the MNLF (Muslim insurgency), not the NPA (New People's Army). It is the festering discontent of the vast majority of our people. There is only one way to meet this threat. Remove its causes. . . . The U.S. Bases will hinder that action.

> For as long as the U.S. Bases stay, that long will the Philippine government remain dependent on the USA whether it be a martial law regime or not, that long will it not be able to act against the wishes of the American government. A real restructuring of our economy and redistribution of our income will hurt U.S. economic interests and those of the Filipino elite partners. The U.S. will oppose such steps—and a dependent administration will be powerless to act in the face of that opposition.[12]

The tragedy that has happened in the past and that seems to have befallen the Filipino people again is the phenomenon of "brother Filipino fighting brother Filipino." The Filipino nationalists in and out of government are under fire. The tragedy is not simply that there is a family feud, but that one of the siblings acts on behalf of an interest outside of the family. The outside party can appear to keep its hands clean and take no responsibility for the dehumanization and death that sucks the lifeblood from a potentially happy family.

There was no American figure directly involved in the killing of an Olalia or an Alejandro. There was no direct American participation on the floor of the constitutional convention to soften the antinuclear provision. A scene I witnessed in an Olongapo bar called Casa Boom Boom symbolizes for me the relationship between the warring parties within the Philippines and the United States.

Casa Boom Boom, an American-owned bar, featured female boxers in addition to the usual attractions of provocative dance and strip tease. We were told beforehand by the local host who brought us to Casa Boom Boom that all the women in the club, whether waitress, cook, hostess, or receptionist, were required to box. If the women didn't put up a good fight, they were docked pay.

Two fragile-looking women were brought into the center

12. Jose W. Diokno, Philippine Civil Liberties Union Circular, 1979.

ring, outfitted in short shorts, scanty tops, and huge boxing gloves. Mr. Hoge, the large, graying, somewhat obese American owner, urged the male members of the audience to keep score. The bell rang and the women started swinging at each other.

As they boxed, Mr. Hoge kept up a running commentary: "Isn't this exciting! Aren't the girls doing a good job? We give them boxing lessons every Saturday." Meanwhile the audience, mostly GIs and their Filipina escorts, laughed, clapped, and generally encouraged the fight to go on. The two women hit and hit each other. They seemed ill-trained in avoiding blows. I noticed that their faces were swelling. Hoge continued his cheery comments. One of the women started to cry and backed into the ropes. Hoge told her to continue. Half the audience jeered her, while her friends among the other fighters tried to encourage her. The tears rolled down her swollen cheeks. Watching these two tiny females beat on each other with their oversized boxing gloves in order to entertain the half-drunk spectators and make money for Mr. Hoge was one of the greatest obscenities I have ever experienced.

This scene was but a mirror of the larger national obscenity. In the tears of the woman boxer, I saw the tears of the widows and orphans who have lost husbands and fathers in the larger civil war raging in the country. In the humiliation and anguish of the woman boxer, I saw the anguish and humiliation of the poor of the Philippines.

The peasants who "reform" the base lands are part of the nationalist movement. They want, in Diokno's words, a "real restructuring of our economy and redistribution of our income." But these nationalist farmers are pursued and killed by the Philippine military and the vigilantes approved by the government. The lethal boxing in the Philippine ring continues.

The bottom line for Mr. Hoge is profit made by entertaining the American sailors. The bottom line for the American administration is retention of their bases in the Philippines. Ronald Reagan is on record in response to the question, "Would you put the future of those bases at risk if it meant standing up for democracy?" His answer was, "One cannot minimize the importance of those bases."

In contrast to the bloodshed and tears of the ongoing deadly boxing game is the tough humanity of a beleaguered people, exemplified by women like April. April and her friends, other hostesses, did not allow their own ability to feel to be taken away from them. The capacity of people under siege to transform suffering is truly a gift of grace.

A precious token of the Filipino ability to transmute violent energy into positive forces is a small brass candleholder that sits in our living room in Chicago. I found it in a Mindanao open marketplace. The candleholder was made by a Muslim brass worker in the southern Philippines from the casing of a 55 mm. artillery shell. The casing could have come from one of two places. It could have come from target practice at Crow Valley Range at Clark Air Base. Here scavengers living around the base risk their own lives by trespassing on the base to retrieve these casings, which they then sell to Muslim traders. The other possible origin of the casing is any of the provinces where fighting is taking place. If so, a real shell—supplied by the U.S. government and paid for by our tax dollars—was aimed at a real person, probably by a member of the Philippine military or paramilitary.

The first time I held the candleholder between my fingers and looked closely at the design, I thought of the passage in Isaiah 2 about beating swords into plowshares and spears into pruning hooks. I touched the design the brass worker had carved on the sides and pondered the significance of this work of art. We sent over a weapon of destruction; they created an instrument of light.

But then I turned the candleholder around and looked at the bottom. I could see the hole where the firing pin had sent the shell on its way to its target. The inside of the beautiful candleholder in my hand might have already killed a peasant. Bullets are an important part of the systematic terrorization intended to deter people from trying to fashion an alternative society where the poorest can eat, send their children to school, have roofs over their heads, and live in peace. I realized that the real parallel to beating swords into plowshares would be to make the shell itself—not just the casing—into a candleholder.

That task would probably best be done in the United States, for as creative and irrepressible as the Filipino response to oppression might be, it is impossible to transform and recreate bullets and bombs while they are still attached to their triggers and controlled by someone else.

11

The New People's Army

WHO ARE THESE PEOPLE ANYWAY?

For three years I watched farm communities thrown off their land, workers locked out of the shop when they organized a strike, squatters evicted from their homes to make way for expanded port facilities or super highways. I followed the economic investigation of multinational agribusiness to its conclusion. I saw the limits of the corporate responsibility movement and shareholders resolutions. I watched well-organized but unarmed farmers lose their land. I took pictures of tribal people in their massive poverty and then stayed with friends in a luxurious housing complex in Manila while working on putting the pictures into a slideshow. The contrast between resplendent living and absolute poverty never ceased to shock me. I visited friends sitting in prison because they were involved in building Basic Christian Communities. I saw the torture marks on the bodies of some prisoners. I attended funerals of slain organizers. I cried more and I prayed more than I ever have in my life. I thought more about life and death, about what is of absolute importance, about what is most precious.

In each experience I asked those involved, "What will you do now?" Often there was silence. Looking back, I think they knew what they would do, but because they knew I was not open to their choice, silence was the only possible answer.

If I were Filipino, what would I do? The desperation of the individual mirrors the desperation of the nation. Daily the life-blood is sucked out of the economy—the soil, the forests, the seas. All the possible natural resources that could be trans-

lated into wealth for the nation are used for the aggrandize-
ment of a few.

How can this be stopped? I remember the many discussions I had with farmers sitting in the shadows of a flickering
kerosene lantern. One farmer's son in Central Luzon, who
dropped out of college after two years because of family financial pressures, described the dilemma succinctly. "This barrio is on the edge of Clark Air Base. We know how huge the
American base is and what powerful weapons they have here.
Our government has to be strong enough to stand up to the
foreign corporations and the U.S. military."

He quickly pointed to his solution, "How will that ever happen? Only if every Filipino supports a nationalist government.
How can a government get that kind of support? Only if the
majority think that the government is helping them survive.
If the government represents the people in the Philippines, it
will represent the farmers and workers and squatters who are
the majority. That means the government program has to be
land and jobs and food. If we Filipinos have that, we will stand
up to anyone who wants to take it from us."

"Yes, but how can we have this kind of government?" his
older companion asked as he joined the conversation. "The
landowners and factory owners and generals and foreign investors will not allow it. We will have to set up our own government to represent us."

By 1980, I decided it was time for me to meet the people
fighting for a representative government. Since I was no longer
working for a church agency at that time, I would not endanger
their programs. My investigation would not heap accusations
of "communist" on them from institutions like the Heritage
Foundation, a conservative think tank based in Washington,
D.C., which has been very influential with the Reagan administration.

Who could help me? Whom should I approach? What is
the process? I decided to ask Elena, a good friend from my
early days in Davao City. She had anticipated this discussion
and had already had me "cleared through channels." She suggested I go to a creative drama seminar in the countryside the
next week. I was disappointed; perhaps she had not understood my request. Nevertheless, I prepared to go since I knew
spending a few weeks in the barrios would not be a waste no
matter what happened.

Elena's husband, Enrique Vasquez, loaned me a pair of his dark pants, a *malong*, and a pair of running shoes, commonly called "adidas." "You'll need the shoes for the climb, the dark pants when you slip in the mud, and the malong for taking a bath," he says. "If the people up there want these items, just leave them there before you return." A malong, used by Muslims in the southern Philippines, is a six-foot-long piece of material sewn together to form a tube. It can be worn as a long wraparound skirt or dress or used to carry children or groceries from the market. Non-Muslims in the progressive movement in Mindanao have adopted and adapted the malong for their own use. It can double as a towel or a blanket at night. It is worn to take a public shower or sponge bath. In recent years the military have seized upon malongs in non-Muslims' belongings as a sign of a "subversive."

The appointed time arrived. Together with Judy (another American woman) and eight Filipino companions—some from Mindanao, some from Manila—I set out one morning by public jeepney. We changed vehicles twice, sat in a house on the outskirts of a town in Davao del Norte until almost noon, left through a window of the house, climbed over a wall, walked through a cemetery, and finally reached a lane where a rented jeepney was waiting for us. Then off we went, over incredibly bad roads, even by Philippine standards.

A few hours later, the jeepney stopped beside a field where two young people were waiting for us under a tree. We began walking through the field and then straight up the hills at almost a ninety-degree angle. The guides fairly skipped along. The rest of us slipped and slid at our own pace. I was not in good physical shape, but soon realized to my great relief that the visitors from Manila were also having difficulty keeping up. The guides carried our bags slung over their shoulders and still managed to make climbing look effortless.

They kept up a relentless pace. "We have two weeks. Why do we have to rush the first day?" I wondered. The Filipinos from Manila brought their own water, which they drank periodically. The guide found spring water for Judy and me. We finally reached a plateau where we could see for miles around. We followed a footpath for a half mile until a clump of bushes and a group of houses came into sight. As we approached the bushes, a middle-aged man, wearing a blue-jean jacket and carrying an M-16, appeared and greeted us. "Maayong Hapon

['Good afternoon' in Cebuano, the local language]. We are about to begin, so please come and join us."

I was stunned at the sight. In the clearing between the houses standing in a casual circle were at least fifty men and women with M-16s and other weapons. Red flags with hammer and sickle were flying from the windows of the houses around us. The assembly broke into singing the "Internationale" in the local dialect. At the end they waved their guns in a salute. I guess Elena did understand what I wanted; she knew she was sending me to more than a creative drama seminar.

Larry, the man who first greeted us, acted as emcee. "We are having a memorial for a dead comrade who was killed last week. That is why we are all together. It is timely that you could be here." Ah, that is why the guides rushed us up the mountain. Then came the introductions—name (first name only, chosen for the occasion), age, where we are from, class background, work, civil status, the purpose of our visit.

The hosts introduced themselves first—all peasants, all young, teenagers or in their twenties, mostly unmarried. Some are in the regular NPA, some in the militias, some are medics, some are in education, a few are message-carriers. Others identified themselves as "masa"—local people who support the NPA.

Then it was the visitors' turn. We all registered "petit-bourgeois" as our class background. The barrio residents asked follow-up questions, particularly of a mestizo-looking male from Manila. Fair-skinned with a long angular nose and soft hands, he was easily a target for their suspicion that he was more than petit-bourgeois. "What does your father do?" someone asked him. "Do you live in Forbes Park?" Forbes Park is an elite residential suburb across from the shopping and commercial center on Ayala Avenue in Makati.

Mestizos, primarily the product of intermarriage between Spanish males and Filipinas during the Spanish colonial period, have often played a treacherous role in Philippine history. The question of identity and loyalty between the conquerors and the conquered during the colonial period parallels the question now of which classes can be trusted not to sell out the revolution. This remains a subject of great concern.

Larry ended the introductions by informing us that the NPA squad would remain in the area to provide protection during the creative drama seminar. "We get up very early to go out and practice maneuvers, but we will serenade you when we leave in the morning."

A creative drama seminar had actually been planned. Youth leaders chosen from various barrios and *sitios* (a smaller unit than a village) congregated for a week of training in form, space, motion, script-writing—the building blocks of drama. Some of our Filipino companions from Manila and from the town were scheduled to conduct the workshops. I stayed at the creative drama seminar for a few days with Judy.

I was used to sleeping on the floor with many people sharing the room, but the sleeping arrangements for the seminar participants were extreme, even for rural Philippines. Large banana leaves, rice sacks, and *benig* (woven mats) were laid on the mud floor downstairs for the drama students. The creative drama leaders and the "American friends" were given the upstairs room. The room was so small that we barely fit lying body by body. Some of us slept on our sides so we wouldn't take up more than our share of the space.

There were no mosquito nets. Malaria, a disease carried by mosquitos, is on the rise in Mindanao, according to the World Health Organization. Some of the visitors brought mosquito lotion, but it is too expensive to be a regular commodity among the people who live here. Mosquito nets are more common since they are a one-time investment—until, of course, the net develops holes. The way our bodies were stacked together, we could have slept three people to a single mosquito net.

In the first week at the creative drama seminar house, we ate only boiled corn and a few tiny dried fish, and drank coffee made from roasted corn. Corn is not as nutritious as rice, but it sits heavier in the stomach so that there is at least the illusion of being full. Elena's husband, who loves good food, had assured me that the people in the NPA areas eat well. "They cook carabao meat [water buffalo] and bake their own bread in solar ovens they construct," he said. He must have visited a different zone. *Zone* is the term used to designate a specific area in which an NPA squad can operate relatively freely.

I was hungry and could feel myself going through caffeine withdrawal. I could hardly wait for the next meal. The corn became more delicious at each sitting. My middle-class way of coping with the hunger pangs was imagining how slim I would be after two weeks of this diet. As I watched the "slim" participants in the drama seminar, it hit me in a new way that they have been hungry their whole lives.

I met with Larry, who clearly emerged, in my mind at least, as the commander, though no one identified him that way. We planned the itinerary for the next weeks, based on my goals. "I want to understand who the NPA really are, how you work to implement your program, what the relationship is between the barrio people and the NPA. I'm sure your contacts told you I am a pacifist," I added.

Larry insisted that Judy and I travel together. For Larry, it was unthinkable that I would not have a companion of my own sex or from my own country. Judy wanted to stay at the seminar with her Filipino boyfriend. He, it seemed, didn't want her at the seminar. I wondered if his discomfort was connected to the villagers' questioning of our mestizo companion on the first day. Would he seem less nationalistic if he had an American girlfriend?

The hardheaded Americans won out in the discussion. Judy remained at the seminar and I began the trek to another village with Erlene, a young woman in the education department of the NPA. She carried a pistol tucked in the waist of her pants. The daughter of a peasant family, Erlene got a job at Stanfilco (Standard Philippine Fruit Company, a subsidiary of Castle and Cooke, which markets Dole bananas). She worked in the packing plant where the bananas are washed in chemicals and packed for shipment overseas. The women working on the "poof machine," which sprays chemicals into the plastic bag of bananas to keep them from rotting or turning yellow until they reach their destination, were always sick. Erlene asked the management about the effects of the chemicals. No satisfactory answers came. Working conditions worsened. She and others decided to start a union at their plant. Soon her life was threatened. Her co-worker was mysteriously killed. "I had to go somewhere. I came up to the hills and joined the NPA."

I realized that Erlene was no stranger to me. Four years before, the story of her attempt at organizing in the packing plant was part of the data my husband and I collected while studying the operations of Castle and Cooke. I probably even asked her then what she thought the solution could be.

We spent the next few days walking, talking, visiting families, attending barrio meetings, bathing in the streams, and sleeping on wooden floors, on bamboo floors, in hammocks. Personal histories meshed with Philippine history meshed with world history to form a kaleidescopic perspective of the NPA.

Only a few miles from the creative drama seminar, other barrio people were hosting a group of thirty college students from the local town. "These are students who have been active in progressive student politics. If there is a military crackdown and they are threatened and need a safe place to come, they can come here. But they should see what it is like first," explained one of the guides.

A slight young man with wire-rim glasses, who looked like he could be a professor of political science from the University of the Philippines, joined the houseful of students. The NPA squad members, surrounded by admiring students, were languidly cleaning their guns. The "professor" spotted me, smiled and sat down on the long narrow bench nearby. "I hear you are a pacifist. What do you think of all the guns around you?" he asked.

I didn't know who the professor was, but he seemed to know about me. Frankly, I was bothered by the students' starry-eyed fawning over the weapons. But instead I said, "I don't know much about guns, but these look very old-fashioned to me. The Philippine military is better equipped. It will be hard to win militarily with only these kind of weapons."

He agreed. "We buy guns and ammunition from soldiers or we take them from the Civilian Home Defense Force or we get them on raids on military or police. Since we get our weapons from the Philippine military, which gets them from the United States, maybe you could get your government to send more modern equipment." He laughed.

The "professor" wanted to know, as did most others I talked to here, about the United States. Do Americans know about the Philippines? What is the political climate? Will there be any change in foreign policy? What happened to the generation of antiwar demonstrators (probably his contemporaries)? Are they critical of Vietnam's invasion and occupation of Kampuchea?

Years later I found out that the "professor" actually heads the Mindanao underground, is a brilliant theoretician, has put together a formidable organization, and cleverly eluded the

military for years. With the exception of the first day of introductions complete with civil status and class background,
most conversations seemed to proceed on intuition here in the
zone. The most help I got from hosts was a two-sentence cap-
sule like, "This is Boy (or Jose or Baby). He/she can tell you
about organizing (or education or farming)."

Erlene reappeared after the discussion with the "professor" and announced, "It is time to take a bath." I joined her in
what felt like an endless hike straight down another ninety-
degree slope. I was thankful for the "adidas" Enrique had insisted that I take along. We followed a stream until it opened
onto some flat rocks. Erlene had brought a small tin can along
to scoop up the water and pour it over herself. She balanced
expertly on the rocks, soaped herself while still wearing her
clothes and then started rinsing with the little tin. She made
it look effortless.

I tried to follow her graceful example, but I slipped on the
rocks, dropped the soap in the rushing stream, and managed
to get my hand caught in my own clothes as I attempted this
modest Filipino method of bathing. I may have washed off a
few layers of tropical sweat in the stream, but by the time we
climbed back up the slope I was again bathed in sweat.

The next morning we were off to a three-day seminar in
another district. "This is an unorganized area," explained Erlene. "I have worked here for six months. I started by identi-
fying a few trusted local people as contacts. I meet with them
and explain our program for dealing with the farmers' problems. They then meet with their friends and neighbors whom
they can trust. The community is now ready for our three-day
course."

About forty people, men and women, old, middle-aged,
young people, and children, gathered under the trees. A Coca-
Cola blackboard was propped up on a table crudely nailed
against a tree. A few children had notebooks and pencils, since
they were designated to take notes for the rest for the community. Most of the farmers here may have had a few years of
schooling, but decided that they write too slowly to take notes
during the sessions.

Erlene herself has completed sixth grade. She handled all
the input for the entire seminar. She began by eliciting from
the farmers the problems they face. They had the pleasure of
seeing their answers on the blackboard. "High prices for in-

puts, low prices for their produce, lack of credit, lack of respect in the town, long distance to market." Most of the concerns were economic.

Erlene deftly arranged the farmers' answers into a pattern and then dealt with the topics one by one. She taught from a worn-looking notebook she carried in her backpack. It contained both the beginners and the advanced course. I was amazed by her ability to build the farmers' agenda into the material she had planned to cover. I asked her later how she was able to dovetail the agendas so well. "This course comes from the farmers. It is based on the movement's experience of listening to the peasants for years," she said. "We have only systematized what they have actually told us to begin with."

By the second day, Erlene had dealt with the problem of feudalism facing the peasants. Landlords own not only the land but sometimes the plow and water buffalo or hand tractor as well. In exchange for loans at low season or sending a child of the tenant to school, the landlord can often demand lifelong loyalty. The relationship is both economically and psychologically exploitative. The farmers themselves supplied the real-life examples for the discussion on feudalism.

Erlene then moved on to the problem of bureaucratic capitalism facing the entire country, explaining how Marcos and his friends in government have enriched themselves through their political positions. Next she tackled the problem of U.S. imperialism by using the example of the high cost of imported pesticides and fertilizers. The farmers themselves pointed to the presence of so many foreign corporations and agribusinesses gobbling land and mineral resources in Mindanao. The U.S. military bases in Luzon and the decadence of the red light district in Manila seem far removed from the farmers here, but it is a part of the Philippine reality Erlene tried to describe and connect to their lives.

She was in the midst of denouncing the immodesty and sexual licentiousness brought by foreign tourists and American servicemen, when two yapping dogs took center stage. The male mounted the female. Everyone laughed and even Erlene visibly relaxed from her lecture stance. After tolerating a few choice comments by some of the more playful members of the group, Erlene turned again to the serious business at hand.

She detailed the connections between the prices of their farm products and American imperialism. By that time, everyone was looking at me. I don't know if that prompted Erlene's addition to the lecture, "I am describing a structure. Not all Americans are bad. There are also good Americans who want to understand our situation."

The seminar was not simply an informational event, conducted in a vacuum. It was one step in a process of organizing and consolidating these barrios and bringing the people into the national project of building another socioeconomic reality. The last session was essentially a call to commitment.

Throughout the seminar, people met outdoors in the yard of the most successful farmer in the area, shifting their positions hourly to stay in the shade as the sun moved across the sky. On the last afternoon of the seminar, a heavy rain began and people scurried to find shelter on the porch of a nearby house. Though by rural subsistence standards it was a large house, the porch could hardly accommodate everyone. People sat on the floor, on the steps, on the railings, huddled together, straining to hear above the almost deafening noise of the pelting rain on the tin roof.

Erlene was ready to make her pitch. The farmers had agreed with the analysis of the three evils of their society—feudalism, bureaucratic capitalism, imperialism. Their personal experience with their landlords attested to the accuracy of Erlene's description of feudalism. They agreed that attempts in the past to overthrow the colonial masters or to make economic changes were subverted by the elite of their own country. They had shared their hopes for a better future for their children. "Nothing will happen, if we don't make it happen," said Erlene. "You can choose to join the millions of other Filipinos who are already working to change our society. But it will not be easy. It will not happen overnight. Many of our comrades have already given their lives."

No one spoke. People looked down or stared into space. A heaviness descended on the group. The rain beat down and the thunderclaps came closer. The scene felt surrealistic to me. Each face mirrored an internal decison-making process. For the first time during my visit here, I felt like an intruder in a private drama.

The seminar concluded and I continued to follow Erlene around day after day. She carried all of her earthly belongings in a backpack—a change of clothes, a flashlight, batteries, a notebook, a pencil, a malong, a few medicines. We were dependent on the hospitality of the barrio people to find a place to sleep at night and food to eat. The vulnerability and the simplicity of this life fascinated me.

As we trudged along, I wondered whether I could give my life to this cause. Could I live this simply, without economic security, to organize pacifists for social change? Could all the sincere church people who abhor violence go to these lengths to propagate their understanding? Would those who disdain excess and advocate pluralism be willing to give their lives to organize according to their vision? What keeps Erlene going?

Erlene is just one of thousands of NPA organizers around the country. The National Democratic Front (NDF), the umbrella organization that includes the Communist Party of the Philippines and the New People's Army, says it has organizations in sixty of the seventy-three provinces in the Philippines. An estimated twelve million people are NDF members or are under NDF influence. In any country and in every generation, there are always a few people who dedicate their lives to the service of others at considerable risk and cost to themselves. The sheer number of Filipinos engaged in this project of changing the basis upon which society rests is astounding.

Erlene and I were halfway through our planned figure-eight loop across the mountain ranges when she took her leave, and Larry and Ram, a new recuit, played "tour guide" for a few days. Ram was a tall, shy teenager, very eager, very enthusiastic about the new life he had chosen. "I wanted to join the NPA to avenge my older brother who was killed by the military a few years ago. But the NPA organizers made me study about our country before they would give me a gun."

Unhurriedly we crossed some of the most beautiful territory I have ever seen. At the top of one hill, we stopped and looked down into a lush green valley and across four distinct sets of mountain ranges. The scenery inspired some personal reminiscences in Larry. He had been in the movement for ten years. Seven years earlier his wife died of complications connected with tuberculosis. He was unable to get to the town for her funeral. He has not seen his six children for almost five years, but hopes his eldest will come to the hills to visit at Christmas. He brushed aside my sympathetic comments about his lack of family life, but I couldn't help imagining Larry in another time bringing home candy for his children and giving them piggyback rides. But instead of scooping up his *bunso* (the youngest child) in his arms after a day of work in the ricefield, or walking the floor at night with a sick child, Larry totes his M-16 everywhere he goes.

The last night of my sojourn in the mountains I was re-united with Judy and Erlene at a house located at the halfway point in the figure-eight loop. We stayed overnight with a friendly, talkative family—father, mother, three teenage daughters, an eleven-year-old son, and several nephews. They were proud of the vegetable and flower garden in the front of the house, the pigs and chickens kept at the side of the house, and the rain water tank that supplied enough water for baths for the family and their guests. It was a relief not to have to walk a mile for bath water.

The daughters especially were shy but strikingly beautiful. As we shared stories and jokes and songs in the evening, I found myself mesmerized by their faces and the way they carried themselves—a fascinating combination of confidence and humility. We all slept together in an upper room that also housed a mimeograph machine and a cabinet of paper.

Ram appeared the next morning to escort us down the mountain to a crossroads where we could catch a public jeepney back to town. He called Judy and me "Ka," which is short for *Kasama*, meaning friend/comrade and is the title of address used by the NPA. Erlene and the others explained that we were "foreign friends," but Ram either did not understand or chose to ignore their correction. He exuded a kind of infinite goodwill as we faced each other to say good-bye. I wished him well in his new life. He nodded gravely. A year later I found out that he was killed by the military only a few days after we said good-bye to him.

Within a few hours I was in Manila, thanks to modern transportation. I stayed with a friend in an elite housing subdivision in Quezon City—four servants, air-conditioning, enough food on the dinner table to feed all the creative drama seminar participants for an entire week. As I wondered how Erlene could carry all the possessions of this household in her backpack, an even more disconcerting piece of news caught my attention.

The *Bulletin Today*, a national English-language daily, published a story about a military operation in several Mindanao provinces. Three NPA were killed, and a mimeograph machine and subversive literature were discovered. The further description clearly fit the family who hosted Judy and me. That can mean only one thing for the daughters. Rape is the military's standard operating procedure in rural areas.

All sorts of thoughts raced through my mind. If only the family had not been involved, the daughters would have been safe. The NPA say they guard people, but their presence makes more problems for the people. I alternated between tears and anger, babbling somewhat incoherently to Jun, a friend who had joined the NPA when he was a student in the 1970s. Jun finally contacted another friend, Vito, and together they tried to process this experience with me.

In the midst of Manila's congested streets, filled with diesel smoke from jeepneys and buses, Jun and Vito and I drove and talked, drove and talked. The dilapidated car sputtered in what sounded like its last gasps, but miraculously it survived the starts and stops of rush-hour traffic.

"We were so unprepared when martial law was declared," said Vito. "Those of us from Mindanao just went up to the hills to live with the farmers and the tribal people. They didn't know us; they didn't trust us. We couldn't speak their langauge. All my companions died of starvation or were killed by natives or by the military.

"I think I only stayed alive because I was arrested. The military surrounded the hut I was in. We had so little ammunition, we decided to surrender. When we went out of the house with our hands up, the military shot us. This is the result," Vito lifted up his dark glasses. His left eye was a mass of red. The story of the first NPA in Mindanao is pitiful. There are only a handful of survivors like Vito to tell it.

In 1977, Jose Maria Sison, a former professor at the University of the Philippines and founder of the Communist Party of the Philippines, and his wife Juliet were arrested. The head of the New People's Army, Kumander Dante, was picked up soon after. Marcos boasted at that time that he had broken the back of the insurgency because both its civilian and military leaders were in custody. Jun viewed the event quite differently. "The new chairman who replaced Sison was an organizational person—exactly what we needed for our development. Sison was the philosopher. He laid the theoretical foundation, for which we are grateful, but we need to move on."

Nothing Jun or Vito said about personal experiences or

NPA history stopped the tears for the young women I had met only a few days previously. Jun finally suggested a trip to Central Luzon, the womb of the Communist-led Hukbalahap resistance as early as the 1930s and of the Communist Party of the Philippines and the New People's Army in the late 1960s. Central Luzon, particularly the province of Pampanga, has a reputation as the hotbed of resistance to foreign occupation and to dictatorship.

December 26, 1968, marked the birth of the Communist Party of the Philippines (CPP) in the province of Pangasinan, straddling northern and central Luzon. The party initially described itself as following Marxist–Leninist–Mao-Tse-Tung Thought, but later quietly dropped the China emphasis. The first communist party in the Philippines, the Partido Komunista ng Pilipinas (PKP), was Soviet related. Jose Maria Sison was originally a member of the PKP, but broke with them before helping to establish the CPP. The PKP continues to exist in the Philippines, but without significant popular support. Conservative think tanks have tried to link the NPA and CPP to the Soviet Union, but in fact the Soviet Union has virtually ignored the CPP throughout most of its history.

I spent several days in the barrio in Pampanga, Central Luzon, where former peasant Huk leader Luis Taruc had been born. Taruc surrendered in 1954, spent many years in jail, and then joined the Marcos government in the Ministry of Agrarian Reform after martial law was declared. In 1981, when Marcos changed the name "martial law" to "constitutional authoritarianism," Luis Taruc invited his fellow farmers from San Monica to Manila for official national government talks. Some farmers from his barrio went, but somewhat dubiously. An old man in the barrio told me, "I sat beside Luis, patted his stomach and said, 'You used to have principles in there. What do you have now? I hope your stomach is not just full of rich food.'"

Another grandfather in the barrio, who had fought with the Huks in the 1940s, spent an afternoon recounting the stories of those days and concluded with the remark, "Now it's the young people, these NPA members, who are really continuing what we began. The old communist party, the PKP, who used to lead us, don't live with us anymore. They just run off to international meetings or stay in Malacanang with the dictator."

In March 1969, the New People's Army was established as

the fighting arm of the Communist Party of the Philippines. The possibility of an army came when the link was made between Sison's organization, composed mainly of students and workers, and the rural peasant army led by the famous Kumander Dante. Dante, born Bernabe Buscayno, the son of a sugar worker, was handed over to the landlord as a day laborer to cut sugarcane because of his family's debts. He joined the Huks as a teenager and rose quickly in the rebel ranks. Many of the early PKP resistance units had degenerated into banditry. Those leaders like Kumander Dante who still had ideals and dreams were looking for a firmer foundation on which to build, and so they joined Sison and his group.

From its meager start in 1969 with 35 defecting Huks and their rusty guns, the New People's Army grew to 25,000 full-time fighters with at least that many in part-time militias in 1985, according to *Liberation*, a publication of the National Democratic Front. The U.S. Senate Foreign Relations Committee Report in 1984 estimated that "the NPA probably can field some 10,000-12,500 full time armed guerrillas and an additional 10,000 part-time militia."[1]

In contrast to the frontier feel of Mindanao, Central Luzon exudes a sense of history and continuity, which carries both strengths and weaknesses. The land is relatively flat. There are no continuous mountains to shelter battalion-size NPA units. The proximity of major military camps like Camp Olivas, as well as a myriad of outposts and the vast military might in nearby Manila make it unwise, if not impossible, for the NPA to emphasize the military aspect of the revolution there.

While there are also proper channels to go through in Central Luzon, Jun's friend Mar, who is a native of the province of Pampanga, simply drove into the area and arranged for me to talk to the farmers. One old wizened farmer said to me, "If you had not come with Mar, I would just tell you, what does an old man like me know about revolution. But Mar is one of our boys. If you are with him, you are OK."

"I am poor, my father was poor, my grandfather was poor.

---

1. William Chapman writes that in 1986 "the NPA had grown to about 20,000 full time and part time guerrillas sharing about 12,000 modern weapons, the party said" (*Inside the Revolution* [W. W. Norton, 1987], p. 110). This is a conservative estimate when compared with other published statements by the party.

For generations we were at the mercy of our landlord's whims. We had to pay—sometimes rice, sometimes our time, sometimes our children. If we objected, the landlord brought out his security guards against us. If we still objected he could call in the government police and military. We had only stones, bolos, homemade weapons against their guns," explained another farmer. "We had no long-range plan about how to bring ourselves out of poverty. We were only resisting because we could not bear it any longer. But it was useless."

"Yes," agreed the old farmer. "We just got poorer. We just got further into debt. We heard in another village that people knew what to do. We invited them to come here and bring their seedlings. They brought rice seedlings, but what has really sprouted here are the seedlings of understanding that they brought. We understand why the country is so rich, but we are so poor. We are fully organized and have brought our seedlings to the other barrios. We are just waiting for the rest of the country to catch up."

One reason the peasants have been so supportive of the NPA is that when it works in an area, some aspect of land reform is launched immediately. The lowest form of struggle is to hide a portion of the harvest to keep rent down. When the peasants are well-enough organized, they confront the landlord to get lower rent or to have the landlord share the land with them. Better wages for day workers are negotiated. If the small landlords are cooperative some compromise arrangement is usually worked out, but the land of intransigent landlords or those who have a reputation for unfairness is confiscated.

The farmers described some of the military harassments they have endured. The oldest farmer showed me a scar on his back from torture he sustained when the military launched a house-to-house search in the barrio looking for the NPA. Others told similiar stories. The teenage women from Mindanao were on my mind.

Finally I ventured my comment, "If the NPA didn't come around here, you wouldn't have this pain and suffering." The old man studied my face and then said, "Do you think that we have no mind of our own? We chose to join this struggle. The NPA are our sons and daughters. The military, not our children, are inflicting the pain. When the military treats us like this, it only steels us to resist more strongly.

"The military has always been here. They didn't just come yesterday. Our landlords sometimes treat us as though we are not human beings. It's easier to put up with it when we know we are fighting for something better," said the old man, who then waited for my response.

It was my turn to stare. The picture of what it means for the people to be the architects of their own future slowly came into focus. Peasants with second-grade education may not map out the entire alternative national economy and social structure, but once they have seen how the plan will benefit them through evidence in their own barrio, they are ready to act. They know by the scars on their bodies that benefits do not come without cost.

I made the only analogy I could think of. "Maybe it's like trying to buy a house in the States instead of renting it. You have to pay every month anyways. It's better to own your own house at the end of the payment period. But the big difference is that in your case, there is no set number of years to pay and no guarantee of ownership in the end. The payments could go on indefinitely. Aren't you afraid of that?" I asked.

"What is the choice? Only to be poor like my father and my grandfather," said one of the younger farmers.

After five hours of discussion my head was spinning with information and my heart was churning with emotion. "Don't you have more questions?" The farmers looked disappointed. They seemed to sense that they were part of my internal drama. While I was lost in thought, they continued the discussion among themselves. The final statement I overheard came from a young farmer who leaned toward his companions and said earnestly, "What's most important is for us to really love each other."

I closed my eyes and shut out the picture of the cane fields in the distance and the bamboo grove immediately behind these men seated on narrow poles that served as benches. Listening to the young farmer's comments, I could almost be back in my childhood Sunday school class, studying 1 John 4:7-8. "Dear friends, let us love one another, because love comes from God. Whoever loves is a child of God and knows God."

As I listened to these farmers in Central Luzon, I remembered earlier conversations with Elena in Mindanao. I had suggested to her that a movie about the Philippines or more efficient lobbying in Washington, D.C., might help her cause here in the Philippines. Why didn't she work in the United States, the source of the guns and the source of the policy that keeps the Philippines poor? "Because liberation won't come from Hollywood or Washington, D.C. It will come from the humble hamlets of our bleeding land," she answered.

When I looked into the farmers' faces, wrinkled through experience and long hours in the sun, and when I listened to their stories, I believed Elena. But when I left the barrio, it became a statement of faith in the face of overwhelming evidence to the contrary. It is like laying odds on David, the young shepherd with a slingshot, instead of Goliath, the giant, who was professionally trained and armed for war. It makes more sense in retrospect to place our bets on David than it would have at the time when David and Goliath actually confronted each other.

Later in the evening I talked to Ka Boy, a short, slight, NPA cadre from the area. He grilled me on my impressions of the Mindanao Front and then made his own comparisons. "They have the terrain to build large units. Where can we hide here— only the sugarcane fields. We have to stay small and focus on education, strong barrio organizations, and economic improvement." This discussion occurred on the third day of my visit. He had ignored me for the first two days, because, he said, "The last American woman visitor asked too many questions about Marx and Engels and Trotsky. I didn't have the theoretical knowledge and I didn't know enough English to answer them."

I asked Boy how he thought the presence of the NPA had affected the life of the peasants. Boy's focus was on the economic livelihood of the peasants and he came alive on this topic. He had a wealth of knowledge on the tip of his tongue— how many tenants in the region, how much land they till, what the production costs are, what they pay the landlord, how much it costs to live for a year, how many crops a year they can plant, what crops will do best, how they could diversify, how they could improve the marketing of products.

"We do thorough social investigations in each barrio before we start any serious organizing," said Boy. The standard procedure is to establish with precision the economic and social status of each family in the barrio in order to determine how to proceed with work. Boy belongs to that strand of the movement which emphasizes economic production and livelihood over ideology and politics. In the early years of organizing, this was not popular and those who advocated more emphasis on production were seen as revisionists. But as the years wore on and the revolution was not just around the corner, it became clear that everyone had to prepare seriously for a protracted struggle.

The majority of Filipinos still live in rural areas and so it is not surprising that the CPP would concentrate its early efforts there. They were following Mao's strategy of organizing the countryside and encircling the cities. But the population is rapidly moving toward the urban areas and even within the countryside the growth of plantations and agro-industrial estates has meant tenants have become workers who earn a daily wage. This shift from a feudal agrarian base to a capitalist base has been the subject of heated debate within the left, both on a theoretical level and in practice as they tried to decide where to deploy cadre and what strategies to employ.

"When you live with the peasants every day and you eat what they eat, you are forced to become very practical in thinking of ways to eradicate the poverty," says Boy. "This is the bottom line of the revolution—a better life for the poor of our country."

"We emphasize self-support and self-reliance," he continued. "We have had too many experiences in our history of strings attached to 'gifts.' While we know we cannot succeed by ourselves and we are grateful for help, we don't want to get caught like Vietnam. This is essentially a nationalist movement."

Then he added with a grin, "Of course, it would be nice to have a well-equipped army so we could secure a safe zone. I'd like to get married and start a family. It will be hard to do while I am on the run."

I never saw Boy again after this conversation. Five years later, Jun told me that despite the hazards, Boy indeed did get married, had two children, and continued to live in Central Luzon.

Jun's predictions in 1987, however, did not bode well for a sedentary family life for Boy. "We expect the next few years to be difficult because of the growing militarization. The majority of the population will live in areas the NPA can't protect. Control will move back and forth between the Manila government and our government. Commerce will be interrupted."

Though Jun was based in Manila, he voiced practical economic concerns similar to Boy's. "Somehow we have to set up our units of production so the people can still make a living with all the fighting going on. We have to be flexible enough to have cooperatives when they are helpful and let go of them when the people don't see the need for them. We won't survive if we can't imagine new methods for economic livelihood and political organization that correspond to people's needs."

More than any other single group within Philippine society, the NPA represents a determined nationalist stance against the U.S. bases and an alternative to U.S. economic domination. This makes it a special target of the U.S. administration. CIA reports and testimony in U.S. congressional hearings during the final Marcos years acknowledged that the NPA had popular support in rural areas.[2] The *San Francisco Examiner*, in a March 23, 1987, report on the $10 million funding for CIA covert operations in the Philippines, said that "the CIA blueprint is the result of increasing alarm over the continued growth of the 19 year old Philippine communist insurgency."

The CIA had achieved their mission against the Philippine communist insurgency in the past. Their operation in the 1950s successfully eliminated the Huk insurgency with a relatively small operating budget. American-sponsored leaders were installed and U.S. economic and strategic interests were enhanced. The Philippine success convinced the United States that it had found a workable pattern for intervention in other countries that did not entail the loss of American lives. However, veteran CIA agent Joseph Smith questioned that assumption. He described the operation as "mistakenly imagined to be workable anywhere, anytime."[3]

In the March 1987 press conference in Davao City, Chief of Staff Fidel Ramos insisted his "total strategy, the Philippine homegrown variety" from the 1950s would fit the bill for the 1980s. A few moments after Ramos's dramatic exit, a Philippine colonel based in Mindanao who also attended the press conference told me, "I was in Vietnam. I think I will send General Ramos a copy of the Pentagon Papers so he can read the results of this program for himself." The Lansdale strategy,

2. Senate Foreign Relations Staff Sub-Committee Report, 1984.
3. Joseph Burkholder Smith, *Portrait of a Cold Warrior* (New York: G. P. Putnam's Sons, 1976), p. 101.

which worked in the Philippines in the 1950s, did not work in Vietnam in the 1960s and 1970s. It was a different time, a different country, a different cast of characters.

The dilemma that faces the Philippine and American administrations is that the Philippines in the 1980s is also a different country. These two governments may be expending time, energy, and money on a military and propaganda enterprise that is not workable. Cory Aquino is not Ramon Magsaysay. Lt. Col. Victor Raphael, former military attaché at the American Embassy in Manila, is not Edward Lansdale. But the most critical difference in terms of success for American low-intensity conflict strategy is that the NPA are not the Huks.

12

The New People's Army

SECOND THOUGHTS

Although being with the people in the barrios and in the New People's Army is a moving experience, coming back into the mainstream tempers one's enthusiasm. As inspired as I am with the simple life, the commitment, and the quiet heroism, second thoughts arise about this whole enterprise. The second thoughts center on three questions—religious and moral questions about violence, the role of faith in the project of social transformation, and the effect of a tightly disciplined structure on creativity and integrity.

The least hint of NPA brutality in media reports raises the spectre of a Gulag archipelago in my mind. I wonder if I have met only liberal NPA members who are not representative of the whole. Or perhaps they really are representative of the kind of people who join the NPA and want to give themselves wholeheartedly and unselfishly to the cause, only later to become capable of ruthless behavior because of the nature of Marxism, the structure of the party, or in response to their experience of severe military repression or abuse.

A discussion of the use of armed struggle to bring about social change is particularly prone to misunderstanding. Filipinos deeply involved in their struggle for economic equality and political participation often interpret westerners' critical questions as support for the status quo. While legally registered citizens' organizations in the Philippines publicly eschew armed struggle as a means to social change, they have nevertheless been accused of supporting the underground. Millions of Filipinos have chosen to work in these open, nonviolent mass organizations, while at the same time many of them refuse to denounce others who have opted for armed resistance.

In the countryside where the military repression is raw and the economic life harsh, some peasants have chosen to participate in the armed struggle as a means to build an alternative society. For a pacifist from the United States to raise questions about the use of violence by impoverished Filipino peasants under siege is an extremely delicate proposition.

How do Christians, who understand the heart of the gospel to be the cross and its symbolism of suffering love, think about and connect to national liberation such movements as the one in the Philippines?

Soon after I sat with landless farmers and walked with guerrillas I was struck by a parable from the Gospel of Matthew that somehow had escaped my attention in previous readings.

> Now what do you think? There once was a man who had two sons. He went to the older one and said, "Son, go to work in the vineyard today." "I don't want to," he answered, but later he changed his mind and went. Then the father went to the other son and said the same thing. "Yes, sir," he answered, but he did not go. Which one of the two did what the father wanted? "The older one," they replied. So Jesus said to them, "I tell you, the tax collectors and prostitutes are going into the kingdom of heaven before you. For John the Baptist came to you and you would not believe him; but the tax collectors and prostitutes believed him. Even when you saw this, you did not later change your minds and believe him." (Matt. 21:28-32)

This story is part of a series of stories that have surprise endings—the people we expect will be the good guys, the upstanding citizens, turn out to be the ones who miss out on the banquet. The stone the builders reject as worthless turns out to be the most important. It becomes the cornerstone for the entire building.

People such as the theologically correct Pharisees who think they rightly belong to the kingdom of God are in for a surprise. "And so I tell you," adds Jesus, "the Kingdom of God will be taken away from you and given to a people who will produce proper fruits" (Matt. 21:43).

As I reread that parable of the two sons, it was very clear that right actions are more valuable than correct words. But I could also hear my junior high Sunday school teacher aghast at my notion that the NPA have correct actions. "That's not what Jesus means by correct actions!" he would say.

Middle-class western religious people adhere to a code of behavior they assume flows out of biblical material. I realized that it was important to examine how environment, class, and cultural influences shaped my ideas about the meaning of Jesus' words. A way to examine my own assumptions was to place them side by side with the assumptions Jesus' listeners brought to the encounters with him.

The people who listened to Jesus' stories also had a body of common experience and knowledge that he must have been playing to as he talked. His Jewish listeners were all raised on the Old Testament law and the prophets. They would have understood the allusion to fruitful action through their reading of the prophets. For example, Micah was straightforward: "What does the Lord require of you? Do justice, love kindness, walk humbly with your God" (Mic. 6:8). Isaiah defined spirituality in terms of acting justly:

> When you lift your hands in prayer, I will not look at you. No matter how much you pray, I will not listen, for your hands are covered in blood. Wash yourselves clean. Stop all this evil and learn to do right. See that justice is done— help those who are oppressed, give orphans their rights, and defend widows. (Isa. 1:15-17)

When Jesus tried to explain his life's mission to his own townspeople, he appealed to the familiar passage from Isaiah 61.

> The Spirit of the Lord is upon me, because he has sent me to proclaim good news to the poor, liberty to the captive, recovery of sight to the blind and to declare the acceptable year of the Lord. (Luke 4:18-19)

Jesus told his listeners that John the Baptist had already pointed out the right path to take in following God's commands. John was concrete in his suggestions.

> The people asked John, "What are we to do then?" He answered, "Whoever has two shirts must give one to the person who has none, and whoever has food must share it."

Some tax collectors came to him to be baptized and they asked him, "Teacher what are we to do?" "Don't collect more than is legal," he told them.

Some soldiers asked him, "What about us? What are we to do?" He said to them, "Don't take money from anyone by force or accuse anyone falsely. Be content with your pay."

People's hopes began to rise and they began to wonder whether John perhaps might be the Messiah. (Luke 3:10-15)

John's commands to share food and clothing and for soldiers to act decently clearly connected to popular expectations of what a messiah should do. Poor people instinctively recognize the essence of God in commands to be fair and equitable.

What many people in the Philippines have decided is that the social changes will not happen because one prophetic voice announces them. They are made inch by inch and row by row through the action of organized people. They must have enough strength so the military will listen when they say, "Don't take money from anyone by force or accuse anyone falsely."

The bottom line of my own religious tradition is the Sermon on the Mount with its commands to go the second mile; turn the other cheek; give your coat to anyone who asks you; and to love your enemies. While Jesus was clearly addressing an occupied people and telling them to carry the packs of the Roman troops a second mile, the fact is that the American people are not in that situation. We are citizens of a country whose worldwide activities bear more of a resemblance to the imperial Roman nation. We still have to identify who threatens us and whom we threaten. We need to identify our enemies before we can love them, before we can go the second mile for them. Whose actions threaten our present lifestyle? When the poor in the Philippines and elsewhere in the world act on their aspirations to eat and provide for their families, they undermine the economic system under which we have prospered. This realization turned the question of the peasants' armed struggle on its head for me.

Heavy with correct words, our western Christian understanding is like the son in Jesus' parable who says yes and then never does what the father asks. We say yes to peace, but our privilege is at the heart of the violence perpetrated upon our sisters and brothers in the Philippines. Decisions on the issues of life and death are best determined by those who are most directly affected by them. These decisions have integrity when they are grounded in actual experience.

The spiritualized veil of correct words through which I was taught to view the world obfuscates the reality of who holds economic and political power. This veil also mystifies our own role in maintaining the status quo through our passivity. For middle-class North Americans to go the second mile will mean focusing on the role of American institutions—business, government, and military—as the source of violence against our enemies, the poor of the Philippines.

This question about Christians and violence is somewhat related to the second question many people pose: Can Christians genuinely participate in a movement for change that is dominated by the left? Will their faith commitment be respected?

Cardinal Sin is voicing a popular consensus when he proclaims, as he has on many occasions, that "Filipinos will never embrace godless communism because we are a Christian nation." Even those Filipinos who remember that a vigorous Muslim minority exists in this "Christian country" point out that Muslims are even more adamantly religious than most Christians in the Philippines.

Are the NPA godless atheists whom the Filipino people will reject on religious grounds? Are people who join the NPA dissuaded from their religious beliefs? I spent a day in the barrios of Central Luzon, talking about religion to NPA members and peasants. A young cadre who grew up in Tondo, one of Manila's most notorious slums, was incredulous that I as a rational, scientific westerner could believe in God. "You know, in the days when people didn't know how lightening or thunder were caused, they worshiped them because they were afraid. Every age creates their own gods to serve their needs."

Others in the group nodded when I talked about the need for humility and a way of viewing our efforts outside of our own ego. One older peasant woman, our hostess for the day, talked about the comfort she felt from saying the rosary. The younger men pointed to the opulence of the church in contrast to their own poverty. Religion clearly had a mixed review in this particular group.

In some barrios in southern Luzon, the *kapilya* (chapel)

was not used for Bible reflection or liturgy. "We just have community meetings in the chapel now. No priest comes here," one of the residents told me.

Though my survey was far from scientific, I found more acceptance of faith as a basis for social action among rural people in Mindanao. However, it was not far from Davao City that a seasoned NPA cadre who came from the island of Luzon challenged me, "Tell me, just what does the Basic Christian Community do for the livelihood of the people? Just how do the Basic Communities protect themselves from the military?"

On the other hand, my friend Sol—a former Mindanao political detainee still under scrutiny by the military, which considers him a hard-core communist—reached a different conclusion. Based on his own experiences with church people, he told me in 1985, "I have observed how church people in great numbers have joined the front lines and stayed there. I came to realize that it was their faith which sustained them. Faith can be a strong enough motivating factor. Like love, it cannot be explained. But it is necessary for life."

Evangelical Christian visitors question what they term *political* involvement of Christians in the Philippines and worry that it will detract from the "simple gospel." These questions spring from an ideological perspective that views Christianity as a series of propositional truths that people must embrace. They read the Bible with these eyes and thus it is very difficult to see God in the suffering and struggle of the poor in the Philippines.

If a religious commitment has shifted from words to actions, the problem of how the people of faith will contribute to social transformation in the Philippines is no longer insoluble. It can be worked out in practice.

Though my inquiries about religion received mixed replies, I found my most serious concern about the National Democratic Front, the New People's Army, and the Communist Party of the Philippines was focused in another direction. The question that persists for me is how there can be enough organization and discipline to effect a truly nationwide change without requiring that level of obedience that dampens people's spirit and creativity. The distortion of the spirit is the most insidious violence against human beings. It can happen in a church structure; it can happen in a Communist Party structure.

In any organization or institution, there is a tension between the group's goals and the respect for individual freedom. This is exacerbated in an organization whose goal is a radical shift in economic and social structures. There is a fundamental tension between the need to be discreet for security reasons (everyone operating on a "need to know" basis) and the importance of people's having some control in molding their lives and society. An individual member who feels a sense of freedom to express personality, skills, and insight will make the best contribution to an organization.

The need for discipline and security and centralized planning, however, can give rise to an unhealthy atmosphere when decisions are not made at the place where they are carried out. If people simply take orders and are not part of the decision-making process, they either become automatons or at some crucial moment may simply withdraw or even betray. That tension is a permanent part of any organized life.

People working in concert to effect a change nationwide need some centralized planning. That requires trust at every level of planning, directing, and executing the decisions. Trust is greatly enhanced if the leadership is competent and broad enough to encompass people with different personalities. But is personal trust enough to counter abuse of power? Even in the American system of checks and balances, it has been possible for illegal and harmful unauthorized activities to go on in the name of "national security."

Is it possible to create a structure where major decision making can be done by the people who will carry out the decisions? Can the local decision making be done in tandem with a larger national plan? Can some form of democratic centralism truly manage to engage the creative participation of the greatest number of people?

The National Democratic Front (NDF) was organized as an umbrella group of organizations almost simultaneously with the organization of the Communist Party of the Philippines (CPP) and the New People's Army (NPA). The army and the party are both member organizations of the National Democratic Front. Unlike in the United States where the Communist Party is legal, the Communist Party in the Philippines is an illegal organization.

In the late 1960s and early 1970s, before Ferdinand Marcos declared martial law, the various member groups within the NDF concentrated on their own organizing. When martial law was declared, member organizations were forced to go underground. Activists scrambled to hold the basic organization together. Many individuals were arrested; others fled to the countryside.

The threads of a united front did not get picked up in earnest until years later. By late 1985, the NDF estimated their influence to extend to more than 20 percent of the population or about twelve million people. Among their member organizations they count a peasants' union, a teachers' union, a students' and youth organization, a women's organization, an organization for Christians, and an artists' union. All these organizations are still considered illegal by the government.

Contrary to the Philippine military's claim in November 1987, legally registered unions, church and human rights groups are not NDF member organizations.

Some thoughtful Filipinos have raised questions about the National Democratic Front structure. "The NDF has difficulty broadening its base because it has been unwilling and unable to accommodate independent organizations. The party has too much influence within the National Democratic Front. A genuinely popular front is made up of organizations which freely choose to band together to accomplish a goal like the dismantling of dictatorship or the building of democracy," a friend named Charlie told me in 1984. Charlie was a party member, but decided to resign a few years ago, not without much soul searching and agony on his part. He still believes in the cause and tries to help out where he can.

The reasons for Charlie's resignation are complex, but I have seen his enthusiasm, his sense of responsibility, and his good judgment on too many occasions not to take his perspective seriously. By 1982 he was warning, "The party is becoming too arrogant. We have to listen more to what people are saying and encourage other perspectives."

"We are doing our best, but everything is so much more complicated now that we are a bigger organization," one party member told me in response to this concern.

Charlie is not alone in his concern. Other Filipinos have quietly dropped out to work at alternative models, while retaining some contact with the party. The tensions were not publicly apparent until the dramatic overthrow of the Marcos dictatorship through elections, the people's power, and American government machinations in February 1986. When Mr. Marcos declared a snap election for February, the party's response was a boycott based on their analysis that Marcos controlled the military, the electoral machinery, the courts, and the media, thus making his victory a foregone conclusion.

The Far Eastern Economic Review reported that the final decision within the party to boycott the election was made by three people and the vote was two to one. According to a source in the NPA, the one dissenting vote against boycott came from the Military Commission, in other words, the NPA. "That shouldn't be so surprising," he said. "We live with the people every day. We are more in touch with them than the technocrats of the revolution are."

In retrospect, the election boycott was a misreading of the people's will and an overestimation of the U.S. level of control. The party acknowledged the mistake publicly, but has paid for it in terms of popular perception.

However, predictions on the bleak future of the Communist Party of the Philippines, the New People's Army, and the National Democratic Front have proven faulty in the past. Mr. Marcos pronounced the insurgency finished in 1977 after Jose Maria Sison was captured, then when Kumander Dante was captured, then again when Boy Morales, alleged head of the NDF, was arrested in 1982.

When Mrs. Aquino finally took power on February 26, 1986, the commentators were sure this spelled disaster for the New People's Army. She issued an amnesty call, but to her surprise very few availed themselves of the opportunity. Her analysis, which mirrored the U.S. State Department analysis, was that most people went to the hills to fight Marcos. As these people would come down, the hard core would then be isolated and easily defeated.

During the cease-fire from December 10, 1986, to February 7, 1987, the Aquino government seemed to be taken by surprise by the extent of popular support for the National Democratic Front. It was clear to me that in practice, many Filipino citizens still saw the NDF structure and program as an appropriate vehicle for achieving national independence and social equality in the Philippines.

A saving grace of the Philippine NDF structure is its ability to accommodate diversity and varying views. Though its critics have painted the Philippine movement for justice as narrow, it has managed to incorporate ideas and strategies that movements in other countries would have split over. The capacity to bend but not break, like the bamboo tree, is the Asian contribution to an organizational model that is essentially based on a western conflictual analysis of society.

Individuals, too, soften the stance of ideological inflexibility through their Asian behavior of keeping in touch with all sides. This is further aided by the fact that many families have a family member in each major force in the country. For example, one Davao-based family I knew boasted an active National Democratic Front member, a government military officer, a priest, and a businessman among its children.

The questions of structure and discipline versus individuality as they apply to the Philippine situation have yet to be fully answered. However, the leisure time and objective distance needed to create a healthy organization is not a luxury available to those immersed in the struggle. The resolution will be hammered out in the crucible of experience and will require the commitment and patience of the best and brightest—if they can stay alive long enough to do it.

13

Agdao Revisited

THE BATTLE FOR THE HEARTS AND MINDS IN THE PHILIPPINES

Agdao, the infamous barrio in Davao City, was our spiritual and geographical home for the majority of our stay in the Philippines in the 1970s. In several return visits, whether alone or with tour groups, I would touch base with the old neighborhood. Each time I returned, I was confronted with a different situation. In 1982, the talk centered on the government policy of "hamletting"—creating free fire zones in the countryside by forcibly moving farmers into barrio or town centers. "Strategic hamlet" was the term coined during the Vietnam War to describe the relocation centers for farmers. The purpose of this strategy was, as the military described it, to "drain the sea, so the fishes could be caught." The sea is the rural people and the fishes are the New People's Army. Some farmers whom the military suspected as hard-core supporters simply left the area. The neighborhood of Agdao in Davao City was one catchment for these evacuees.

I visited the province of Davao del Norte, which borders Davao City, with Virgilio Montecastro, a longtime friend. Persistent reports of hamletting reached Davao City through evacuees from the province of Davao del Norte. We drove Vir's bright yellow jeep through tracks that served as roads, through creek beds, and across streams to reach the remote barrios outside of Davao City. Along the way, we noticed the shells of small houses, abandoned by their inhabitants.

We stopped to walk through one abandoned *sitio* (a cluster of houses smaller than a barrio). The place felt eerie—houses, gardens, but no people. We heard some noise and followed it, and found one old man hanging *abaca* (plant fibre out of which both rope and clothing is made) over the fence railing in front of his house. "Why are you still here?" we asked. "I don't want to leave my place and lose my crops. The military told us they couldn't guarantee my safety—that this is a free fire zone. I'm an old man. I am ready to die." I looked at the deep lines etched in his face, each one a testimony to hardship and endurance.

That evening Vir and I stood at the edge of the barrio and watched the lines of farmers and their work animals slowly walking up the hill toward the schoolhouse where they were billeted. Men, women, and children climbed the hill, looking exhausted. They didn't bother to stop or smile for the flash cameras waiting for them. The military allowed them to go back to their farms during the day, but a sunset to sunrise curfew meant that the farmers had approximately twelve hours in which to walk five kilometers to the fields, work in the fields, and then walk five kilometers back to the barrio center to arrive before sunset, which in the tropics is about six P.M.

Usually farmers work on the fields in the cool of the early morning. By nine or ten o'clock, the sun is already unbearably hot and within a few hours of being directly overhead. Because the Davao farmers had to walk a few hours to reach their fields, they were forced to work far into the heat of the day in order to be ready to start back home in time to beat the curfew. In happier times and places, I had tried my hand at harvesting in the rice fields. It took only a few minutes of constant bending to cut each individual stalk to realize how exhausting the work can be, even without the extended daily hike.

The next morning we visited the schoolhouse. Sleeping mats were already folded and placed in a corner, cooking pots lined up outside on open fires. Most of the farmers left just before sunrise to get to their fields. The priest, Ely Bianchi, asked Nina, an older woman, to show us the cemetery. Bianchi, an Italian priest of imposing physical stature who has lived in the Philippines for many years, explained, "When the farmers were forced to come to the barrio center, it was the rainy season. A few children had measles and with the families living so close together in the schoolhouse, the measles spread. Poor diet and not enough potable water exacerbated the problem and soon some of the children, especially the babies, died."

Our guide, Nina, the grandmother of one of the dead children, met us at the cemetery. Several mothers were kneeling beside fresh graves, placing flowers at the foot of handmade crosses on which each child's name, date of birth and of death was crudely inscribed. The simple grave markers were interspersed with larger wooden structures, a poor rural version of a mausoleum. Nina led me up a hill past other vaults for the dead along the curved incline. When we reached the top, she gestured silently toward the rows and rows of small white crosses. I walked between the uneven rows and read the crosses—three-month-old babies, two-year olds, a few six-year olds. All children, all dead within a few weeks.

I looked up at Nina. She was standing with one of her granddaughters, hands behind her back, staring into the distance. I wanted to walk over and hold her. Instead I started taking pictures of the crosses. There are hundreds of Ninas, standing forlorn at the graves of their children and grandchildren; they comfort each other in the immediate moment. The best comfort I could offer would be to help get the news out. Through my tears, I tried to remember that the impact of the moment could be multiplied through the eye of the camera.

Some observers pointed to a possible relationship between a recent election for the Batasang Pambansa, the Philippine National Assembly, and the fact that the people in this area boycotted the national election for Assembly representatives. The government concluded that the people were organized in solid opposition to the Marcos regime. Other observers pointed to the economic interest of some military officers, who, after they moved the farmers off the land, set up their own plantations for fast-growing trees used for fuel.

When international attention focused on the hamlet strategy in Davao del Norte, the government changed the description of the original plan somewhat. They claimed that the shifts were permanent and insisted that the farmers really wanted to resettle in the town centers. That claim stretches the imagination. Why would any farmer want to spend most of his day walking to and from his fields? Since pre-Hispanic times, Filipinos have lived in scattered settlements.

The Spanish colonizers had tried to resettle the Filipinos into compact villages like they had in Mexico and Peru, but the progress was slow. Archbishop Garcia Serrano observed in 1622,

> Although it is impossible to deny that the natives would be better instructed and would live in a more orderly way if the small villages [barrios] were to be reduced to the capital [poblacion] . . . they consider it such an affliction to leave their little houses where they were born and have been reared, their fields and their other comforts of life, that it could only be attained with difficulty. . . . Thus has the experience of assembling the people into communities in Nueva Espana proved.[1]

Though the views on the reason for the military action in Davao varied, the progression of events for the farmers in this province over the years was painfully clear. The people faced economic hardship and attempted to build alternatives. I watched their efforts to band together through Basic Christian Communities. The government response to civilian initiatives was repression and the abuse of their human rights. I saw the demolition of their houses and their crops at gunpoint. This depressing scenario seemed to play itself out in an endless cycle with increasing fervor. It would have come as no surprise to me if the farmers had decided to join or support the NPA, although I had no evidence that this was the case with the farmers I met.

When I revisited Davao City in 1984 and 1985, people were focused on the Welga ng Bayan (National Strike) in the hope that a series of concerted strikes nationwide could bring the Marcos regime to an end through sheer economic pressure. Participants who formed the backbone of the strike came from neighborhoods like Agdao. An added pressure in Agdao at the time was a grass roots battle for control of the community between Wilfredo "Baby" Aquino, a notorious barrio captain with his armed goons, and the urban NPA actively organizing in the neighborhoods.

Through the years I noted how stolidly people in Agdao and other communities responded to whatever came their way. They seemed unflinching—in the face of military raids, zoning operations, demolitions, fires, and evacuations. Since

---

1. Emma Helen Blair and James Alexander Robertson, *The Philippine Islands*, vol. 5: *1493–1803* (Cleveland: A. H. Clark, 1903), p. 233.

I had on many occasions witnessed the courage of the Davaoe-nos, I was unprepared for the level of fear and paralysis I saw among the residents when I returned in March 1987. What I found in Davao was shocking, especially in contrast to the openness and democratic space I had just observed in Manila.

On the evening of March 8, 1987, I attended a spellbind-ing show at the gala Cultural Center on Manila Bay. Karl Gas-par, a well-known Filipino churchworker and former political detainee in Davao, together with other Redemptorist seminar-ians, presented a reflection on the theology of struggle and its place in the Philippines. The program included song, dance, and dialogue, and made use of banners, streamers, and flags. During the Marcos years, some of the songs and stories were heard only in the barrios or in street demonstrations. Mesmer-ized, I sat in my comfortable seat in the genteel atmosphere of the air-conditioned center while the actors shouted out their longing for freedom and justice. During the Marcos period people could not have imagined performing in this great hall.

Two hours after the performance, I took a Philippine Air-lines night flight to Davao City. From the moment I stepped off the airplane, I felt tension in the air. Friends I had known for years seemed almost unable to discuss what had happened. Electronics expert/photographer Vir Montecastro, who in the past had a ready explanation for social phenomena, just kept repeating, "I don't know why there is so much fear; I don't know why people seem paralyzed. I am trying to find out myself."

Agdao, the urban poor neighborhood that had launched my husband, Gene, and me into an understanding of the Phil-ippine reality, was inaccessible. A group of armed vigilantes also claimed Agdao as their formation center. Calling them-selves *Alsa Masa* (rising masses), they controlled the area, brandishing their M-16s at checkpoints to keep out unwel-come visitors. The vigilantes from Agdao quickly proliferated and new groups had formed and set up checkpoints on roads leading into most urban poor communities in the city.

Paramilitary units in and of themselves are not new in the Philippines. Armed groups, "lost commands," and fanatic re-ligious sects, for which the military denied responsibility, roamed the countryside during the Marcos era. In his capac-ity as head of the Philippine Constabulary, Fidel Ramos formed the Civilian Home Defense Forces (CHDF) in the 1970s. The CHDF were often pointed to as the most notorious human rights abusers by such watchdog organizations as Amnesty International.

In its final human rights report before Marcos fell, the New York based Lawyers Committee for Human Rights described the CHDF as "one of the worst human rights violators in the Philippines." Their report, published in December of 1985, charges that "on numerous occasions, CHDF units in search of suspected subversives have left non-combatant civilians dead in their wake."

According to the new Philippine constitution, ratified in February 1987, the CHDF must be disbanded. One colonel, active in military intelligence for twenty years in Mindanao, told me, "Even if Mrs. Aquino orders us to dismantle and disarm the CHDF, I am not sure we will be able to do it. These paramilitary units have taken on a life of their own." And then he added, "The CHDF was never that helpful in defeating the insurgency; their abuses just turned the people against us. They should have been dismantled long ago, but it may be too late now."

The newest phenomenon is the vigilante groups springing up "spontaneously" all over the country as a "buffer between the people and the abusive New People's Army," to quote Chief of Staff Fidel Ramos. The armed vigilante groups, which formed in Agdao, soon proliferated across Davao City and then across the country.

The vigilantes now operate in almost all the urban poor communities in Davao. The core members are often local criminals and thugs in the community or out of school, unemployed youth. They are armed by the military, although in the beginning of their meteoric rise the military denied any connection with them. But a secret memo, written in December 1986 by Col. Franco Calida, head of the Davao Metropolitan District Command of the Philippine Constabulary, states that "the truth is that the Alsa Masa movement is being utilized by the military as a vehicle in campaigning to win the hearts and minds of the populace."

Mrs. Aquino endorsed the concept of unarmed vigilantes during a visit to Davao City in March. She said that unarmed citizens groups are a "concrete manifestation of people power and an effective weapon against communism without the use of firearms." A few days after the Philippine national daily papers quoted her statement of approval, they published a picture of two "unarmed" vigilantes, one holding a knife in his hand, the other holding the head of one of their victims.

In a return visit to Agdao in October 1987, President Aquino went one step further and endorsed the armed groups as well. Speaking before four thousand Alsa Masa members, Mrs. Aquino told them, "We look to you as an example. . . . While other regions are experiencing problems in fighting the insurgency, you here . . . have set the example."[2]

Secretary of State George Schultz, in a visit to the Philippines in June 1987, said, "As far as citizens groups are concerned, as I understand it, they are being organized within the framework of governmental authority. They are not sort of free-floating vigilante groups. And President Aquino has supported that approach and we support what she is standing for."

However, also in June 1987, Defense Minister Rafael Ileto said, "Alsa Masa is not part of the military—so we're not accountable for them. Lt. Col. Franco Calida is not leading the Alsa Masa. He is indirectly cooperating, but he is not in control. If an Alsa Masa kills a man, Calida cannot be tried for command responsibility. They're not integrated with the military; they're ordinary citizens. If they kill, then the police should file a case against them in civilian court."[3]

This confusion of civilian and military roles and who is finally responsible for the behavior of armed civilians creates a reign of terror.

Still, the severity of what was happening in Davao did not hit me until I visited a longtime friend, Leonora, in another urban poor barrio where the vigilantes were also active. Leonora was one of the first churchworkers Gene and I met in 1977 when we first arrived in Davao. A few years before, she had founded a Montessori kindergarten in this urban poor community of Panacan. One of the first things Leonora confided when I arrived at her house was, "I have never been so afraid during martial law as I am now."

I remembered Enrique Vasquez's words in 1977 when he began introducing us to churchworkers in Davao City: "Leonora's whole family is committed, even the dog." Leonora and her family had worked for human rights even before mar-

2. Carol Arguillas, "Cory Backs Alsa Masa," *Manila Chronicle*, 24 October 1987, p. 1.

3. Philippine News and Features news service, 8 June 1987, p. 2.

tial law was declared in 1972. She bravely stood up to the Marcos military on numerous occasions in the past. One night, for example, a large military contingent surrounded her family's house. Leonora went outside alone, invited the military men to come in, offered them coffee, and kept her composure throughout the visit. If this woman is afraid, there must be something to fear.

Leonora guided me surreptitiously from her home to the Montessori school, which was actually a simple wooden house on stilts that the parents helped construct. We watched Norma, the lead teacher, gather the children together in one corner for a story and action songs. The children glanced shyly in our direction between songs and quickly looked away when I smiled at them from across the room.

Soon the children dispersed to their tables, eagerly taking up the few crayons available, to begin their coloring exercise. Leonora explained her fear. In June 1986, a military person from a local camp befriended a group of unemployed youth who hung around the Panacan community. The officer supplied them with spending money, marijuana, and, later on, arms. The youth, some of whom are only fifteen years old, are now roaming through the community with guns and grenades. They visit the homes to persuade the people to support them. "They sit there and toss their grenades up and down as they talk. These children have no training in the use of arms," says Leonora.

Leonora then told me that Norma is number one on the local Alsa Masa hit list. I looked across the room at this soft-spoken, middle-aged woman as she leaned over to admire a child's drawing. What could Norma possibly have done to be the object of the counterinsurgency drive?

Norma traces her trouble to May 1986, when a woman active in human rights work was murdered and another seriously injured in this community. Norma took the initiative to call a community meeting to plan for pursuing justice for the victims with the help of the mayor, the police, and military. "We felt that there was military involvement and it was important to bring the perpetrators of the crime to justice," she recalls. In the ensuing months as she pursued the case, the Alsa Masa came into being and focused on her as their number one enemy.

Unlike some other communities where the core of the vigilantes are hardened criminals, Norma's protagonists were teenagers. "I hid for a long time until finally I thought, why am I hiding? These are just children." She sent a message to them, asking for a meeting.

In Davao in the past years, many local communities were visited or organized by the New People's Army. Often local people fed NPA members or let them sleep overnight. At least one member of the local vigilante group had done that. Norma confronted him, "You are pointing your finger at me, saying I am a communist. But what I did, you did. We both know that before your armed group began, the NPA had already withdrawn from this neighborhood. Your group is not a protection from the NPA and you know that I am not a communist. So stop harassing me."

The harassment has not stopped, but Norma is now walking around the community and she is still alive. But she is the exception. For the most part the people of Davao City have complied with the vigilante demands. In other communities I visited, many people like Norma have already been killed.

A few days after visiting Leonora and Norma, my friend Vir and I drove his bright yellow jeep with its huge press sticker through the urban poor community of Exodus and noticed a streamer announcing an Alsa Masa checkpoint. Opposite the streamer, in a small wooden structure, sat three young men ostentatiously exhibiting their M-16s. They noticed my camera, called me over and asked me to take their pictures. I smiled weakly and pressed the shutter. "Will we be in *Newsweek*?" one asked.

In some urban barrios, the Alsa Masa have forced each household to register its members with the organization. Households that refused to register or to contribute financially to the Alsa Masa were marked with an "X." Anyone in the area not accounted for was suspect. I was shown a registration certificate from one community that indicated that a three-year-old child was an NPA surrendered.

In the community of Ma-a (jokingly referred to in the past as Ma-anagua), residents noticed the heading at the top of the registry list read, "NPA Surrenderees." Everyone consented to have their name on the list except one older woman, the mother of Karl Gaspar, whose presentation I had viewed at the Manila Cultural Center just days before. Mrs. Gaspar refused to sign, saying she had never been a combatant. Though she declined publicly, no one dared follow her lead.

Davao City is often singled out as the bellwether for political direction, a laboratory for social experiments in the Philippines. It is a vibrant bustling port that handles agricultural export products from the neighboring provinces. Davaoenos are properly proud of their cultural diversity and their frontier pioneering spirit. When my husband and I lived in Davao, I was amused to hear people speaking about Manila with as much suspicion as Chicagoans view New York and Washington, D.C. "The Manilans think they are the center, but the real action is here."

In the late 1970s, people in Manila talked about Davao in hushed tones, as a wild and woolly city where violence and armed encounters were commonplace. Those of us who lived there did not find the reality as frightening as it seemed to those who read reports about the city. In 1987, however, it felt like Davao had turned into a Manilan's worst nightmare—inexplicable violence, outside the bounds of control of the duly constituted authorities.

How did this happen? Why did it happen? In the course of interviews and observations, I realized that the struggle to win the acquiescence, if not the hearts and minds, of the citizens was being waged at the neighborhood and barrio level in Davao. Various institutions of society were utilized or at least neutralized in this attempt to pressure Davao residents to think and act differently. The support of the media, the compliance of the church hierarchy, and the cooperation of the local civilian government structures and business people were important ingredients in helping the military to achieve their goal.

For example, Davao City disk jockey Jun Pala plays a crucial role in the strategy of the counterinsurgency campaign. Pala works at a radio station formerly owned by a Marcos crony, which was sequestered under the Aquino government. "We will exhibit your heads in the plaza," he told critics in a March 1987 broadcast. "Just one order to our anticommunist forces, your head will be cut off. Damn you, your brains will be scattered in the streets."

Every day for four hours, Pala spews out similar threats and tirades against Maryknoll and Redemptorist priests, against Assumption, Carmelite, and Good Shepherd nuns, against city council members, human rights workers, and social development agencies. Pala caused a mass evacuation of an outlying barrio in February 1987 by announcing that the place would be bombed.

Local and national broadcast ethics committees have issued cease and desist orders. He ignores all orders. When I was in Davao in March 1987, Col. Honesta Isleta, the spokesman for Chief of Staff Fidel Ramos and head of the national broadcast ethics committee, called a press conference in Davao City to explain the steps he had taken to try to stop Pala. When he ordered Pala to come to a hearing, Isleta received letters of complaint from Colonel Calida and other Davao military leaders for his "persecution of Pala." A prominent Davao businessman and a Davao lawyer, recently elected to Congress, interceded on Pala's behalf. Both men had a somewhat liberal reputation during the Marcos era, but seemed to have no difficulty in supporting Pala's outrageous behavior, in the name of anticommunism.

Isleta appealed to General Ramos to intercede. Ramos treated the charges as a squabble between brothers and told them to "work it out."

Why didn't Ramos support Isleta in his attempt to rein in Pala? An officer in the Central Command in Manila told me, "You have to understand that the Philippine Constabulary [PC] is Ramos's baby. Ramos depends on the PC officers' support for his power. He needs Colonel Calida's support. If Calida intervenes on Pala's behalf, it doesn't matter if Pala is acting illegally or not."

Pala went so far as to warn Isleta over the airwaves that he could expect to be in a coffin if he continued his complaints. Isleta, whom Aquino's executive secretary Joker Arroyo publicly called the "Goebbels of the Philippines," became a pathetic figure at the Davao press conference. He appealed to members of the media to help him deal with Pala. The chairman of the Davao broadcast ethics committee responded strongly, "You sir, have the military strength to deal with this man. We are only citizens with no arms and you expect us to be braver than you."

In addition to the media contribution to the growth of the vigilante movement, the church in Davao also played a role in the build-up by its willingness to tolerate the vigilante violence.

The Catholic church in Mindanao generally has been the most progressive in the country and open to the winds of change from Vatican II. Programs for the establishment of

Basic Christian Communities and lay leadership are encouraged or at least granted in response to pressure from below. A notable exception in Mindanao is the Davao City diocese, presided over by Archbishop Antonio Mabutas.

Mabutas has long been a foe of the direction church social action took in Mindanao—empowerment of the poor and marginalized. Such work in the city is done either through religious orders or through independent institutions. Mabutas focuses on sacramental matters and church building projects. In fact, his cathedral building drive in Davao was headed a few years ago by the wife of Antonio Floreindo, the chief Marcos crony in Davao, who escaped from the Philippines soon after Mr. Marcos fled.

Mabutas's associate in Davao City, Bishop Patricio Alo, is a vocal supporter of vigilantism. "On the moral side," he says, "people have the right to defend themselves. The communists will kill anybody who is an obstacle to their movement." Mabutas has also spoken in favor of the vigilantes, but warned that "we must work with the military and government officials who could discipline them."[4] Mabutas's consistently weak-kneed support of church human rights and social action workers under fire in the archdiocese has undoubtedly emboldened the military and Jun Pala in their attacks.

On the national church scene, Cardinal Sin, archbishop of Manila, issued strong warnings against any "political involvement" of sisters and priests. This statement followed his active role in the removal of Marcos. What Sin meant, of course, was "political involvement" with the left. He had been able to collaborate critically with the Marcos dictatorship and has actively supported Aquino.

Sin's clampdown sent ripples through the church structures. Religious superiors withdrew members of their orders who were active in Davao City, ostensibly for their own safety. The result was that priests and nuns who had been playing a pivotal role in the protection of human rights have been removed from the scene of the struggle. Their presence might have deterred or at least retarded the pell-mell rush into violent chaos.

Though the influential Catholic Bishops' Conference of the Philippines has tried to skirt the issue of the vigilantes, Car-

4. *Philippine Agenda* (Manila: Crossroads Publications, 1987), p. 2.

dinal Sin said in November 1987 that he backed armed vigilante groups organized purely for self-defense against communist guerrillas.

The local civilian government structures have reacted in somewhat the same manner as the church structures. By February 1987, the Davao City Council had already set aside 180,000 pesos of the mayor's discretionary fund to pay for supplies for the Alsa Masa. Two council members who objected and questioned what kind of supplies were to be purchased became the object of Jun Pala's public broadcast accusations of communism.

Luz Ilagan, one of the dissenting council members, is a professor and department head at the local Jesuit university, Ateneo de Davao. She became part of the city council during the period of "democratic space" soon after Mrs. Aquino was elected in 1986. When I talked with her in Davao in March, she seemed desperate. "The cause-oriented groups projected me into this position. I have tried to stand up for the truth, but now I feel like I am all alone. Every day, I hear my name on the radio. I tell my husband, I tell the human rights groups, we have to do something, but everyone is scared or confused."

In addition to the media, the church, and the local government, the "total strategy to defeat communism" also relied on the Chinese business community in Davao City. Chinese businesses are typically grocery and hardware stores, restaurants, warehouses, rice and corn mills. This traditionally conservative group initially helped to fund the Alsa Masa. Their support was probably important in the beginning since all parts of government, including the military, were strapped for cash.

However, there were already indications in February of 1987 that some Chinese businesses were disillusioned with the Alsa Masa and realized that this motley group could not provide protection for them. In the past, many Davao businesses paid taxes to NPA collectors. These same collectors changed sides and began collecting for the Alsa Masa. An NPA source in Davao told me, "We made a serious mistake in allowing marginally responsible people in the poor communities to collect money for us. Without proper orientation, they were undependable. Whether through threat or reward it was easy for them to change sides. Some of them were probably with the military all along."

Colonel Calida, in his secret December 1986 memo, acknowledged that there may be problems with vigilante members: "It is a fact that some of the Alsa Masa members have criminal and other derogatory records. Being in depressed areas and considered to be living below the poverty level, we cannot expect that they should strictly adhere to the moral values in the same way as those who belong to the middle and upper class of our society."

The Filipino business people and professionals seem to have resigned themselves to the growth of vigilante groups and military operations. The urban middle class helped to bring Mrs. Aquino into power and have nothing to gain at the moment by contradicting her when she publicly supports the vigilante groups.

The constant barrage of anticommunist propaganda on the radio is coupled with the free movement of armed citizen vigilantes who pinpoint and sometimes kill those they label subversives. This has virtually paralyzed community health and welfare and development work in the urban poor communities. Social development and human rights agencies were at a standstill in Davao when I visited them in March 1987.

This is particularly critical when the military conducts actions that cause mass evacuations. In late February 1987, for example, the military carried out operations and aerial bombings in the outlying barrios of Davao City. Over ten thousand people fled their homes because their barrios were directly hit, because they saw bombings in neighboring barrios, or because they heard Jun Pala threaten bombings in their barrios on the radio.

Evacuees are not new in Davao City. In the past, social development agencies would move swiftly to provide relief goods to the families and human rights agencies would pressure the military to allow the families to return to their homes as quickly as possible. However, in March the tension was so high in the city that most development workers and local journalists were afraid to go to the evacuation centers. I accompanied a small group of Filipino journalists and medical personnel to one evacuation center set up in a banana plantation just outside of the city. We drove in a vehicle supplied by "Cory's Crusaders," a group of upper-middle-class housewives who had worked in Mrs. Aquino's presidential campaign. "They are our safety ticket into the evacuation center," said the nun who briefed our delegation before we met the Crusaders.

After a dusty half-hour ride to the banana plantation, we arrived at a dismal sight—a large tent set up beside a cement platform around which hundreds of children, old people, mothers, and fathers sat or stood. The usual smiles were absent. Forlorn and suspicious looks greeted us.

Before we had a chance to talk to the people, Cory's Crusaders announced that they had to return to the city. They hopped in their car and roared off, leaving us with the evacuees, the military liaison officer, and several banana plantation employees.

Sanitation was virtually nonexistent at the center. One small faucet was the only source of clean drinking water. Some children were sick with measles and there was fear of an epidemic spreading among the hundreds of children in such close quarters. "The army gave us food," said one young mother, "but it is only enough for three days. After that we don't know what we will do." I tried to question the public relations army officer who was mingling with the evacuees about how long they would have to stay and who really supplied the food. He skillfully dodged the questions and suggested I talk with his commanding officer—who was not there.

An old man described his feelings when he saw the bombs falling on a neighboring barrio—fear, panic, a sense of imminent death. Within an hour, his entire village had packed up and left the area. Some younger men told me that their corn crops were ready to be harvested, but the army would not allow them to go back. "What will you do if you can't harvest the crop?" I asked. "Eat grass, I guess," one of them replied.

"Do you think Mrs. Aquino would help you, if you could contact her?" I ask. They looked at each other, shrugged their shoulders, and gave me a withering look.

In the meantime, the children noticed the cameras and were eager to pose for pictures. They bunched together and gave the pro-Cory sign—index finger pointed up, thumb straight out to form an "L." The "L" stands for *Laban* (to fight), the name of the political party under whose banner Mrs. Aquino's late husband, Benigno, ran for office from his jail cell in 1978. It became the Cory symbol during the 1986 presidential campaign. What an irony, I thought—the evacuee children, homeless because of Cory's military policy, giving an enthusiastic endorsement of the president. Later on, when I developed the film and printed the picture, I noticed that the children in the back row had slanted their hands so that the "L" looked more like a gun.

Evacuees in other centers around the city were not as lucky as the ones we interviewed. Journalists who visited the centers reported people sleeping on empty rice sacks on the ground with no overhead cover. Responsibility for the evacuees was vaguely distributed between the civilian government and the military.

It was during my futile attempt to visit Agdao in 1987 that it dawned on me what a fearsome challenge faces Mrs. Aquino. A successful campaign for the hearts and minds of the people must include economic improvement. In a country where 60 percent of the population still lives in the rural area, this will mean a commitment to a comprehensive land reform program that would alter the social relations within the country and affect international economic trade relations. Some of the basic forces who support or consent to her leadership at this point—the United States government, the Philippine military, foreign corporations, and Filipino landowners—would balk at these changes.

In the meantime, the children of the Philippines must pay with their lives for this economic inequity. On an average, four hundred Filipino preschool children die every day, mostly of such preventable and curable diseases as diarrhea, pneumonia, and measles, according to recent UNICEF statistics. The desperation of the urban poor, the rural landless, and the small tenant farmers who see their children dying will continue to fuel the armed resistance.

I realized, as I felt the tension in Davao City, that if the Aquino administration cannot fulfill a commitment to land reform, they will have to make sure that the media, the church, human rights groups, and local civilian governmental institutions do not get in the way of military counterinsurgency action. This kind of control will be possible only through a national scenario much like the one being played out in Davao. However, even that level of chaos and violence does not guarantee control by the forces fomenting the chaos.

Some of the more thoughtful government military commanders question the strategy applied in Davao City. A succinct description of the current situation and prospects for the future comes from a Philippine Armed Forces colonel in Mindanao: "General Ramos says the roots of the insurgency are economic, but then he applies a military solution. We are employing the same strategy as the Americans did in Vietnam. So we will probably end up with the same result here as the Americans did in Vietnam."

In addition to the action of the military, the civilian government, some of the media, and the acquiescence of the church and middle-class professionals, yet another factor allowed for the unprecedented growth of the vigilante movement in Davao City. The National Democratic Front and New People's Army must shoulder some of the responsibility for the confusion. Views on their level of culpability vary between simple errors in judgment, which they themselves acknowledge, to the more fundamental problem of their implementation of democratic centralism.

A deep disappointment for those supporting the movement for liberation came in the form of a nightmare of brutal killings within the NPA in Mindanao over a period of time from 1985 to 1987. Some of the most pernicious activity took place in the barrio we had called home, Agdao, and thus made it doubly difficult to digest.

Though the stories vary, some common elements are agreed upon. For several years, anywhere from three to ten, depending on the source, government military intelligence agents had infiltrated the NPA in several areas of Mindanao. Some infiltrators, known as deep penetration agents (DPA) or "zombies," had reached the highest levels of the organization and were influencing decision making. Some shot NPA members from behind during operations. Others simply passed on information. Some recruited their own units within the NPA. When it became apparent that there was large-scale infiltration, some NPA leaders panicked. It was not clear who was who. Investigative committees were set up, but evidently some government agents were able to get on the committees themselves. The result was confusion, paralysis, and panic, which led to NPA killing NPA.

One former sister who had joined the NPA in Agusan several years ago told me that no one from her unit was left. "There was a time when I cried every night. I just couldn't believe that people I had eaten, slept, and worked with for so many years could really be government agents. The barrio people kept asking me 'What is happening? Why are the comrades killing each other?'"

The process of trying to detect informers caused suspicion and mistrust within the ranks, which greatly weakened the movement in Davao City. Attempts were made to root out the agents without adequately informing the community residents about what was happening. The NPA moved out of areas of Davao soon after the election in February 1986. This left a power vacuum in the communities as well as a confused and truamatized population.

In March 1987 I talked to Janie, a representative from the National Democratic Front involved in trying to untangle the Davao City mess. "It took us a long time to figure out who we could put on an investigative committee. We also made a big mistake by not sitting down with residents in the organized areas to explain. They became confused. Of course, we wrote a paper," Janie smiled, self-consciously. The movement is notorious for writing papers. "A paper does not take the place of face-to-face discussions. Our investigative committee is slow because we don't want to convict anyone without sufficient evidence, so we are now rechecking everything the first committee did. Our greatest concern is that this never happen again."

"How can you live with people day in and day out, engaged in such intensive work, and not suspect that something was not right?" I was incredulous. "Well, in retrospect," she replied, "we now see that what we thought were simply personal failings and lack of personal discipline was something much more. It was just outside of our framework to think that there was such a massive organizational infiltration."

While I was in Davao City in March 1987, Col. Franco Calida was holding public exhumations of skeletons he claimed were NPA victims. During Ramos's visit to Davao, he was treated to the spectacle of shelves of skeletons, which Colonel Calida displayed with obvious gusto. The stench of the skeletons was unbearable and even Ramos turned his head in thinly disguised nausea during the viewing. A month later, Calida held a mass funeral for over a hundred victims, complete with a printed memorial pamphlet modeled on the brochures printed for the victims of government atrocities in the past.

"Our new committee has checked and rechecked all the records. There is no way that all those bodies are NPA victims. We know where our people are. We can only take responsibility for seven or eight of Colonel Calida's show skeletons. We believe the others must be victims of military salvagings, and victims of deep penetration agents. When the DPA's realized that we were on to them, they began a slaughter before they gave themselves up to the military, pretending to be NPA surrenderees," Janie told me.

In July 1987, after the purge, Sol, a party member based in Davao, added his voice to the others raised for reform. He wanted to make sure such an undisciplined killing spree could not happen again. He said, "It should be stressed that the DPAs instigated and encouraged the slaughter. No doubt some genuine members did their own killings, too, but it would have been less frightening if there had been no intrigues. I don't mean to lightly dismiss this. Whether DPA or not, the party's image has been tarnished and we must by word and deed declare, 'never again!'"

Sol shared Janie's concern that some government agents may have survived the purge. Unmasking them will be necessary, but even so, Sol insists, "There must be some civilized ground rules. Guilt must be established beyond reasonable doubt because death is forever. Any hysterical accusation, any attempt at hasty trials, getting confessions through torture, or overeagerness to execute spies should be viewed with suspicion as a DPA operation. The person calling for harsh measures should be investigated. At least that will prevent DPAs from killing or instigating killing. It will stop any indiscriminate killings and reduce spies to mere conduits of information. That is still damaging, of course, but no more internal and external slaughter!"

As we sat in the elegant dining room of a Chinese hotel in Davao, I asked Janie what I should tell people in America about this harsh episode. She looked me squarely in the eye and said firmly, "The truth."

What is the "truth"? Ten years ago my husband and I lived in a relatively peaceful barrio called Agdao. We slowly became aware of the injustice perpetrated on our friends, like Alfredo, who was arrested for working for a different "version" of society, and Lita, whose family lost their farm to an agribusiness conglomerate. We watched the urban poor of Davao City organize Basic Christian Communities. We saw those communities disrupted by bulldozers. We witnessed the Agdao residents in the front lines of the Davao City People's Strike, standing unarmed against a military equipped with M-16s, tear gas, and tanks.

The truth is that the violence done to the people of Agdao was not only economic and military, it was also spiritual. It wounded people's hope and undercut their vitality. The commitment to slow, painstaking step-by-step organizing, which had built a sure, firm base in other parts of the country, was abandoned. Instead, Davao City became a test site for direct organizing by armed NPA units. Traditionally, unarmed political organizers open up a new location over a period of years. "We are able to organize much more quickly when we begin with armed NPA in the area," boasted one local organizer a few years ago. "We are surprised ourselves how fast a neighborhood can be organized."

But some activists had questioned the process from the beginning. Jesse, a longtime organizer, told me, "It takes a long time to develop a leader and it takes even longer to develop a solid community commitment. We will pay for taking shortcuts. Just because people can mouth the right lines does not mean they have integrated the new knowledge with the selflessness needed to accomplish their goals. Just because a new organization has a name does not mean that it can withstand pressure."

The truth is that institutionalized violence of economic hardship and direct military violence escalated over the past ten years in Agdao. The Marcos troops, the paramilitary, and the NPA organizing units finally culminated in the Alsa Masa vigilantes here. I remembered that ten years ago Marcos tried to institute a form of vigilantism—the Barangay Brigades. They withered within a month in Agdao. The confidence to stand up against the capricious violence of the state comes from being solidly rooted. It comes from being part of a healthy web of relationships within the community and between communities. The Alsa Masa are taking much longer than a month to wither.

After ten years, the truth is that the same guiding questions and the same plumb line remain. Where are the significant signs of hope? What serves the needs of the majority in the country—the poor and marginalized?

14

The Struggle for Humanity

Intense violence and counterviolence, the outgrowth of economic and political structural problems, dominate the Philippine headlines. But behind the attention-grabbing headlines, many Filipinos are stubbornly pursuing a more humane path through the middle of the problems and the rampant violence. What stands out most clearly on the Philippine social landscape are the courage and persistence of ordinary Filipinos living in extraordinary times. The commitment to a deeper humanity emerges from every sector of society—both rural and urban—and crosses class, job, profession, and gender lines.

Amid the chaos and violence, in spite of some betrayals, bitterness, and weariness, committed peasants, workers, women, church and human rights workers, youth and students, and national political leaders faithfully continue to fulfill their charge to build a better society. What keeps them going? How, under such adverse conditions, can they keep working, while we in the United States shrink from scenes of poverty and numb ourselves with sitcoms, football games, and consumerism? Examining the human and creative side of the Philippine struggle might give us some clues to this perseverance.

Throughout Philippine history, the peasants have born the greatest burden—political disenfranchisement, human rights abuses, economic hardship. It could be argued that they have contributed more than any other sector in society to the national economy. The organized peasants have made and are continuing to make a valuable contribution in standing up against militarism while at the same time fashioning a new model for development.

I have been touched on more than one occasion by expressions of enduring creativity under dangerous and difficult conditions. For example, in 1984 I joined a fact-finding mission in Quezon province, south of Manila on the island of Luzon. This area had weathered year after year of military offensives. A group of doctors, students, concerned professionals, human rights documentation workers, and church people hiked through the mountains for six hours, some of it at night, through creek beds and up slippery slopes, to reach Barrio Malaya. *Malaya* means "freedom" in Tagalog.

Hundreds of barrio people were waiting and they applauded as we descended the last slope. Despite the fact that there was no electricity in this remote barrio, the people had rigged together a system of battery-operated loudspeakers attached to various trees, so as we entered the clearing we were greeted by the clear firm notes of Filipino freedom songs. Gigantic red welcome signs fastened to the roof of the schoolhouse and waving in the breeze added to this moment of high drama.

Before our official duties began—gathering testimony of human rights abuses—we, of course, were fed. This is traditional hospitality anywhere in the Philippines. What struck me in Barrio Malaya was the graciousness with which the ritual was observed by people who were obviously on the margins of society economically and geographically.

Children, men, and women wore faded, threadbare clothing. Those who weren't barefoot walked around in rubber thongs that had been worn down almost paper thin. It is customary in the Philippines to dress up for visitors. On other occasions, when I visited rural barrios unannounced, I noticed that residents in tattered clothing would reappear in newer attire as the minutes and hours passed. The people of Barrio Malaya were expecting us and it was obvious they were putting forward their best.

Our hosts received us on the veranda of the small schoolhouse, supplied us with steaming cups of coffee, and gave us a restful space of time to recover from our long hike. Then they led us to the back of the building where a long table was covered with banana leaves. Wildflowers at each place setting adorned this fresh green "tablecloth." Steaming bowls of newly hulled mountain rice, chicken soup, and fried pork with greens were strategically placed along the table.

A friend who runs a catering service for select groups in the United States once told me that 95 percent of the success of a catered meal depends on appearance. I knew no one in Barrio Malaya had graduated from catering school, but someone in the village had an artistic sense. Steaming soup was elegantly served up by shy young men, ladeled into the scratched plastic cups omnipresent in barrios across the Philippines. They moved deftly around the table making sure everyone was taken care of, their timing as impeccable as any star waiter in the finest establishment. Amy Vanderbilt or Miss Manners could not have planned or executed a more genteel dinner party than we experienced in Barrio Malaya.

Residents from neighboring barrios, who had arrived earlier in preparation to give their testimony, joined in the meal. Barrio Malaya hosts must have fed five hundred people that afternoon.

But it was after the meal that the real drama began. The people who came to testify arranged themselves behind signs painted in red on white rice sacks. The fact-finding delegation sat on the schoolhouse veranda looking out over the field.

Behind the sign "Biktima ng salvaging" (victims of salvaging) stood the relatives of those who had been summarily executed by the military. "Victims of forced surrender" are those who were rounded up by the military and forced to surrender as New People's Army members so their pictures could be taken with their hands raised. This helped boost the regional military reputation in the eyes of Central Command in Manila. After their "surrender" the men were released. "Victims of forced evacuation," numbering about one hundred, bunched themselves around their sign. Victims of harassment and victims of torture each had their own rice sack signs.

As we looked out over the field, a clear pictorial view of the human rights situation faced us. With no electricity, there is of course no television nor video presentation, but the human mural spread across the field before us was as effective as any movie I have seen. Not only was there an artistic caterer in the community, there must also have been a choreographer.

After we were given the pictorial overview, the most serious cases of human rights abuse were presented to the entire group by the victims or by the families of the victims if the victim was dead. Our fact-finding mission then divided into four groups and for the next six hours listened to person after person telling a story of abuse. The sun went down. The lanterns were lit. The stories continued. Will they never stop? I could hardly bear to hear one more story. The stories were remarkably similar, but each one was told in a distinctive manner. Some witnesses were shy. Some provided embellishments and colorful detail. Others told the event flatly—all verbs, no adjectives.

After the last story was told and supper was eaten, visitors and barrio hosts again gathered in the field to entertain each other. The barrio officials gave their usual speeches of welcome; then the music and skits began. The students in the delegation who had diligently taken notes all afternoon transformed the barrio peoples' stories into a series of interlocking dramas. The spectator response was electrifying—cheers, claps, sighs, laughter, shouts of recognition at certain points.

The students from Manila were quite pleased with themselves and the result of their work. Then the barrio folks presented their songs and dramatic readings to a hushed audience. Later one of the students in the delegation told me, "We are a cultural team from the university, but these barrio people know more songs than we do. They have gone much deeper than we have. When they sing about justice and freedom, you can feel their experience in every word."

Not every rural community in the Philippines displays the same level of creativity as Barrio Malaya, but they all share one enduring quality expressed in different ways—graciousness and human generosity. It may be a reflection of the beauty of nature around them and the more relaxed pace of rural life. However, I discovered the same selfless spirit in the industrial setting among the organized workers.

One young woman of generous spirit whose image remains in my mind is Evangeline Academia, who works in the Lotus Export Company at the Bataan Export Processing Zone (BEPZ) in Central Luzon. Evangeline is from a peasant family and she came to BEPZ in the hope of improving her lot in life and sending money home to her subsistence farm family. Over 80 percent of the twenty-six thousand workers at the BEPZ on Luzon are women, almost all under twenty-five years of age. BEPZ, also known as the Zone, is home for sixty transnational corporations, which bring in materials, use Philippine labor, and export all the goods produced there.

Women participate in large numbers in the Philippine workforce and are preferred by some companies because of their ability to do precise hand and eye work. Employers also hope they will prove to be obedient and uncomplaining. However, many women at BEPZ are active unionists and form the backbone of the national women's division within the Philippine's militant national labor movement, the Kilusang Mayo Uno or May First Movement.

I met Evangeline when I joined a Philippine ecumenical fact-finding mission set up to investigate the killing of two workers and the wounding of thirty-three others in a picket line at the BEPZ on January 31, 1987. From documents and eyewitness accounts, our investigative team pieced together the event and the circumstances leading up to it.

After nine months of dialogue with Zone officials and a march to Malacanang Palace with petitions bearing ten thousand signatures and still no positive results, the workers decided to strike. They based their demands on Mrs. Aquino's May Day speech in 1986, when she promised to abolish repressive labor laws, provide job security, and integrate the cost of living grant into the actual wage on which benefits and overtime are computed.

The strike, which began on January 27, became stronger each day. Eighty percent of all workers in the Zone stayed away from their jobs. The transport drivers joined in a sympathy strike. A province-wide Welgang Bayan (Peoples Strike) was launched. The fishermen joined, demanding that they be allowed to stay and fish in the area despite the growing industrialization. The students joined, demanding a library. The youth group, KADENA, joined, demanding recreational facilities for youth. The vendors joined, protesting the privatization of the public market in Mariveles, the town adjacent to the Zone.

On January 30, Zone administrator Jaime Guerrero, who was also a member of the government negotiating panel during the peace talks, together with the local police chief, the minister of labor, and the mayor met with the workers' representatives. The panel agreed that the workers' demands were legitimate. They also promised that there would be no harassment at the three barricades the workers had set up at intervals along the road to the factories.

The very next day, four military trucks, two fire trucks, and a jeep of military men appeared and through a combination of threat, waterhose, and truncheon destroyed the barricades and forced the workers to retreat to the bridge leading to the town of Mariveles. For two hours the fire trucks, using an inexhaustible supply of water from the river, hosed the workers on the bridge. Military reinforcements arrived. Power lines were cut so that there was a communication blackout to the town. Two helicopters hovered above. According to affidavits by bystanders, at one-thirty in the afternoon police charged at the workers with truncheons. At the same time, a blast of rapid gunfire came from under the bridge and from the surrounding hills. Two people were killed and seven wounded through gunfire. Twenty-six were wounded by the truncheons.

Our fact-finding team, sent by the Manila-based Ecumenical Movement for Justice and Peace (EMJP), spoke surreptitiously with Evangeline Academia, age twenty-one, in the town of Mariveles, outside of the Zone. The military had coincidentally called all the wounded workers to the military camp on the same day as the team arrived to take their testimony.

Evangeline balanced her hand, hidden in a huge bandaged cast, on her lap, and told her story. "Because of our friendly negotiations with the government panel on January 30, I thought it would be peaceful, so I didn't go to the barricades the next morning. But then I heard there was trouble so my friend and I went to check. By that time the barricades were broken down, so we joined the strikers on the bridge."

Her face tilted down, she was the very image of docility. "I saw the helicopters up above and I was afraid. But," she explained quietly, "I was also ashamed to leave my co-workers there, bearing the brunt of the water cannon, since I am an official of the union. So I joined them.

"Before we knew it, the soldiers started attacking with truncheons. The strike leaders yelled at us to lie down, so we did. I felt shock and fear—no pain. I was only conscious that I was lying on top of a man." She stopped, looked at the fact-finding team, a little embarrassed. Her demeanor was modest. I could understand why an employer looking at Evangeline would think he had a docile, eager, and obedient worker. Her story, however, belied her appearance.

"When the shooting stopped, I noticed my clothes were ripped off and my left hand was limp and bleeding. I ran from the bridge to another friend's house, got some water to drink, then boarded a tricycle for the clinic." A tricycle is a motor-bike with a seat and roof attached for passengers, used as public transportation, especially in smaller towns. "They told me at the clinic that my hand couldn't be repaired there. I walked to another clinic, but there was no doctor. None of the public jeeps would stop.

"I saw one blue jeep with wounded people piled like pigs in it but I didn't take it because I was scared the military would stop it. I finally found another jeep with only four wounded and it went to the BEPZ hospital. I had to wait in the emergency room because there were more serious cases. Finally the nurse injected pain reliever, wrapped my hand in clothing to stop the bleeding. They X-rayed my hand but told me I would have to transfer to the public hospital, a forty-five-minute drive away. I felt so weak. Before I passed out, I told my friend, 'No matter what, don't let them cut off my hand. I need it for work.'

"My friend told me that the doctor at the public hospital wanted to amputate, but she said no, so he worked for four hours, trying to mend my hand. I will need another operation. The doctor doesn't know if my hand will ever function nor-mally." Evangeline ended her testimony with a question punc-tuated by the fierce look in her brown eyes, "Will there ever be anyone who looks after the workers?"

Evangeline had thought she would be able to contribute to her peasant family by getting a regular salary as a worker. What are the possibilities for a young woman like Evangeline in the barrio? If her family is allowed to stay on the land, she could marry a farmer and do double duty in the home and in the fields. If her family loses the land or finds it impossible to make a living on its small acreage, she could go to the nearest town or city and look for work in a factory, department store, or restaurant, usually at less than the minimum wage. Many young women, like Evangeline, take that option.

In 1984 I stayed in a farming community in Agusan del Sur, just outside of Butuan, Mindanao, to get a better grasp of the rural women's situation. The men, eager to entertain, showed me the rice fields and explained in detail the cost of inputs like fertilizer and pesticides, of renting a hand tiller, and of irrigation so that the "miracle rice" developed at the In-ternational Rice Research Institute in Los Banos, Philippines, will grow miraculously. "We men meet regularly to discuss farming and economic problems," they told me.

In the evening, it is traditional for everyone to gather together and "have a sharing" as they term this kind of informal discussion that actually has a purpose. During the sharing, I asked if there was a women's group in the barrio. The women, seated at the edges of the room, shook their heads. One of the more talkative men offered the comment that "the women are too jealous; they can't get along with each other."

I looked around the room and remembered some of what I had read about women's roles in Philippine history. Before the Spanish colonial period, women in this Pacific archipelago were active in decision making in social, economic, and political life. Women could administer their own property, were entitled to inheritance, and could retain property rights before and after marriage. In the native pre-Hispanic religion, women played a central role as priestesses. They presided over religious ceremonies, communicated with the spirits, and undertook counseling, healing, and prophesying the future.

The imposed Spanish colonial culture turned the tide against women. Spanish law, derived from the Code of Roman Law, stressed male superiority and emphasized that women belonged at home. They were forbidden to transact business without their husbands' knowledge and approval or to dispose of their own property. Myths of the helpless woman dependent on male gallantry were propagated. Spain's 350-year occupation fanned a double standard and contradictory image of women—saintly Virgin Mary juxtaposed with Eve, the sexual temptress.

The American colonial experience reinforced economic control by men, although more women were brought into the work force. The public education system, the Protestant work ethic, and emphasis on individual salvation all carried potential seeds of egalitarianism. However, these features of American colonialism did not make as strong an impression as the hundreds of years of Spanish Catholicism's emphasis on passivity and piety. The Protestant religion with its emphasis on the Word supported a more rational approach to religion and life as opposed to the color and imagery of Spanish Catholic liturgical life. This helped to undercut further the reverenced healing authority held by women in the pre-Hispanic religions.

Aspects of native pre-Hispanic culture have been masked

by the onslaught of colonial culture. The enculturation of the people as a whole facilitated the acceptance of economic and political structures from the west. These structures heightened and sometimes further created inequality between men and women.

I thought of this colonial legacy as I watched the faces of the men and women in that Butuan barrio. The women remained silent, not answering the public charge of jealousy. However, as soon as the meeting was over, they quickly surrounded me. "We want you to know why we don't have a women's group," said Mely, the oldest in the group. Plump, slightly stooped, work and worry lines in her face, she looked at me with blazing eyes, "We do the housework and the marketing, look after our children and help in the fields. By the end of the day we are exhausted. We are not jealous of each other; we are tired."

A younger woman about Evangeline's age took over the explanation. "Our husbands want to meet in the evening or they want to go see a movie in town. I have only young children, so I have to stay home and look after them." My hostess for the week, a quiet, emaciated-looking woman, added, "When we are frustrated we go to Mely's to talk. She gives us good advice."

That remark reminded the women of past incidents and activated a flurry of further discussion and rollicking laughter among them. Their life was hard, not only because they were poor but also because of expectations upon them as women, but it was clear to me that they enjoyed each others' company. They had found ways to support each other. Suddenly remembering that I was still there, Mely turned to me and said, "We want to be organized as women. . . . Maybe the next time you come and visit us, we will be."

Despite being enmeshed in a colonial and patriarchal social structure, notable women have broken from that traditional mold. Philippine colonial history is dotted with stories of strong women who took leadership in the resistance against rulers. Gabriela Silang is probably the best known. In the eighteenth century she formed an army of two thousand men after her husband, Diego, was killed, to fight the Spaniards with homemade muskets, blowguns, and arrows. Gabriela was finally captured and hanged in full view of what remained of her following. She died for a revolution against Spain that was not to succeed until a hundred years later.

Another heroine in the fight against the Spaniards was Tandang Sora, as she was popularly known. Widowed at an early age, with six children to raise, she was implicated by the Spaniards in nationalist activities preceding the revolution. Tandang Sora was exiled until she was eighty years old. When she returned to the Philippines, she immediately began to organize reading and discussion sessions and to provide shelter for revolutionaries who were wounded in battle.

In addition to individual heroism and locally managed resistance, there has also been cooperative work and organizing on a national scale among women. For example, in 1937, during what is known as the Commonwealth period of American colonialism, women won the fight for suffrage. They mounted a campaign in which they got almost a million Filipinos to ratify the amendment to give them the vote.

In the 1960s students became a formidable political force through such movements as Kabataang Makabayan (Nationalist Youth). The University of the Philippines became a hotbed of student radicalism designed to seek major changes in Philippine society. A young female studying mass communications, Lorena Barros, was one of the organizers of the women's group, Makibaka (Fight Back). Makibaka protested decadent activities like the Miss Universe Pageant and other beauty contests. When the group was forced to go underground, they moved to the hinterlands of Quezon province to continue their struggle. Barros and some of her companions were killed in 1976 in an encounter with government military troops. Like Gabriela Silang and Tandang Sora, Lorena Barros did not live to see the fruits of her labor.

However, Makibaka apparently flourished quietly as an underground organization. During the brief democratic space that existed early in the Aquino administration, Makibaka sponsored several press conferences in 1987 to remind the public of its presence, albeit subterranean.

The flowering of legal women's organizations began in 1984 under the aegis of "Gabriela." Gabriela forms the umbrella for a national coalition of peasant women, urban poor, women workers, tribal women, women religious, and professional women from the middle and upper middle class. The organization was named in honor of the eighteenth-century Filipina heroine, Gabriela Silang. Some of the women involved in its leadership had been in the militant nationalist movement for many years before they began to focus their energies directly on the oppression of women.

During the past ten years, I have been privileged to meet and learn from Filipina women, both those in Gabriela member-organizations and those struggling on their own. Evangeline is a special person; Mely is a special person; but these women are not isolated examples. A host of strong and committed women live across the country. Each woman's story is particular to her, but the common thread that runs through all of the stories is the courage and grace of the women under pressure.

Hilda Narciso is an active "parliamentarian of the streets" whose face comes into focus when I think of courage and persistence under pressure. Hilda, a former teacher, was thirty-two years old and single when she was arrested on March 24, 1983, in Davao City. She was delivering a package to a German pastor who was scheduled to leave for Europe shortly. She was just one among many who were arrested when they tried to bid farewell to him.

Hilda was blindfolded and taken to a "safehouse" where soldiers accused her of being a communist. Ironically, a safehouse is a safe place not for the arrestee but for the military, to question and torture suspects outside of the official military premises. A motel room or house often serves as the "safehouse." Hilda was raped by one soldier and sexually abused by several others. Two days later she was transferred from the safehouse to the military's Camp Catitipan in Davao City.

Hilda demanded and was promised a medical exam on April 6, but instead she was flown to Manila and taken to a military hospital there. Efforts by her lawyer to obtain a full medical examination with an independent doctor present were unsuccessful until May 20, almost two months after Hilda was arrested. The military doctor, Maj. Felicisimo del Rosario, noted healed lacerations on her cervix, but made no conclusions regarding their cause.[1]

Despite repeated requests by her lawyer and by supportive church groups, the Armed Forces of the Philippines made no effort to gather any further evidence about the rape. Hilda Narciso's lawyer filed a formal complaint on July 19, 1983,

---

1. "Salvaging Democracy: Human Rights in the Philippines," report by the Lawyers Committee for Human Rights, New York, 1985.

with the judge advocate general for that region, requesting a line-up so that Hilda could identify the rapist by sight. Two months later, on September 22, Hilda's attorney, Emelina Quintillan, and representatives of various women's groups met with the Davao regional commander, Gen. Dionisio Tan-Gatue, who then agreed to reopen the case. Tan-Gatue later concluded that some of the men involved in the incident had not been under his command, so he could not conduct the investigation. The case was forwarded to his superiors in Manila. These kinds of delaying tactics continued for years.

Hilda's case became a cause célèbre among women's organizations in the Philippines and abroad because she was one of the first female detainees to admit publicly to being raped and to insist that her rapists be brought to trial. Rape is a standard operating procedure used to intimidate and break down women detainees, according to Task Force Detainees, the human rights documentation agency of the Association of Major Religious Superiors.

Most Filipinas feel ashamed of having been raped and feel even more ashamed of discussing it publicly, so very few cases are ever brought to light. Added to this cultural factor was the fact that during martial law it was impossible to win such a case since the military reigned supreme and the courts complied with the dictator's wishes. Hilda's persistence was extraordinary.

I met Hilda in October 1984, a year and half after her ordeal. We talked in the safety of a convent in Manila. She still trembled as she recounted her story, tears welled up in her eyes, and she stopped periodically to compose herself. She showed me a skin rash on her arms that appears when she is tense and nervous.

"People can't understand why it is taking me so long to recover. I don't understand either. I have always been a strong person, but I feel so vulnerable," she said. "A lot of women's groups invite me to speak. I look brave when I speak publicly, but then I am terrified when I am alone. And I still don't like to relate to men at all, even the ones who are kind."

Hilda was discouraged with the legal route. "Nothing is accomplished this way, so I have to find other methods. The women's groups have chosen the extra-legal path of letters, vigils, and demonstrations. I am now gathering data on other women who are in the same predicament as I am. I have already interviewed ten and plan for at least fifty more. They really pour out their hearts to me because they sense I know what they are going through. If I can show that mine was not the only case, there may be more hope of stopping this practice. But," she sighed, "it is so hard to hear these stories every day. I am exhausted after only one interview."

It strikes me that Hilda has actually initiated a self-help support group for rape victims. Through her seeking justice for the victims, Hilda is managing to furnish the psychological support needed to recover from the trauma of the experience. This emotional support is gained, however, at the risk of military revenge against the women who are naming their rapists.

As Hilda exemplifies the determination of women political detainees, I think of Fr. Rudy Romano as a compelling example of the hundreds of dedicated priests around the archipelago who are forging a new theology in the everyday practice of their vocation.

I was able to talk at length with Father Rudy in 1984 at the Redemptorist Convento (priests quarters), located on the spacious and elegant cathedral grounds in Cebu City, central Philippines. At that point he was hiding in the convento because the military had threatened his life. Their threat was in reaction to his support for the laborers involved in a recent general strike in the city.

Father Romano is a tough, loquacious priest from the island of Samar. Early in our conversation he reminded me that people from Samar are famous as strong warriors. One question started him on a stream of thoughts that ranged from personal reminiscences to statements of faith and ruminations on the role of the church and Christian leaders in troubled times.

"The church's role," he began, pushing his half-finished plate to the side, "is to facilitate the surfacing of leaders. Through the Bible-sharing the people realize that God is in them, and they come to realize their own value and dignity. Good leaders are selfless and clear thinking. But I worry about the church, because she is always a step behind the people. If the church maintains a middle or reactionary course, the people will build their own church.

"Now, how does the state work?" Rudy leaned across the table, but I knew he was not really asking me. He was just preparing to launch into another topic. "The state survives through deception. When people are no longer deceived, the state has to resort to violence. Less people are deceived now in this country, so that is why there is so much militarization and so many human rights abuses."

Father Rudy had been immersed in work with the poor in Cebu for years. As a result, he was well known by the local military. Since 1971, his religious order, the Redemptorists, have worked in the poor parishes around Cebu, encouraging the growth of Basic Christian Communities. When the workers were on the picket line he was there to say mass for them. When the squatters marched, he spoke at their rallies.

In 1979 Father Rudy was arrested for speaking at a human rights rally. The military turned water cannons on the assembled people to disperse them. Five intelligence men removed Father Rudy from the scene and stuffed him into their car. In the struggle his soutana was torn and his glasses smashed. "Remember, I am from Samar. We are fighters." he said. Rudy was taken to the military camp with the soldiers pointing their weapons at him as the sirens blared. Soon the sisters, seminarians, and urban poor surrounded the camp. He was released but subpoenaed to come to court on charges of assembling without a permit and resisting arrest.

Father Rudy's daring spirit and his groundedness in the culture enabled him to find a creative resolution to the court case. He wrote a letter, threatening to put a curse on the generals if they would have the nerve to try a priest. He then affixed the signature of the Catholic Defenders, a powerful conservative organization within the church set up to defend the traditional creed and institution. The curse, *gaba*, is a powerful tool, especially among a population where the traditional Spanish Catholicism is deeply rooted. Father Rudy got on his motorbike in the middle of the night and dropped copies of the letter in prominent places. The generals never showed up in court.

After the ill-fated court case, Father Rudy discovered that the military was planning a raid of religious institutions. Through a friend in the media, he managed to proclaim that fact on the radio and in the newspapers. Pre-empted by the headlines, the military had no choice but to give up the plan. After meeting Father Rudy and hearing other people's stories about him, there was no doubt in my mind that the local military commanders must have spent a lot of time plotting a suitable revenge for this indefatigable man.

In the precarious human rights context of the Philippines, I had learned to soak up each word in an encounter with a compelling person, because there was no guarantee of meeting the person alive again. Father Rudy was that kind of individual, but in the physical surroundings of the stately cathedral in Cebu, I thought of him then as inviolable.

Father Rudy's final reflections before we parted were about Jesus. "You know Jesus only lasted three years. He was trying to lead the people to understand themselves, but they were not ready yet. That's what did him in."

On May 11, 1985, six months after our encounter, the news was telexed to the United States human rights organizations—"Rudy Romano is missing!"

The motorcycle he was riding in Cebu City was stopped. Several plainclothes armed men forced him into their car, the license plate of which was traced to a military vehicle. His religious order, the church, and his friends in the Philippines and abroad searched and pressured the military for clues to his whereabouts. Rumors were rampant. He is alive, but his tongue is cut out. He is dead. He is alive, but the torture has driven him crazy. Days, weeks, months went by. Each Friday the bells are rung for him at the cathedral in Cebu. Officials from the Vatican and European parliaments made inquiries with no result.

The flicker of hope had almost been extinguished when Marcos was driven out of office. Hope was again ignited. If Father Rudy was really dead, at least his friends could be shown where his body was, so they could arrange for a proper burial service. Despite the heightened pressure based on the belief that the Aquino government could coax the answer from the military, no news has yet been uncovered. The military men identified as Rudy Romano's kidnappers were found not guilty in a Cebu court in 1987 and released.

Like Rudy Romano's friends, Hilda Narciso entertained no hope of successfully pursuing her case in the courts under the Aquino administration. Even the trial of the president's late husband's murderers lagged because witnesses were afraid. The military establishment itself might become unhinged if the culprits behind the actual soldiers who fired the gun were identified.

"But, of course, I am still trying to push the case," Hilda told me in 1987. Father Romano's friends still toll the bell for

Rudy in Cebu, waiting for the open moment when the truth will be found.

If any single human being has stood publicly in the way of a government move to reduce emphasis on human rights, it was former Philippine senator Jose W. Diokno. Diokno died from cancer a month after the cease fire was terminated between the government and the NDF in February 1987. A monumental figure in Philippine politics, Diokno, known affectionately to his friends as "Pepe," came from the upper class.

He was an uncompromising nationalist, which led to his imprisonment when Marcos declared martial law. His prison experience convinced him of the need for free legal assistance for the detainees, which he began providing in 1974 when he was released.

Diokno served on the government negotiating panel during the peace talks and was appointed to the Presidential Commission for Human Rights until his failing health forced him to give up both posts. To the end of his life, his home remained a center where those active in the struggle for peace and justice could gather and get his counsel.

The attendance at Diokno's week-long funeral in early March was a testimony to the diversity of people with whom he worked. Tribal people from northern Luzon danced their traditional dances late into the evening. Various national organizations held ongoing masses and prayers for him. Bishop Antonio Fortich came from the island of Negros to concelebrate the funeral mass. Thousands of people came to view the body. The side and back of the entire church were filled with wreaths. I walked around and read the cards—everyone from Dole Philippines to nationalist human rights organizations had sent their regards.

Mrs. Aquino spoke at a special service attended by foreign diplomats, government officials, human rights workers, antinuclear activists, and the urban poor. Meanwhile, the peasants union chose that exact time to gather in the courtyard outside the church to begin their march to commemorate the Mendiola farmers' massacre, which had happened a few weeks earlier. The farmers marched out of the main gate of the churchyard, banners waving, only moments before Mrs. Aquino's limousine pulled in at the side of the church.

In her speech, President Aquino reminisced about her own husband's death, about Diokno's connection to her family, and his help to all others in need. "What really would have made Pepe happy," said one Maryknoll nun who worked closely with Diokno, "would have been for President Aquino to use the occasion to announce a new offer to break the impasse between her government and the National Democratic Front."

While no one person is the determinative factor in any situation, Diokno's passing from the scene at such a delicate time meant one less influential person to keep a foot on the brake in hopes of averting civil war. The events of the weeks immediately following his death moved the country more quickly toward polarization.

Diokno was a famous voice for nationalism. Many Philippine students are equally vociferous, but much less widely known. The students were the earliest supporters of the struggle of the farmers and workers. In what is referred to as the "first quarter storm"—the student protests in early 1971—students linked with worker and peasant unions. Many of those students became the backbone of the nationalist movement and were forced to go underground after the declaration of martial law in 1972. Student life usually lasts four years and then the graduates join the work force. In many ways, student activism on college campuses has functioned as a training ground that supplied leaders for other organizations within society.

Leandro Alejandro is one example of a student leader who went on to take responsibility in the national struggle. I knew "Lean" as a gentle, soft-spoken, very bright young man who had a special gift in relating to all kinds of people of all ages. Leandro's overriding concern and commitment was to the poor and marginalized in Philippine society. He was elected Student Council president of the University of the Philippines in 1983 and in that capacity helped to bring the students into contact with the problems of other groups in society.

For example, when the peasants union came to Manila in 1983 to press their demands at the Ministry of Agriculture and were forcibly dispersed, they took shelter in a convent where Leandro and other student leaders were meeting. Lean tried to dialogue with the police who surrounded the convent and in the process was arrested and jailed for several months.

In 1985, though he was only twenty-five years old, Leandro became the secretary general of a national coalition of student, worker, peasant, and professional groups called Bayan. During the Marcos era, Alejandro took the lead in organizing nationwide unarmed people's strikes to bring the Marcos government to its knees. He became a well-known figure to the military.

After Mrs. Aquino came to power, Lean responded to her call to join the political process in the country. He ran for Congress in the May 1987 elections with the Alliance for New Politics, a political movement that emphasizes nationalist issues like land reform and the dismantling of the U.S. military bases. Leandro was outspent, harassed by goons, and defeated at the polls.

Less than four months later, on September 19, 1987, Lean was shot in the face at close range in front of the Bayan office in Metro Manila by gunmen believed to be linked to the Philippine military. He was just returning from a press conference at the Philippine National Press Club in which he announced a rally to be held on September 21, the anniversary of the declaration of martial law by Ferdinand Marcos in 1972. The purpose of the rally was to protest the rising militarism in the Philippines and to urge President Aquino to assert more control over her military. Alejandro's assassination took place only three weeks after an attempted military coup against the Aquino government.

Most Philippine analysts conclude that Alejandro was killed by right-wing military or paramilitary forces. A few days before the assassination, Col. Honesto Isleta, Philippine Armed Forces information officer, had named Lean and other Bayan officials as targets for arrest.

Only a year and a half before his assassination, Leandro had married Lidynaida Nacpil, an active women's leader. Their daughter was seven months old when Lean was killed. In a statement at his funeral in Manila, Lidy said, "Every tear that we shed is a drop into the flood that shall sweep us to victory." Lidy, who is from a well-known Methodist family in the Philippines, began an international speaking tour less than two months after Lean's murder. She was asked in a public forum in Chicago in November 1987 whether she wanted justice for Lean. She replied simply, "What is more important is that we continue what he was doing—working for justice for all in our country."

The Amnesty International Reports throughout the martial law years were filled with stories of tortures, killings, massacres, preventative detentions, detentions without trial. Other international investigative bodies also filed similar reports at the United Nations and published documents in various countries.

The most consistent and reliable Philippine documentation agency for human rights is the Task Force Detainees (TFD), set up in 1974 by the Association of Major Religious Superiors of the Philippines. A nationwide agency with dozens of documentation centers and hundreds of workers, TFD collects and collates data on human rights abuses, helps victims of abuses, advocates for the release of detainees, and has spawned various organizations to work on specialized areas of abuse. Until Marcos was ousted, TFD data was used by the U.S. Department of State in their annual human rights report. In 1986 the Task Force was nominated for the Nobel Peace prize.

Many unassuming human rights "troops" around the country work hard and take risks daily to stand against abuse. Of these brave people nationwide, best known is Sr. Mariani Dimaranan, a diminutive Franciscan nun in a gray habit. She has doggedly kept at the job of human rights documentation and advocacy on behalf of the victims and their families since 1974.

When martial law was declared, Sister Mariani was jailed for almost three months in a cell with twenty others. There they shared the food, their clothes, and their lives. "That experience showed me how selfless these activists were. They put me to shame. I, a nun, who supposedly was to lead the way in selflessness, learned so much from these people the government was calling communists," Mariani told a group of nuns in Chicago in November 1986 during a nationwide speaking tour sponsored by the American Friends Service Committee.

For many years, Sister Mariani taught and worked in the administration of St. Joseph's College, run by the Franciscan order. After martial law was declared in 1972 and many students, teachers, organizers, workers, and farmers were imprisoned, it became clear to the church that an apostolate for the care of detainees should be developed. When the Task Force for Detainees was founded in 1974, Sister Mariani began as its director and continues to the present in that capacity. During her visit to Chicago in 1986, she mused, "Friends moved into other areas of work, and I wondered if I should, but somehow human rights always seemed the right pursuit for me." Nevertheless she devoured the theology books at her host's house and ordered an *Interpreter's Dictionary of the Bible* and other theological materials to be sent back to the Philippines.

In 1986, President Aquino appointed Sister Mariani to the newly formed Presidential Committee on Human Rights (PCHR). Aquino commissioned the PCHR to investigate complaints of human rights violations and report their findings to the president and to the public. Sister Mariani functioned in two jobs, retaining her position with the TFD, but working every morning at the University of Life, which houses the PCHR. "I no longer have time to go to bed with a theology book these days. I just fall asleep exhausted every night," she said. Mariani is sixty-three years old, but doesn't seem anywhere near retirement.

Despite its best intentions, the PCHR had a backlog of cases of abuses from the past regime and thus had difficulty dealing with the current abuses. It had no prosecution capabilities; it simply recommended cases for prosecution. To date none of those cases has been successfully prosecuted.

During Sister Mariani's speaking tour in the United States, she was subjected to tough questioning by human rights activists who for years had petitioned the Marcos government or alerted their congressional representatives to abuses and lobbied against aid to the dictator. "Why have no cases been prosecuted? Why is the committee so slow? Has the president put restrictions on you?" Mariani gamely tried to answer, finding herself for the first time in her human rights career on the side of defending the government.

Four months after her American speaking tour, I visited Sister Mariani in her TFD office on the grounds of the Religious of the Virgin Mary Convent in Quezon City. Since Mariani's visit in Chicago, Rolando Olalia, the well-known labor leader and chairperson of the progressive political party, Partido ng Bayan, had been brutally murdered; twenty-two farmers had been killed at Mendiola Bridge; the workers on the picket line at Bataan Export Processing Zone had been shot at with two killed and thirty-three wounded; and seventeen peasants had been massacred in Lupao, Nueva Ecija.

Members of the PCHR, helpless to respond, had tried to resign, but Mrs. Aquino called them to a special meeting and persuaded them to stick with her. In the meantime the stories of brutal murders by civilian vigilante groups in Davao began hitting the Manila papers. Mrs. Aquino supported Chief of Staff Fidel Ramos, who said the vigilantes were an important part of the counterinsurgency strategy.

Sister Mariani sat behind her wooden desk, the fading sunlight poking through the small window in her cubicle as she held her head with her hands, "Oh, the lady president is so hard to defend . . . and she is so hard to criticize." She paused and said wearily, "What will we do? During Marcos's time, these kind of massacres and atrocities would mean thousands of people demonstrating on the street. People are dying and now everyone seems paralyzed."

I felt like I was witnessing the dark night of the soul. Any response I could think of seemed inadequate to the gravity of the moment. "What about Amnesty International? What about the Lawyers Committee for Human Rights? What about the International Jurists Commission? What about all the groups who used to come to the Philippines to document human rights abuses? Where are they?" Only a year before, Sister Mariani and the Task Force Detainees had been nominated for the Nobel Peace Prize. Surely these influential people and groups had not ceased to be concerned about the rights of ordinary Filipinos.

She gave me a hopeless look and then, in her typical fashion, Sister Mariani cut the heaviness by announcing that we needed ice cream. She swept out of her little office, gathered up the visitors in the waiting room and escorted us all to the Magnolia ice cream parlor for banana splits.

When I got back to North America, it became clearer to me what Sister Mariani was up against in the struggle to make the protection of human rights a reality during the first years of the Aquino administration. All the world had witnessed the heroic Filipino people defeat a dictator, standing up against tanks and guns. They were inspired by the tiny woman in yellow who embodied democracy. The woman in yellow was finally in the presidential office, so all should be well with the Philippine world and international attention could shift elsewhere.

A deeper look would have revealed the basic forces still intact—the military, the elite of the country, the American government. Because the usual international eye is set up for cursory glances around the globe at best, the actual situation in the field was achingly difficult to transmit accurately. That was Sister Mariani's burden.

Any mention of evil still lurking in Aquino's Philippine paradise immediately placed the bearer of bad tidings under suspicion as either pro-Marcos or pro-communist. Indeed, that is how Mrs. Aquino herself played the game, calling for help against the fascist right and the totalitarian left. The Sister Marianis who cried "Look here. People are suffering" under the new administration as they did in the old were ignored at best. In the case of Sister Mariani and the Task Force Detainees, an international attack to discredit them was attempted. For example, in May 1987, Heritage Foundation, the right-wing think tank based in Washington, D.C., circulated a paper entitled "The International Anti-Aquino Network: Threat to Philippine Democracy," in which Sister Mariani was fingered as a threat.

In fact the threats may be in the opposite direction. TFD documentation units in Cagayan Valley, home of Juan Ponce Enrile, were disbanded in 1987 because workers' lives were in jeopardy. Even the TFD unit in Manila transferred offices as a security precaution. These kinds of incidents also happened during the Marcos government, but at that time they received widespread attention and concern, especially abroad. Many of the international organizations or groups that acted as human rights advocates in the past drew back from any activity they thought might be interpreted as undercutting President Aquino. Lost from the discussion seemed to be the idea of the importance of checks and balances in a democracy, where questions are interpreted as a contribution to building something better.

In some sense, the human rights work in 1987 was set back to where it was in 1974 when the Task Force Detainees was born. It is a monumental task to start up the international wheel of human rights concern once it has ground to a halt.[2] However, there is one major difference in restarting the international groups—and that has to do with the work in the Philippines itself. In 1987, there is not merely one task force mandated by the religious sector, but rather an organizational

2. Finally in 1988, several human rights organizations, including Amnesty International and the Lawyers Committee for Human Rights, published reports that are critical of the human rights situation in the Philippines under Aquino.

alliance of human rights advocates that represents the legal and medical professions, various religious denominations, women's groups, and trade unions. Not only have the number of people and organizations increased, but the patient day-to-day work throughout the years has also created a body of experience that can be built on to face new situations.

A good example of this sophistication based on years of experience is the excellent work done by the Philippine Alliance of Human Rights Advocates (PAHRA) in hosting the independent fact-finding delegation led by former Attorney-General Ramsey Clark in May 1987. In the space of one week, PAHRA was able to provide the fact-finding mission with resource persons and local guides in various areas of the country and arrange appointments with victims, church persons, military personnel, and government representatives. They also organized an international press conference in Manila for the delegation that received wide coverage.

Despite their experience of uneven international support, especially during the early days of the Aquino administration, Filipino human rights advocates value and seek after international aid in their endeavor. Thanks to the persistence of Sr. Mariani Dimaranan throughout the years, the local Philippine base for human rights work is solid.

I glimpsed this combination of persistence and humanity again during a three-day women's walk to the Bataan Nuclear Plant, over one hundred kilometers from Manila. The plant has since been mothballed by the Aquino administration, but in 1984, residents in the area were terrified that it would go on line. The reactor itself had safety problems. The site was on an earthquake fault on the slope of an active volcano in an area subject to tidal waves. Even the Marcos-appointed mayors of the neighboring towns were opposed to the plant.

The women led the march through Central Luzon and at each town local demonstrators greeted the marchers and escorted them to the town plaza. I rode in the journalist jeepney, which sported a bright yellow MEDIA sign front and back. During the three-day march I realized that the men and women of the press on this trip were no ordinary writers and photographers. They worked cooperatively. I sensed no competition between them. Granted, they rode in the media jeepney while most of the participants walked, but they did share in the meager food and lodging (the floor of a school gymnasium one night and benches of a church the next night) of the rallyists. I found out later that a few of them had been political detainees themselves at one time.

After two days of walking under the hot sun and holding public meetings late into the night, the exhausted women headed toward their grand finale. Homemade torches flaming, they began to march into the night, led by two former beauty queens turned social activists, Maita Gomez and Nelia Sancho.

Ominous storm clouds in the afternoon developed into an evening thunderstorm that quickly extinguished the torches. The rain lashed against the plastic protective sheet hung over the back of our open jeepney. Each time the wind lifted the plastic covering, I glimpsed the resolute faces of Maita and the other women walking behind the jeepney. They were gasping for breath against the downpour, as water literally streamed down their faces.

Then suddenly someone yelled and the procession stopped. A young man shaking with the cold was stuffed into our already overcrowded vehicle. One of the Filipino photographers quickly put away his camera equipment and hauled a towel and T-shirt from his bag. The photographer removed the wet shirt from the shaking figure, tenderly swabbed him with his towel and offered him a dry T-shirt. His instinctive act of human kindness shamed me, because all I could think about at the time was my own discomfort—no space for my legs in the cramped vehicle, damp and cold clothing, rain spilling through the pathetic plastic covers.

As I watched this display of compassion from a member of the working press I remembered the words of Carolina Malay, National Democratic Front spokesperson, as she described what happened to men and women in the movement. "One difference is that the men cry more easily and the women cry less than their counterparts in the broader Philippine society."

The development of courageous women and compassionate men is a historic undertaking. It is even more impressive because it is done in the context of poverty and militarization where the leisure psychologically necessary to process internal change is not available. However, this change may not be so much a conscious goal as a by-product of honestly working together on the pressing needs of economic and physical survival.

The stories of courage and grace of individuals and communities in the Philippines are endless. Some of these vignettes have described relatively well-known Filipinos—Senator Jose Diokno and Sr. Mariani Dimaranan have traveled and spoken abroad in North America and Europe. Though still quite young, Lean Alejandro gained prominence nationally in the years before he was killed. Others—like Evangeline and Mely, the residents of barrio Malaya, and the young photographer on the women's march—are known only to their friends and co-workers.

The courage, commitment, and persistence of so many Filipinos in a chaotic and violent time is a truly remarkable gift. What are their sources of strength? What compels them to continue? Each of the women, men, and groups mentioned share some similarities. They all live in a context where it is virtually impossible to ignore the problems. Immersion in the situation is a powerful stimulant to action. The positive qualities within the culture itself also help to sustain the work and smooth the difficulties—generosity, creativity, and hospitality.

Another source of support within the Philippines is the existence of a national people's movement. There is no need to be a lone heroic figure, which is energy-draining and cannot be sustained forever. Each person knows that her or his work contributes to a larger cause. Each person knows that the liberation of the entire country does not rest on her or him alone. Mely, for example, nurtured her friends with one eye on the possibility of organizing a women's group in her little barrio to link with the national women's movement.

The women's movement can build on sources of strength from the culture itself—the stories of pre-Hispanic women's characteristics and the contributions of Filipina women through history. The stereotypical description of Filipinas used by corporate employers or foreign sex customers is deceptive. Gracious, generous, and gentle women are described as "docile, eager, and obedient." That fundamental error is not only an insult to women in the Philippines but denies access to any understanding of their alternative style of behavior.

One of their alternative strengths is the stamina that arises from a sense of companionship. Hilda Narciso fought the odds on her rape case, not simply for herself and by herself, but with other women and for other women. That in itself was a psychologically healing experience. Evangeline jumped into the fray of the strike because she could not abandon her co-workers. That decision cost her her job and probably the use of her hand.

A sense of one's proper role within the struggle can also provide the motivation to continue. This is especially true for the middle class and professionals who might have the option of walking away from a difficult situation even in a place like the Philippines. Fr. Rudy Romano knew he held power as a priest and was convinced he should use it to protect the people against the military. Jose Diokno used his position as a national figure to work with and on behalf of the marginalized.

Strange as it may seem in a discussion about persistence and tenacity, the ability to draw back and take a "sabbatical" is part of the strategy for the long haul. Sister Mariani's insistence on ice cream in the middle of a critical discussion and her flights into theological treatises are a healthy way of drawing back in order to go forward.

All of the people and groups mentioned share another common characteristic—a vision of the future that keeps short-term, personal goals from dictating their actions. Leandro Alejandro and thousands of other nationalists, human rights advocates, union and peasant leaders, and church workers have laid their lives on the line to oppose this new phase of militarism in the Philippines. Lidy, Lean Alejandro's widow, did not call for revenge after his death, but for a strengthened commitment to the goals of a just society.

Another common characteristic, embodied for me in the young photojournalist who shared his clothing, is the gift of empathy. This may be the most basic and needed characteristic for the long haul. Because he knew that he would not like to be cold and wet, he instinctively cared for the cold, wet, and exhausted human being who was thrust into our jeepney.

These human beings, ordinary Filipinos acting out of empathy, are ultimately the reason for our hope. The struggle of sincere, vulnerable people against great odds provides inspiration for others to become involved as well. Lidy Nacpil-Alejandro expressed it well: "Every tear that we shed is a drop into the flood that shall sweep us to victory." That kind of commitment in the midst of personal loss and sorrow is an expression of hope for all of humanity.

15

The Choices We Face

Any visitor to the Philippines who meets with active church people cannot help but be impressed with the commitment and courage displayed across all denominational lines. Throughout the colonial period, throughout martial law, and now in the era of low-intensity conflict, somehow the flowers continue to bloom despite the typhoons.

A typical conversation between Filipino host and international guest toward the end of a visit in the country is a variation on this theme. "What will you do in your country, now that you have seen our life here in the Philippines?" "Do you have any suggestions for us? Tell us how you manage to remain hopeful in the face of such great odds here in the Philippines."

"You have to find your own way—discover what is appropriate in your setting, just like we had to here. We had a lot of imported wisdom from the United States and Europe, but we had to stop being awed by outside advice. What works elsewhere doesn't necessarily translate into something useful here."

Despite these disclaimers there is an eagerness on the part of Filipino church and human rights workers to talk about America, Americans, and their links to events in the Philippines. Liberation theology or theology of struggle grows well in the soil of the Third World, but what is a liberating gospel for those caught in the affluent belly of the American beast?

Theologian, poet, and activist Ed de la Torre tells Americans to reread the foundational story of liberation for Jews and Christians found in the Old Testament. The Book of Exodus records Moses and Aaron's organizing efforts and Israel's escape from slavery in Egypt after generations of oppression.

De la Torre advises, "Don't read from the point of view of Pharaoh; after all you are not the rulers in America. Read from the point of view of the Egyptian people. When will the Egyptians realize they too are oppressed? When they have to make the bricks themselves because the Israelite slaves aren't making them anymore. Then the question for the Egyptians becomes, when will they themselves be freed from Pharaoh's clutches?"

The liberation of Filipinos is intimately connected to the liberation of Americans. Solidarity is not an act of charity because we feel sorry for suffering people. If the Israelites can free themselves from the pharaoh, it will hasten the day that the Egyptians too must take on the pharaoh. Egyptians with a short-term view will think it is to their advantage to have another race work as slaves to make their bricks. But ultimately the pharaoh will not be satisfied only with what the slaves can provide; the Egyptian citizens will be squeezed as well. To keep the slaves in line, more weapons will be needed. The citizens will be put to work to pay for the weapons.

The Filipinos employed in "brickmaking" for the pharaoh—those whose cheap labor provides bananas and pineapples, tennis shoes, clothing, and electronic equipment—are engaged in a struggle right now to gain the power to redirect the profits from the bricks for their own welfare. The question for the Americans is not, as one agribusiness executive put it— "Are you willing to pay more for your bananas in the supermarket?" Rather, the question is, "Are you willing to struggle with the pharaohs so that the profits and savings accrue more evenly and benefit producers and consumers, not only the managers and the investors?"

As a result of the "brickmakers'" struggle, deepening rifts and class divisions are leading to greater violence in Filipino society. In fact, these can be resolved only within the country. Uncaring and greedy people are as prevalent in the Philippines as in any society. However, the internal problems have been exacerbated by a violent foreign presence over the past 450 years. The internal tensions at this historical point in time are being blown out of manageable proportion by the constant interference of the Philippine government's closest ally—the

United States. Departure of the United States does not guarantee that there will be a healthy resolution of problems in the Philippines. *But continued American presence in the manner in which we have acted since the turn of the century does guarantee more bloodshed, violence, and inequality.*

The story of the Philippines and the struggle of sisters and brothers there comes full circle to rest with us here in North America. *Our task as Americans is to remove our country's negative influence and unwarranted interference in Philippine affairs.* We can call on our government to apply the goals inherent in our country's birth to the relationship to the Philippines—self-determination, local control, and a respect for the decision of the majority. However, no one is under the illusion that the CIA, Pentagon, or White House will follow a politics of empathy of their own volition.

In a participatory democracy, the initiative to change the direction of our foreign policy will come from the citizens who carry this concern. We have a responsibility as members of a society in which, at least theoretically, the citizens have a role in decision making. It is through concerted citizen effort that policy or legislative changes eventually take place.

Those who help to plan American military policy are sensitive to the effect of American public opinion on the success of their plans. George Tanham, former president of Rand Corporation and counterinsurgency expert, draws a clear connection between U.S. operations in the Third World and citizen response in the United States:

> To me, our most pressing problem is not in the Third World, but here at home, in the struggle for the minds of the people. . . . Propaganda and organizations are not enough. We must have a purpose and we must integrate the purpose of special operations, psychological operations, shows of military force, economic programs and all the rest. If we lose our own citizens, we will not have much going for us anywhere else in the world.[1]

The American government strategy in the Philippines and elsewhere is to wear down those who are working for economic equality and inclusion of all in the political decision-making

1. Quoted by Sara Miles, "The War at Home," North American Committee on Latin America's Report on the Americas, April-May 1986, p. 40.

process. This strategy is projected to take a long time and designed to be done in a low-profile manner so as not to attract American public attention. Pentagon theorists now say that the mistake in Vietnam was not the fact of intervention, but the commitment of U.S. troops. The presence of U.S. troops and corresponding American media cameras inhibited the success of the total counterinsurgency effort.

Many military theorists are concerned that the American population and American soldiers will stand in the way of future successful military operations.

> The enemy's political-social structure must be identified and captured or eliminated and the political and psychological instruments of the revolution must be destroyed. *The strategy is not likely to be in accord with democratic norms or compatible with conventional military posture. Support and assistance for the offensive phase of counterrevolution are likely to create political and moral dilemmas for Americans, both in the domestic political sphere and in the military.*
>
> American military personnel are in an extremely untenable moral and ethical position if they are engaged in offensive counter-revolutionary operations. While such actions may have some acceptance as part of covert operations conducted by U.S. intelligence agencies, political and military difficulties arise when they involve other agencies and institutions.[2]

Each person in the United States is vital to the success of modern, low-intensity conflict wars. Contra guerrillas and national armies supported by the U.S. government will never win with guns, nuclear stockpiles, or fortifications unless the people are behind them. Millions of people will die in these all-out grass roots wars, but every effort will be made to convince the American people that the crusade is indispensable to our national security.

This strategy of a quiet, all-out war designed to escape the anger of a skeptical American public is not just a political issue. It becomes a spiritual issue for all of us when we recognize how we are instruments of this modern warfare. If by

2. Sam C. Sarkesian, "Low-Intensity Conflict: Concepts, Principles and Policy Guidelines," *Air University Review* 36 (January-February 1985): 5.

our silence or resigned and plaintive sighs we give permission for our lives to be used in this way, our notion of spirit, of God, and of our independent ability to think and act will be fundamentally warped.

We may theoretically know that low-intensity conflict is a long-term strategy designed to wear people down, but on a spiritual level, we often cling to the assumption that a decisive moment will occur in a dramatic battle of good and evil. Like instant coffee, we hope that the battle will be instantly dissolved. America's aggression is not simply limited to bad foreign policy and economic policies. Evil encompasses more than low-intensity warfare: it reflects a national spirituality that is self-destructing and does not know it.

Pacifists in the United States face a formidable challenge. It is probably more difficult to be a pacifist in the United States than in almost any other country. Our government's militarism and repression seeps into every aspect of our lives because our personal lives are intricately knitted into the structures of our society. We fund our government's militarism when we pay taxes and when we pay our telephone bill. The weapons manufactured in our country through government contracts and sold to other countries are used in the grass roots wars in which civilians are the main victims. Many large corporations that produce consumer items are also involved in some aspect of weapons production. Our purchase of those consumer items help keep those companies going.

In addition to direct killing, we must also consider our part in the slow death that occurs through malnutrition, overwork, and poor sanitary conditions. The underpaid workers in multinational corporations and the farmers who cannot grow rice, corn, and vegetables to eat because their land is used to grow luxury fruit for export cannot provide adequately for their children. They will watch their children suffer from malnutrition-related diseases.

Recognizing this connection is a way of coming face to face with evil. It is almost more insidious because the activity is one step removed from our immediate purview and thus is sanitized. To espouse nonviolence and live responsibly locally is an extremely costly commitment. It is almost impossible to live in the United States and not finance America's military exploits.

Some American citizens refuse to pay that portion of their tax which goes to war costs. The figure varies between 40 and

60 percent of the national budget. This is because some military budget items are hidden—for example, in the Department of Energy, where taxes pay for the construction of plutonium triggers for bombs made at Rocky Flats in Colorado. On the other hand, veterans' benefits, which come out of the Pentagon budget, are basically for retirement, education, health, and rehabilitative services. Most people would want to pay for these.

As residents in this imperial nation, we face not only economic and military entanglement. We are also subject to the spiritual desolation that results from our collective pathology. When my husband, Gene, and I returned to the United States after living in the Philippines, I was struck by the emphasis on psychological health and the amount of effort and energy poured into that endeavor in this country. People told us they did not want to hear about the Philippines because they felt overwhelmed by their own personal or family problems.

In our first years of re-entry, I too felt overwhelmed and puzzled by what I considered a cold social environment in North America. That is not how I had remembered life here. The irony is that as a culture we seem more frank and explicit in terms of expressing emotions than Filipinos, but sometimes too many words obscure meaning and scuttle genuine intimacy. The hospitable and engaging atmosphere of the Philippines had introduced a different standard for human interaction. The ordeal of my first few years back in North America helped me to understand that the frantic activity or misty romanticism of so many people here is a result of a deep dissatisfaction and longing that is not attributable to their individual experience alone.

A Filipino friend pointed out some reasons for the incongruity. After several years of hosting foreign visitors on study tours in the Philippines, Al Manrique, a Filipino artist and student of human nature, concluded, "The West promotes a highly individualistic competitive society and spirit of domination. The effect of this capitalistic, profit-first economy in the cultural or spiritual psyche of westerners is basically the holding back of anything personal or emotional. Some westerners hold back because they cannot fathom the intensity of feeling of total engagement."

However, the difference in relating is not simply a cultural or economic phenomenon. It also correlates with the fact that great numbers of people in the Philippines have chosen to struggle for a vision that is larger than their day-to-day life. That commitment releases energy and creativity.

The last twenty years of struggle have forced realism upon the participants. The romanticism of the 1960s' youth who joined the nationalist movement en masse with the hope of bringing in the new day quickly has been steeled and tempered. Theologian and former political prisoner, Ed de la Torre, one of those who have undergone this process, says, "We desire to focus on the ambiguities and difficulties of the struggle for liberation, rather than the romantic vision, because we are in the midst of nitty gritty problems daily in the course of our struggle to liberate ourselves and our country."

These twenty years of struggle have also intensified human relationships. Manrique describes the situation: "We struggle in the midst of chaos and terror to find order, justice, peace, and liberation. We hold to solidarity as one of our basic arms in the struggle. We have no time to measure, but we have plenty of time to plunge deeper into total engagement, not only with our sisters and brothers, but also with our enemies."

Over a period of ten years, I could see in Filipino friends some important internal changes as a result of their commitment to struggle for a goal together with others. Part of it was a change from an absorption on the personal to a concern for the social. Paradoxically, that change in focus created a firmer, deeper individual.

In contrast, in our North American society, our individualistic vision easily becomes impaired. We become inebriated with the subtle values of our society, which flow through our bloodstream like alcohol. We are not even aware that it is part of us. Our first task is to "dry out," so we can think clearly and walk in a straight line.

Part of the detoxification process is to examine the internal obstacles that keep us apart from each other and thus unable to take concerted action with sisters and brothers in the Philippines and elsewhere. It helps if we can recognize the compulsive anxiety that pushes our country to build massive armaments and stockpile them in order to be prepared. This need for millions of explosive metal "safety nets" arises from a spirit of fear and dis-ease. Where do these fears and questions originate?

Questions can develop from unchallenged assumptions about how a social order should be set up or who is capable of doing so. Pictures of united and determined people on the street in the Philippines or South Korea or elsewhere may only seem like a "mob" as we sit in our easy chairs watching the six o'clock news. This assessment often comes from a lack of experience in cross-cultural or cross-class situations. It is easy to become suspicious of people and situations when they are totally new. Fears can spring from an aversion to seeing or being part of a scene raw with sweat and dirt.

Questions can also serve as a smokescreen to avoid inconvenience to ourselves if we start opening ourselves to the implications of what we are seeing and hearing. Many hesitations arise from a fear of facing personal changes. The gulf between what a visitor to the Philippine barrios faces and the visitor's family, friends, and vocation at home may be too overwhelming.

In the midst of the American emphasis on public relations and truth through image, it is easy to lose one's way. "How can we pierce through illusions," asks Manrique, "except by breaking them with truth in its most brutal form?" Truth force, the power of accurate perceptions spoken simply, is like an antidote to the sickness of our society. It brings a transcendent element into the mundane details of life. Its effect is to enhance and enlarge life, as a dried prune soaked in water becomes larger and softer.

It is crucial for us to understand intellectually and emotionally what is happening to Filipino farmers, workers, and women as a result of the actions our government takes in the name of security. If we have heard the testimonies of those who suffer and struggle or seen the effects of injustice with our own eyes, then there is no turning back. To be solidly engaged with others means we share both their joys and sorrows, their certainty and doubts.

Work in this area is not simply a temporary deviation from our life plans; it will entail a long-term commitment that impinges on every life choice we make—lifestyle, work, friends. It is important to bring to the crisis in the Philippines—as anywhere in the world—a time line that is not too short. It may require all of our lifetime as well as our children's and their children's.

It comes down to a decision to develop our life according to the politics of empathy. This may be the one realistic hope we have of surviving as a people and as a globe. Our security rests in our openness to others. Our survival and the survival of sisters and brothers in the Philippines and elsewhere depends on our being able to sense our interconnectedness.

When we first returned from Asia, Gene and I traveled for eight months in Canada and the United States, listening to local concerns and telling stories about the Philippines. We met many hard-working, sincere people who were disheartened and felt isolated in their work for justice, but they continued nevertheless. While they witnessed to their belief that a more equitable world is possible, they still asked, "What difference does my little action make, anyway? Is there any hope?" Ironically, from the experience and insight of the very people who questioned the efficacy of their work, we hammered out our hope, our strategy, and our connectedness in North America.

We hope for all people to have the power to make choices for themselves, to take control over their own lives, and to be responsible for their own decisions. That would include what they eat, what they wear, what they do each day, where they work, and how they relate to their families and their neighbors.

This is a reasonable hope, but it is not yet realized. People who choose to be healthy and well nourished are poor, sick, and malnourished. People who choose to work are unemployed. People who choose to farm are driven off their land in the Philippines and in Canada and in the United States. One major obstacle in the way of people's directing their lives is that the control of resources and ways of making wealth is not equitably held, neither in the Philippines nor in North America.

In our political system, members of the American Congress or Canadian Parliament are somewhat accountable to the citizens. However, in our economic system, large corporations and banks are accountable to a select group of board members or stockholders whose major concern is short-term profit rather than the fair distribution of goods and services. At this point, the political process basically upholds the present economic arrangement.

The problem of the United States' negative interference in the Philippines is connected to the essential character of the society here. Our goal is not simply a cut in military aid to a repressive military. We may win one vote on one country and yet not make a dent in the essential way our government and other institutions relate around the world.

Before a change can be made, enough people must want that change. Alternative newspapers and journals, public radio and television can provide necessary information to illustrate the need for a change. So can tours to countries like the Philippines to meet sisters and brothers there and hear from them directly. Journals, forums, and study conferences will not mobilize great masses of people, but they help to lay the groundwork for a new climate of opinion in which specific changes are possible. Sooner or later, the information in alternative journals finds its way into the mainstream media. The first questions about U.S. involvement in Vietnam were raised in mimeographed flyer form.

In addition to information, emphasis on an individual simplified lifestyle prepares us to view the world differently. It helps to have a supportive, cohesive community when we simplify our life and struggle on behalf of others. Our own individual change in lifestyle tells us we do not need everything the advertisements tell us we need. Our grouping together tells us that cooperation with others is possible. A change in lifestyle or joining a community is not an end in itself. These actions, however, can free us to think more creatively about how to bring more and more of our lives under our own control.

The traditional institutions in which to work for change in society are legislative bodies and the courts. Working in the electoral arena to introduce a politic of empathy will only make sense if we already have a committed grass roots movement going in the direction of liberation and justice. Can we ask our elected representatives to risk their security to try to curb corporate power if we ourselves have not shunned their seduction? Court rulings often reflect the prevailing climate of opinion. That brings us back to the importance of a large mass of people, knowledgeable and ready to act on their convictions.

It is clear in the Philippines and it became increasingly clear to us as we re-entered American society that economic inequity is not correctable through the traditional political process. Direct confrontation with the economic powers, whether in the Philippines or in North America or elsewhere, is unavoidable. This will require strong investigative research on individual corporations as well as the development of a comprehensive understanding of the patterns of international economic control. Most people's eyes glaze over when the International Monetary Fund or transfer pricing is mentioned.

Our Filipino friends have discovered that their everyday life is linked to these larger institutions and economic practices. It is a life-and-death matter to them to acquire a solid understanding.

If we are to commit ourselves to restrain our government's negative influence and interference in the Philippines and its resulting blight on this country, we must make some necessary preparations. Even after we have made a basic commitment to confront our government and other institutions in our country, a host of new questions will face us as we move more deeply into engaging in this struggle.

How can we develop the internal strength to sustain our long-term commitment to the politics of empathy? How can we maximize the strengths we do have, so we can contribute most fully and effectively to the goal of peace and justice?

Some of the sources of strength that sustain people in the Philippines are also available to us. However, to appropriate some of them will require a more concerted effort on our part, given the socially alienated environment in the west.

The Philippines provides a national context in which it is virtually impossible for citizens to ignore the problems. Immersion in the situation with virtually no options but to stand and fight is a powerful stimulant to action. A member of the middle class in a country like the United States has more options for personal advancement, and thus the choice to struggle for equality and fairness for all is not quite so compelling. However, a long view of where we are headed if we continue our present direction tells us that there is no other option but to struggle for a more sane approach to international relations.

A growing number of groups within North America are left with few economic options, just as in the Philippines. The parallels between the Philippine situation and the American situation are becoming more apparent. For example, Gene and I presented programs throughout rural Iowa on the role of multinational agribusiness in the Philippines. One Sunday evening in a church basement just outside of Iowa City, we showed our slideshow on Castle and Cooke (Dole) with its emphasis on the plight of small farmers contracted to Dole. Before I could turn on the lights after the slideshow, a voice yelled in the darkness, "That's our story. That is what is happening to us farmers in Iowa."

A sense of one's proper role within the struggle can also provide the motivation to continue, especially for the middle class and professionals who might have the option of walking away from a difficult situation even in a place like the Philippines. In western countries where the middle class forms a large percentage of the population, the question of appropriate contribution to the overall struggle is crucial. Tackling local issues is sometimes the best way of genuinely connecting to people elsewhere.

For example, in Warman, Saskatchewan, the dairy farms of Mennonite farmers were threatened by the proposed construction of a uranium refinery plant. The farmers and their supporters made it clear that they opposed the construction on environmental, ecological, economic, social, and moral grounds. Hundreds of residents packed the federal hearing in January 1980 in the little town of Martensville every day despite the thirty-degree below zero temperatures. Everyone from children to grandparents testified. College students wheeled in a solar oven, presented alternatives to nuclear energy, and produced a homemade loaf of bread from the oven for the panel members. One farm housewife, her voice cracking with stage fright, set jars of berries and milk in front of the federal panel from Ottawa and begged them not to allow the destruction of her farm and its produce. An elderly church leader hobbled to the stand and in broken English explained the history of the Mennonites, their pacifism, and their calling to be faithful stewards of God's earth.

Saskatchewan premier Edward Blakeney accused the Mennonites of being selfish, telling them that their intransigence was dooming Third World people like Filipinos to poverty. The Philippine government was planning to purchase the uranium from Saskatchewan for use at the Bataan Nuclear Plant, north of Manila. Leaders of the concerned citizens of Warman contacted us. Are we really dooming Filipinos to poverty, they wanted to know. At the hearing, I described the Filipino opposition to the Bataan Nuclear Plant, based on both safety and economic factors.

The Warman people's creative resistance in sub-zero weather reminded me of the Filipina women's three-day march against the Bataan Nuclear Plant in pelting rain. "I feel very close to the Filipinos," said one Warman participant later, "even though I have never been there. We and they are working for survival. We are lending support by confronting the same forces in our own country."

Another very important source of strength is the presence of companions in the work. Filipinos in the movement for justice know that there is no need to be a lone heroic figure. Not only is this energy-draining, but it can't be sustained forever. Each person's work contributes to the larger cause. That sense of companionship with others provides the stamina to continue. Filipino artist Al Manrique explains that "the oppressed have nothing else, but to engage with each other totally. This is their strength. They have a long history of openness to engage totally with anybody primarily because there is a need for solidarity."

Patience and unselfishness are characteristics that have helped to build a strong, united effort in the Philippines. Filipinos do not have a monopoly on these traits, but the life-and-death questions and circumstances of the work help to minimize the more selfish impulses of the persons involved. The patient step-by-step organizing at the barrio level has gone on virtually unnoticed by the outside world or even the elite of the country for twenty years. It has been done by people who cannot even use their own names. The scrambling for credit that often goes on in work in the United States is not possible there.

The reward for those involved is that the day is hastened when everyone will be fed, clothed, housed, and educated. The goals of the people are to be free, to dance, sing, paint, create, make love, eat, and have shelter. They look forward to the time when the Philippines as a nation will be able to create its own expression of society where each citizen can enjoy life in peace.

That is not to deny that conflict does erupt in the Philippines which can be attributed more to ego needs than to honest difference in policy. However, examples of selflessness help to gather more selfless action. That kind of generosity can be nurtured by remembering to "keep our eyes on the prize." Building a spirituality of empathy to sustain us for the long haul involves clarifying our own core of values. What is of ultimate worth? What are we willing to die for? What are we willing to live and struggle for? A deeply embedded vision of the future also keeps short-term personal goals from dominating our decisions about what constitutes effective action.

If we test our desires and needs and impulses against the life-and-death issues of economic inequity, for example, some of our selfishness will evaporate. My experience in the Philippines helped me to understand that people can deepen their spiritual life through acts of compassion and works of justice. Often healing and reconstruction of personal life or family relationships happens in spite of our efforts and not according to the schedule that we plan—truly by the grace of God.

The Philippine church of the people in its material poverty has come to a rich understanding of the strength that proceeds from integrity. Karl Gaspar, now a Redemptorist brother serving in the barrio of Candelaria in Bukidnon, Mindanao, described his life with the peasants there in his Christmas 1987 letter to friends:

> Living with the people in the context of the mission—I move from one house to another and sleep under a different roof each night—provides me with a perspective that I find most empowering. The people are poor but they are capable of total giving. They seem powerless but there is an integrity in their response to life. They may be perceived as devoid of hope given their pathetic situation, but the irony of it all is that they provide me with a rich reservoir of hope. Indeed the poor will inherit the earth.

The committed poor in the Philippines hold up a mirror for both the middle-class Filipinos and the "do-gooder" westerners to view themselves and their fears more clearly. It is almost like the story of the rich young ruler who came to Jesus and told him he had kept all the commandments and done everything prescribed by law, but knew he lacked something for liberation. Jesus told him, "Go sell all your possessions, give the money to the poor." The ruler could not face the prospect of such vulnerability and sadly backed down from his commitment to liberation.

If we turn away from that mirror, we may keep our friends, our family, our possessions, and our job intact, but we will lose the energy, health, and joy that comes from sincere struggle. Our humanity is diminished and the future is jeopardized when any of us pull back. Like the rich young ruler, once there is clarity about the problem, we face the responsibility of making choices.

It is customary in the Philippines to have a party, a *despi-*

dida, to say good-bye to someone who is leaving the office, the city, or the country. When Gene and I left Davao City after two years, we were given a despidida. After the songs and the gifts and the ice cream, friends shared reflections on the past two years' observations and advice for the future.

The most memorable words came from a quiet, somewhat shy staff member who worked in community development. We had not really learned to know him well during our stay. When it was his turn to comment, he simply said, "Thank you for not coming here to convert us or to tell us co-ops or miracle rice or multi-cropping are the answer to our problems. Thank you for choosing to just come and be with us."

Karl Gaspar, the director of the agency where we worked, completed the despidida reflections with his challenge, "Now as you go to your own country, we ask you to keep vigil with us. Continue to be our companions along the road to justice and freedom."

To become companions on the journey toward justice is a choice that confronts all of us. Part of the joy of taking this road is the privilege of walking with many courageous and creative people who have already been walking for a long time. Choosing this journey is the first step; our ongoing challenge is to be worthy companions.

16

Memo

TO: THE UNITED STATES ADMINISTRATION
RE: FOREIGN POLICY GUIDELINES TO
    ACHIEVE OUR GOALS IN THE PHILIPPINES

The current American foreign policy in the Philippines is forcing the best and brightest leaders in that country to choose between the legitimate interests of their nation and the priorities of the United States. It may be in our best interests to redefine our long-term strategy in the Philippines in accordance with our constitutional and historical values in order to retain the full respect and friendship of the Filipino people and their leaders.

History and Current U.S. Goals in the Philippines

The United States has related to the Philippine nation since the turn of this century. The Philippines became the first U.S. colony in 1898. It has been our closest ally in the Pacific since 1946. At this juncture in history, it is imperative to assess realistically both the internal situation in the Philippines and the basis of our current policy toward that country.

    U.S. president Theodore Roosevelt predicted in 1902 that "the 19th Century was the century of Europe, the 20th, the century of America. The next century will be the Pacific Century." The main aims of the U.S. government in the Pacific at the turn of the century were economic: to secure the Philippines as a market, as a source of raw materials, and as a military strong point from which to penetrate the markets of China.

Though the particulars have changed somewhat, our interests in the Philippines remain economic and military. In order for us to achieve our interests, the Philippine population must have stability and some measure of prosperity.

Assessment of Philippine Stability and Prosperity

Despite improvements during the Marcos years in such infrastructure items as roads and bridges and such development projects as hydroelectric power, the per capita caloric intake of Filipinos continues to be one of the lowest in Asia. The Gross National Product has increased and the economic growth rate has been positive for the past two years. However, the actual purchasing power of citizens has not increased. The Philippines will not be a useful market for our goods if the citizens' purchasing power is not increased.

The Philippine government's $28 billion foreign debt was incurred while following advice of the International Monetary Fund. That debt now functions as a time bomb. If the Philippine government reneges on its payments, it will, with other Third World debtor nations, destabilize our banking institutions here in the United States. If, on the other hand, the government tries to keep up with its payments, it must take the money from already impoverished citizens. This will contribute to social instability and lack of money for purchasing U.S. manufactured goods and services. Neither option is in our long-term interest.

At the same time, nationalist sentiment and activism has extended into every aspect of Philippine life. For example, in August 1987 there was an overwhelming public rejection of the oil price increase designed to raise more money for the government's foreign debts. The strike included not only the urban poor and the bus and jeepney drivers but also public transportation companies, middle-class consumers, and Philippine oil dealers.

In addition, the military activities of the New People's Army (NPA) reflect a growing citizen support that has extended to the urban areas. NPA assassination squads could probably not carry off their bold attacks without a disciplined support network. The streets have been cordoned off and extra security details have been set up in Manila. Though the police have arrested persons, it seems that those actually responsible have eluded capture.

Failure of our Foreign Policy

Our interest in the Philippines is connected to its strategic importance in the region. This memo concerns our policy in the Philippines, but because that country is basic to our global policy, it has to be reviewed in the larger context of our foreign policy goals.

Our international relations have been conducted with the goal of defeating communism and thus ensuring American security. Political commitments based on this premise have resulted in positioning our troops to endure military humiliations such as the bombing of our marines in Lebanon and the bombing of ships in the Persian Gulf. Despite the amount of money and weapons expended, we are more isolated internationally and thus less secure than we have ever been. American civilians, too, endure hostility from citizens of other nations and are less secure than ever when traveling abroad.

In the Philippines, as elsewhere, we have pursued our premier form of policy initiative—the rollback of communism. Our preoccupation with defeating communism may have obscured our judgment of character. We have received numerous reports of U.S. government-related covert involvement in supporting and training vigilantes and death squads as long as they call themselves "anticommunist." In the name of fighting communism, we may well have helped to unleash chaotic military and paramilitary violence in the Philippines.

If we choose to try to defeat the nationalist movement in the Philippines, we will have to expend every effort in psychological operations and stepped-up covert action in addition to massive military power. To continue in this direction can only result in further military and economic insecurity and isolation. An alternative direction is to construct another framework from which to see and achieve our interest and position in the Philippines.

Guidelines for a Successful Foreign Policy

A reasonable guideline for our foreign policy will derive from the basic values of our nation. Our nation was born out of the struggle against Britain for local control; our nation grew up with the commitment to fashion our own future and destiny. If we review our own experience, it will be easier to recognize that other nations are experiencing a similar process. We know how it feels as a nation to be thwarted in our resolve. Thus we can respect the right of other nations to proceed in their own fashion toward democracy, general welfare, and domestic tranquility.

This approach can also be described as a politic of empathy. Local control, majority rule, and self-determination are conservative and basic values that can guide our foreign policy initiatives and our relations with other nations. We did not achieve the best result on our first try. It took many decades and generations of struggle to abolish slavery, to guarantee universal suffrage, and to adopt other amendments of civil rights and liberties to our constitution. We surely respect that right in other nations to determine their own destiny.

Implications for the Philippines

Much of our spoken policy should continue to be spoken and to be followed: support for democracy, fair play, freedom, and human rights. However, both the privatized foreign policy and the covert government and military destabilization must stop.

At the turn of this century, Presidents McKinley and Theodore Roosevelt moved into the Philippines in order to reach the markets of China. Between then and now, China has gone through a revolution and has experimented with its economic and social system in an attempt to feed its citizens. The world has not fallen apart. The United States has remained strong. We have adjusted to China's social experiment. Just as it is possible to adjust foreign relations with a large country, it is also possible with a smaller country.

The Filipino people may decide to tailor their economic and social system to fit and meet basic needs in their country. If we apply the politics of empathy and our own American experience, we see that it is necessary for them to follow a suitable, if not identical, path in order to feed their citizenry and boost their income. We may have to adjust some of our present practices and policies to accommodate the realities in the Philippines. But, ultimately, citizens with more purchasing power and a country with less foreign debt is healthier for us.

We recommend a ban on CIA covert operations and any private U.S. activities in the Philippines to destabilize that government. We do not fear grass roots nationalist groups. The Filipino in the barrio is not our enemy unless we define him that way. His aspirations for a decent life are not subversive unless we define them as such. The nationalists who do not want our military installations on their soil are not our enemies unless we define them as our enemies. If the majority of local people decide they need land reform and higher wages, the U.S. does not have to fund the military to shoot them. Individual freedom to choose and respect for the choice of the majority are, after all, American commitments.

We do not have to get caught in supporting the repression of human beings if we apply the politics of empathy. As a nation, we can choose to build a foreign policy on some of our solid and trusted values and thus retain our self-respect.

Helpful Reading on the Philippines

Bello, Walden. *Creating the Third Force: The US and Low Intensity Conflict in the Philippines.* San Francisco: Institute for Food and Development Policy, 1987.

Bonner, Raymond. *Waltzing with a Dictator: The Marcoses and the Making of American Policy.* New York: Times Books, 1987.

Chapman, William. *Inside the Philippine Revolution: NPA and Its Struggle for Power.* New York: W. W. Norton, 1987.

Gaspar, Karl. *How Long? Prison Reflections from the Philippines.* Ed. Helen Graham and Breda Noonan S.S.C. Maryknoll, N.Y.: Orbis Books, 1985.

Schirmer, Daniel B., and Stephen Rosskamm Shalom. *The Philippines Reader: A History of Colonialism, Neocolonialism, Dictatorship and Resistance.* Boston: South End Press, 1987.

Index